Wittgenstein's Family Letters

Wittgenstein 1947 © Cambridge Archive.

ALSO AVAILABLE FROM BLOOMSBURY

Dialectic of the Ladder: Wittgenstein, the 'Tractatus' and Modernism,
by Ben Ware
Portraits of Wittgenstein, edited by F.A. Flowers III and Ian Ground
Wittgenstein, Religion and Ethics, by Mikel Burley
Wittgenstein's Secret Diaries, by Dinda L. Gorlée

Wittgenstein's Family Letters

Corresponding with Ludwig

EDITED WITH AN
INTRODUCTION BY
BRIAN MCGUINNESS
TRANSLATED BY
PETER WINSLOW

BLOOMSBURY ACADEMIC
LONDON • NEW YORK • OXFORD • NEW DELHI • SYDNEY

BLOOMSBURY ACADEMIC
Bloomsbury Publishing Plc
50 Bedford Square, London, WC1B 3DP, UK
1385 Broadway, New York, NY 10018, USA

BLOOMSBURY, BLOOMSBURY ACADEMIC and the Diana logo
are trademarks of Bloomsbury Publishing Plc

First published in Great Britain 2019
Paperback edition published 2020

Copyright © Brian McGuinness, 2019, 2020

Cover design: Clare Turner
Cover image: Kurt, Paul, Hermine, Max, Leopoldine, Helene,
Ludwig – Neuwaldegg 1917 © The Brenner-Archiv.

Brian McGuinness has asserted his right under the Copyright, Designs
and Patents Act, 1988, to be identified as Editor of this work.

For legal purposes the Acknowledgements on p. ix constitute an extension
of this copyright page.

Bloomsbury Publishing Plc does not have any control over, or responsibility for, any
third-party websites referred to or in this book. All internet addresses given in this
book were correct at the time of going to press. The author and publisher regret
any inconvenience caused if addresses have changed or sites have ceased to
exist, but can accept no responsibility for any such changes.

A catalogue record for this book is available from the British Library.

A catalog record for this book is a available from the Library of Congress.

ISBN: HB: 978-1-4742-9813-1
        PB: 978-1-3501-6281-5
        ePDF: 978-1-4742-9811-7
        eBook: 978-1-4742-9814-8

Typeset by RefineCatch Limited, Bungay, Suffolk

To find out more about our authors and books visit www.bloomsbury.com
and sign up for our newsletters.

Contents

List of Illustrations

Acknowledgements

The editor here builds on a previous smaller selection of family letters published in 1996 by Hölder-Pichler-Tempsky Verlag, one of whose principal editors was Frau Maria Ascher Corsetti. She has helped me also with counsel and I thank her in the first place. That edition appeared in the Schriftenreihe der Wittgenstein-Gesellschaft and its current President Dr Friedrich Stadler has been kindly supportive of the appearance of this second extended edition.

Of the family members who at that earlier time provided letters and illustrations alas only Dr Andreas Sjögren survives. He has generously provided yet more material, particularly photographic. I thank Dr Stephan Stockert for the permission to reissue this family correspondence collection and to Dr Florian Stockert for his continuous support and availability to answer questions regarding the family history. I owe a debt to the generosity of Francoise and Pierre Stonborough who have given me free access to their private photo archive. Mr Louis Wittgenstein made available to the Brenner-Archiv in Innsbruck letters exchanged between his father Paul and his uncle Ludwig, a most important addition to this selection. The Brenner-Archiv itself, guided by its director Dr Ulrike Tanzer and two of its senior associates, Professors Allan Janik and Josef Mitterer, has been an invaluable resource. There I could consult the material presented in the Gesamtbriefwechsel (on which I myself have worked, now used by kind permission of electronic publisher InteLex) and have access to Ludwig Wittgenstein's Collection of Nonsense, items from which also appear (signalized as such/with due warning) in these pages. For the exploitation of the Archiv I have had the ready assistance of Dr Joseph Wang and Dr Anton Unterkircher. On military matters in particular I have had help from the extremely well-informed Dr Martin Pilch of Vienna. For general control of texts, translation and biography I could not have had better help than that of Dr Joachim Schulte with his unrivalled knowledge of the Ludwig Wittgenstein corpus, help unstintingly given throughout a lifetime. My work would not have been possible without the help of my Siena assistant, dottoressa Mariangela Faso.

This volume has been produced almost in tandem with a German version edited by Frau Radmila Schweitzer of the Wittgenstein-Initiative in Vienna, whom obviously I have constantly consulted. We have both profited much from the exceptional attention that Colleen Coalter of Bloomsbury has devoted to this edition. I am extremely grateful to these ladies. One might say there are here three editors, or four, counting Dr Schulte. In such circumstances it will not be a surprise that our translator, Mr Peter Winslow, has had to show patience as well as persistence in the exceptionally difficult task of producing a colloquial, or rather epistolary, translation. We hope it has turned out well.

Siena, May 2018

People and Places

People

Rudolf von Alt (1812–1905) his daughter Louise presented Hermine with a female head painted by her father, an eminent Viennese painter best known for town- and landscapes.

Mima Bacher friend of Hermine's from a family associated with Karl Wittgenstein, who became an important member of the family; her first son, **Arvid Sjögren**, married Helene's youngest daughter Clara Salzer; her second son, **Talla**, married Marguerite Respinger, previously regarded as his fiancée by Ludwig.

Hermann Bahr (1863–1934) Austrian writer, playwright, director, and critic.

Adolf Busch (1891–1952) violinist of international fame.

Eugen D'Albert (1864–1932) pianist and composer.

Michael Drobil (1877–1958) academic sculptor and member of the Wiener Secession, another of the close friends made by Wittgenstein as prisoner of war.

Paul Engelmann (1891–1965) architect and student of Adolf Loos, thanks to whom Ludwig met him when he went to the artillery school in Olmütz in 1916, Engelmann remained a devoted disciple. Emigrated to Palestine in the 1930s.

Ludwig von Ficker (1880–1967) editor and publisher of the cultural magazine *Der Brenner*.

Marie Fillunger (1850–1930) Austrian singer, a frequent guest at the Wittgenstein's home. Recommended by Johannes Brahms, she was a friend of the Schumann family and in particular the companion of Eugenie Schumann.

Gottlob Frege (1848–1925) the German mathematician and philosopher, whom Wittgenstein considered his chief inspiration.

Ernst Geiger (1912–1970) student of Ludwig's in Puchberg until 1924; he remained a protégé of the Wittgenstein siblings for a long time and gave them more than just typical difficulties, until finally good relations were established.

Ludwig Grodzinsky an ordnance officer, Wittgenstein's superior in Krakow in 1914.

Anton Groller (d. 1945) administrator for the family, especially valued during their 1938–9 troubles.

Hermann Hänsel son of Ludwig Hänsel, often advised by the Wittgenstein family. He became an eminent forest scientist.

Ludwig Hänsel one of three close friends that Wittgenstein made when a prisoner of war in Cassino, he became director of a Gymnasium. Wittgenstein often stayed with his family.

Hugo Heller (1870–1923) book dealer, organized numerous readings and concerts.

Rudolf Koder (1902–1977) elementary school teacher, and later school director, whom Ludwig met in Puchberg. Koder became a life-long friend of Ludwig's and indeed of the entire family.

Josef Labor (1842–1924) Bohemian composer, organist and family friend of the Wittgensteins, who was blind from birth and lived in Vienna from 1868 until his death in 1924.

Helene Lecher (1965–1929) a friend of Hermine's who directed a day-care refuge for malnourished and ailing children.

Rosine Menzel (ca. 1863–1920) accompanist, friend of both Labor and the Wittgensteins.

Johannes Müller (1864–1949) evangelical religious writer.

Moritz Nähr (1859–1945) family friend and family photographer.

Julie von Paic housekeeper and daughter of a Serbian general.

Ellen Pinsent (1866–1949) mother of Ludwig's friend David Pinsent, prominent in mental health reform.

Louise Pollitzer family friend. Because of her Jewish ancestry, she went to America – with Gretl's help – during the Nazi period.

Heinrich Postl from Puchberg am Schneeberg, where he played music with both Ludwig and Koder, was part of the Wittgenstein and Stonborough families' domestic staff from 1928 to 1971.

F.P. Ramsey (1903–1930) many-sided mathematician, logician and philosopher, the original translator of Ludwig's *Tractatus*. Later, in September 1923, he visited Puchberg for two weeks to discuss the ideas of the book.

Marie Röger-Soldat (1863–1955) and **Marie Baumayer (1851–1931)** were musical friends of the house, a violinist and pianist respectively. Both were admired and counselled by Brahms and Clara Schumann.

Bertrand Russell (1872–1970) the British philosopher, Wittgenstein's first teacher at Cambridge from 1912.

Mitze Salzer a relation of Ludwig's brother-in-law Max Salzer and a close friend of Hermine's.

Fräulein Staake (d. 1945) Pianist, who frequently came to the Wittgenstein family home to play duets with members of the family.

Elsa Stradal (d. 1945) a singer with whom Wittgenstein's mother played music.

Max Veilchenfeld and **Wilhelm Kux** bank directors and former colleagues of Karl Wittgenstein.

Places

Alleegasse

A street in the fourth district of Vienna, renamed Argentinierstrasse after 1921, but the family continued to use the old name. Number 16 was an impressive nineteenth-century town house, purchased by Karl Wittgenstein. It was inherited by Hermine and Paul but remained the centre of family activities and used for their musical recitals.

Hochreit

A large country estate in Lower Austria purchased by Karl Wittgenstein. It was inherited by Hermine, though Helena and her family became co-proprietors. There was a large stone house and a number of frame houses as well as much accommodation for estate workers.

Innsbruck

Home to Ludwig von Ficker, publisher of the magazine *Der Brenner*, now also of the Brenner Archive.

Kundmanngasse

A street in the third district of Vienna where Margaret Wittgenstein purchased an entire city block, in which Ludwig and his friend Paul Engelmann built for her a modern house planned to the last detail.

Neuwaldegg

A district, outside Vienna at the time, where Karl Wittgenstein purchased and adapted a villa for between seasons use. Its park rose sharply from the road and stretched into the Vienna woods, Ludwig was born in the house in 1889 and in 1914 he there met Ludwig von Ficker.

Olmütz

An historic town in Moravia, at this time largely German in population, seat of an archbishopric. Ludwig came here to train as an artillery officer in 1916 and met a group, largely Jewish, of culturally and intellectually interested young men who had an important influence on his development. One of them was Paul Engelmann.

Otterthal

A village in Lower Austria, where Ludwig was school master for two years.

Puchberg

First of the Lower Austria villages in which Ludwig taught. Here he met Rudolph Koder and Fr. Neururer.

Trattenbach

A village in Lower Austria, where Ludwig was school master for two years.

The House of Wittgenstein

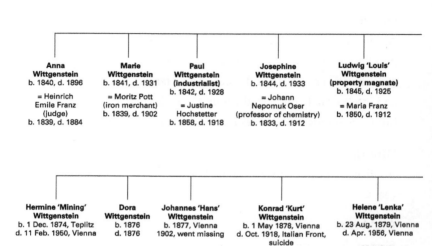

| Anna Wittgenstein b. 1840, d. 1896 = Heinrich Emile Franz (judge) b. 1839, d. 1884 | Marie Wittgenstein b. 1841, d. 1931 = Moritz Pott (iron merchant) b. 1839, d. 1902 | Paul Wittgenstein (industrialist) b. 1842, d. 1928 = Justine Hochstetter b. 1858, d. 1918 | Josephine Wittgenstein b. 1844, d. 1933 = Johann Nepomuk Oser (professor of chemistry) b. 1833, d. 1912 | Ludwig 'Louis' Wittgenstein (property magnate) b. 1845, d. 1925 = Maria Franz b. 1850, d. 1912 |

| Hermine 'Mining' Wittgenstein b. 1 Dec. 1874, Teplitz d. 11 Feb. 1950, Vienna | Dora Wittgenstein b. 1876 d. 1876 | Johannes 'Hans' Wittgenstein b. 1877, Vienna 1902, went missing | Konrad 'Kurt' Wittgenstein b. 1 May 1878, Vienna d. Oct. 1918, Italian Front, suicide | Helene 'Lenka' Wittgenstein b. 23 Aug. 1879, Vienna d. Apr. 1956, Vienna = Max Salzer (government official) b. 3 Mar. 1868, Vienna d. 28 Apr. 1941, Vienna |

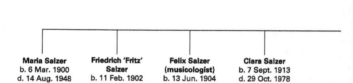

| Maria Salzer b. 6 Mar. 1900 d. 14 Aug. 1948 | Friedrich 'Fritz' Salzer b. 11 Feb. 1902 d. 22 Jul. 1922 | Felix Salzer (musicologist) b. 13 Jun. 1904 d. 12 Aug. 1986 | Clara Salzer b. 7 Sept. 1913 d. 29 Oct. 1978 = Arvid Sjögren |

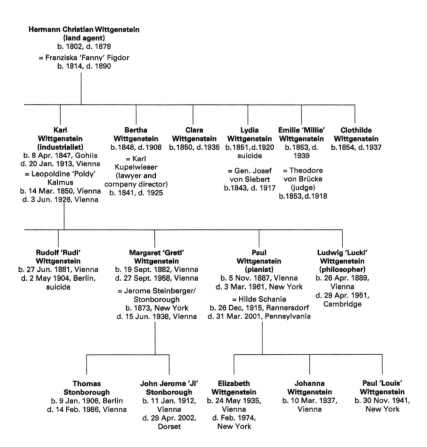

Hermann Christian Wittgenstein
(land agent)
b. 1802, d. 1878

= Franziska 'Fanny' Figdor
b. 1814, d. 1890

Karl Wittgenstein
(industrialist)
b. 8 Apr. 1847, Gohlis
d. 20 Jan. 1913, Vienna
= Leopoldine 'Poldy' Kalmus
b. 14 Mar. 1850, Vienna
d. 3 Jun. 1926, Vienna

Bertha Wittgenstein
b. 1848, d. 1908
= Karl Kupelwieser
(lawyer and company director)
b. 1841, d. 1925

Clara Wittgenstein
b. 1850, d. 1935

Lydia Wittgenstein
b. 1851, d. 1920
suicide
= Gen. Josef von Siebert
b. 1843, d. 1917

Emilie 'Millie' Wittgenstein
b. 1853, d. 1939
= Theodore von Brücke
(judge)
b. 1853, d. 1918

Clothilde Wittgenstein
b. 1854, d. 1937

Rudolf 'Rudi' Wittgenstein
b. 27 Jun. 1881, Vienna
d. 2 May 1904, Berlin, suicide

Margaret 'Gretl' Wittgenstein
b. 19 Sept. 1882, Vienna
d. 27 Sept. 1958, Vienna
= Jerome Steinberger/ Stonborough
b. 1873, New York
d. 15 Jun. 1938, Vienna

Paul Wittgenstein
(pianist)
b. 5 Nov. 1887, Vienna
d. 3 Mar. 1961, New York
= Hilde Schania
b. 26 Dec, 1915, Rannersdorf
d. 31 Mar. 2001, Pennsylvania

Ludwig 'Lucki' Wittgenstein
(philosopher)
b. 26 Apr. 1889, Vienna
d. 29 Apr. 1951, Cambridge

Thomas Stonborough
b. 9 Jan. 1906, Berlin
d. 14 Feb. 1986, Vienna

John Jerome 'Ji' Stonborough
b. 11 Jan. 1912, Vienna
d. 29 Apr. 2002, Dorset

Elizabeth Wittgenstein
b. 24 May 1935, Vienna
d. Feb. 1974, New York

Johanna Wittgenstein
b. 10 Mar. 1937, Vienna

Paul 'Louis' Wittgenstein
b. 30 Nov. 1941, New York

Introduction

BRIAN McGUINNESS

The Wittgensteins were a family that might well have figured in one of the nineteenth century sagas they read, modelled themselves on, quoted and recommended. They were a family that, because of their wealth and self-confidence, were able to create their own world, their own support-system, their own values – persons of every degree, artists, musicians, students, friends and associates of every kind were invited, protected, employed, subsidized, absorbed. Wittgenstein brought his friends into the family and they usually became the friends and protégés of everyone – Paul Engelmann, the architect; Ludwig Hänsel, the friend Wittgenstein made as a prisoner of war; Rudolf Koder, the lifelong friend Wittgenstein met as a school teacher – they all became friends of the family. He found friends there too and at least once, in Marguerite Respinger, a sweetheart. This is what he was – not a follower of any one creed but a Wittgenstein.

There he found and helped to create the ethos of always doing the hard thing, the intolerance of anything perceived as moral weakness, strongest when a close relative was involved. 'The older generation', one of his nephews told me, 'didn't stop short of the other person's conscience.' Potential weakness might be recognized, but they were slow to think that laying a person's faults clear would not be sufficient to make him amend them. Such were Margaret

Stonborough's or, to use Ludwig's name for her, Gretl's dressings down of her brother Paul, and no doubt of many others. And at the end, when a person had to be broken with because he had done the easy thing – the comfortable, the self-interested, sometimes merely the obvious thing – there was a certain attitude of 'Ah well . . .'.

A severe world then, with a sword over the gate, but an Eden none the less, marked by warmth and love and confidence: these were the positive aspects of the candour that sometimes wounded. And all seemed, was made to seem, unforced and natural. It was a rarefied moral universe, but much else as well, and those taken into it were usually captivated immediately. How many became admirers, like Frank Ramsey, of Gretl; how many found on the Hochreith, the family's country estate, a hospitality reminiscent of Victorian times. In the same way a chance meeting with Wittgenstein on a train would convince Gilbert Pattisson that he had met an extraordinary man. Pattisson later became a constant companion on holidays and managed Ludwig's modest finances.

The moral basis of this universe was not distinct from the intellectual, the cultural, the artistic. Taste was not second to, but integral with, the moral sense. Pictures, furniture, drawing, and, above all, music were expressions of a single ideal. Drawing could be honest, pictures ethical, the piano could be played with due restraint, the furnishing of a house could do one good. But intellectually strenuous too. Some rational occupation was required and conversation could be exacting. From childhood there had always been intellectual pursuits, psychological games, a simple code, theatricals often self-composed, exchange of reading, passages marked for special attention. Most of these have left their traces in Wittgenstein's philosophical examples, his diary and, as we see here, in correspondence with his family.

Seated centre Helene, to her (stage-) left Gretl, at her feet children Ji and Clara © The Stonborough Family.

Descriptions of this world have been given by Karl Menger in his memoirs,[1] and by Engelmann too.[2] Respinger describes for her grandchildren both the marvels she found in it and the demands it made on her – a fairy-tale setting of splendours and miseries, boxes at the opera, animated gatherings, jewels, recitals, buffets, with on the other hand good works among the hopeless poor of Vienna and serious walks with the compelling figure of our Wittgenstein, tweed-jacketed and open-necked whatever the occasion.[3] Cecilia Sjögren relates the family's relation to music and the arts.[4] Wittgenstein's

[1] Karl Menger, *Reminiscences of the Vienna Circle*, Dordrecht and Boston, Kluwer, 1994.

[2] Paul Engelmann, *Letters from Ludwig Wittgenstein with a Memoir*, Oxford, Basil Blackwell, 1967.

[3] Marguerite Sjögren, *Granny et son temps*, privately printed, Neufchatel, 1982.

[4] Cecilia Sjögren, 'Die Familie' in *Wittgenstein: Biographie, Philosophie, Praxis*, Secession Exhibition Catalogue, Vienna, 1989, pp. 98–117.

building of a house for Gretl (in many respects a joint project with her) has been analysed in detail by Paul Wijdeveld.[5] The structure of the clientele illumined by the correspondence between members of the family and Ludwig Hänsel.[6]

Ludwig Wittgenstein

There can be no doubt then that the Wittgenstein who twice came to a rather sceptical Cambridge to work could say with the hero,

> I am come not from darkness and suffering,
> but from splendour and delight

but like that hero he brought with him problems enough for his hosts and for himself. For he carried everywhere with him the preoccupations of the moral universe sketched above. His rejection of some features of it – the renunciation of his fortune, his wish at times not to be identified as a member of a rich and powerful family – in a sense resembled his because they stemmed, paradoxically, from his determination to make his own world and in particular to forge his own character. In a yet fuller sense than his father he was to be a 'self-made man'.[7] We see this in his determination to root out real or

---

[5] Paul Wijdeveld, *Ludwig Wittgenstein: Architect*, London and New York, Thames and Hudson, 1994.

[6] *Ludwig Wittgenstein–Ludwig Hänsel: Eine Freundschaft*, ed. Ilse Somavilla and others, Innsbruck, Haymon-Verlag, 1994. The replies by Hänsel have been pruned of what was thought embarrassing.

[7] Karl Wittgenstein's essays (reprinted in *Politico-Economic Writings*, ed. J. C. Nyíri, Amsterdam/Philadelphia, John Benjamins, 1984) show this to have been his ideal, largely fulfilled, though family connections and at times family investments (amply repaid) were the springboard. Much the same is true of his father, Hermann Christian, who made a like claim.

imagined defects of character – cowardice, laziness, tendency to take refuge in lies. 'Cambridge is bad for many people because it is airless,' he told pupils or followers, 'but I produce my own oxygen.' He assembled his own court: 'Good human beings are what I collect' he told one protégé, in which project he was sometimes, though of course not always, successful.[8]

This programme gives sense to his exclamation, 'Of course I want to be perfect!', gives sense also to the rules for the minutiae of life in his circle as well as to the agonizing over major decisions.[9] Here is the true locus outside philosophy for the construction of language-games, of imagined activities and for the rejection of private language.

From such a programme, paradoxes and failures were inseparable. An obvious one is that he often felt forced to retreat into isolation. More generally, the insistence on naturalness led almost inevitably to occasional artificiality, insincerity, exaggeration. Naturalness is the hardest of qualities to force. Thus he created for himself the figure of Wittgenstein the teetotaller, the old maid, the virgin, the shunner of great houses. It was alleviated of course by a frequent self-disparagement and by his obvious familiarity with the grander life that he rejected.

Severity, as with himself, so with his disciples and friends, was not to be avoided. One pupil, after a particularly hard struggle, wrote, 'I'm tired of his going about laying down the moral law . . . And yet there is a very great deal in him to love.'[10] Everyone realized that these aspects were indivisible. The earnestness was an essential part of his charm.

---

[8] Gretl even said: 'All Lucki's swans are geese.' But then finding swans was not the point.

[9] In his own family, for example, they ranged from problems about how to organize their Christmas celebrations to the proper reaction to the Nazi occupation.

[10] Alice Ambrose, *Wittgenstein in Cambridge*, ed. B. McGuiness, Chichester, Wiley-Blackwell, 2012, p. 242.

Christmas in the Alleegasse, Ludwig the sole diner in informal dress.

Was he happy? This is perhaps the wrong question to ask. There is not a standard happiness against which his life can be measured. He himself asked in his First World War notebooks whether we have any more right to wish a person happiness than to wish him misfortune: the most we can say is, Live happily! – which in context means something like, Live your life with the right attitude![11] Happiness, on this view, is not something found in life but something put into it. After the First World War it was his own life he was insisting on living. His last words, 'Tell them I've had a wonderful life', are also puzzling only if we ignore this conviction of his.

---

[11] Entry for 29 July 1916 (L. Wittgenstein, *Notebooks 1914–1916* (really 1914–1917), Oxford, Blackwell, 1961, 1979, p. 78:

> It is generally assumed that it is bad to wish another unhappiness. Can that be right? Can it be worse than to wish him happiness?
> It all seems to depend, so to speak, on *how* one wishes.
> It seems one can't say more than, Live happily!

The Wittgenstein Family: Karl and Leopoldine and the brothers

The letters published here give some idea of the resemblances within the family but also of the differences. These differences are evident even in the account, on the whole defensive and celebratory, given by his sister Hermine in her *Family Memories*[12] written in 1948, in the Vienna of *The Third Man*, when a renaissance of Austria could only dimly be foreseen. She gave much space to an earlier generation, the eleven children born in the mid-nineteenth century to Hermann Wittgenstein and Fanny Figdor. The most successful of these, though perhaps the most difficult in his youth, was the father of the generation we are concerned with, the steel magnate Karl. Karl's children too were remarkable, especially the youngest two, Paul and Ludwig, musician and philosopher respectively, for whom the family is chiefly remembered today. The correspondence between them is published here for the first time in English while a selection from that with the sisters appeared in an earlier German edition.

Three other sons died in or before the First World War. The mother of all of them was Leopoldine Kalmus – among the consorts of the siblings the only Catholic and the only one with some Jewish ancestry (a point of adventitious importance at a later stage). Above all she was a person of exquisite, even excessive, sensibility, great musicality, complete impracticality and (apparently) total subjection to her omnicompetent and most affectionate husband. The model proposed for the daughters was, for its time and when kept within rational bounds, possible to follow, but it was not easy to be a son of theirs.[13]

---

[12] Published in German containing much material about the family, ed. I. Somavilla, 2014. For a general account of the family see my *Young Ludwig*, Oxford, Clarendon Press, 2005 (a re-issue), Chapter 1.

[13] The two sides of this heritage, as it affected Ludwig, are adumbrated in my *Approaches to Wittgenstein*, London, Routledge, 2002, pp. 160ff.

Two suicides by the elder sons at the beginning of the century showed this – Johannes, a potential musical genius, recognized as such by Brahms, and Rudolf, a chemistry student in Berlin, who modelled his death on Otto Weininger's. A third suicide followed at the end of the war and was always attributed to motives of honour – Kurt's Hungarian troops would not follow orders, but there are indications in wartime correspondence, when he was detained in the United States on business, of concern about his stability: he is still the same, as childish as ever, says his mother. She feared that he might feel slighted at the end of the war if his brothers had served (in fact they had been wounded and maimed) and he not. She was relieved that he returned in time to go the Front – such were mothers in that war; such at any rate was she.[14] So the light-hearted Kurt, who played so engagingly in their four-handed musical evenings, died, for all we can see, pointlessly.

It seems that their father imposed expectations that these sons could neither meet nor reject and that their mother, while not opposing these, imposed conflicting ones of her own. Specifically Karl wanted his sons to follow a technical profession, but more generally his example required that they be capable of some considerable achievement. Paul says that Ludwig alone had the technical abilities of their father and we can see that only Paul and Ludwig matched the father in achievement. Perhaps they matched him in strength of character too. Like the father both were relatively undistinguished, at times even unsatisfactory pupils, as children but then rapidly acquired, almost for themselves, the knowledge and abilities that they decided they required.

---

[14] The mother's correspondence with Ludwig can be read in Ludwig Wittgenstein, *Gesamtbriefwechsel*, Innsbruck Electronic Edition, 2005 in the 'Past Masters' series of InteLex. References to Kurt can easily be found there, but see also the further footnote on Kurt below.

Like the father both at times went through enormous struggles – Karl when he ran away from home to America, Paul when he lost his arm and yet determined to continue his career as a pianist. Ludwig struggled all his life both from the elusiveness, the extreme difficulty, of his subject matter and from the torments which his own temperament and conscience inflicted on him: there is a well-known story of Bertrand Russell's, who, seeing him deeply distressed, asked him whether he was thinking about logic or his sins – 'both!' was the reply.[15] Paul seems to have suppressed inward conflicts more successfully, at any rate Ludwig's occasional reminiscences represent his brother as the stronger character in childhood, while in himself Ludwig in retrospect found cowardice, laziness,[16] and a tendency to lie. During their war service both brothers exhibited a courage or recklessness in battle that amazed their comrades. With these qualities there went a degree of ability that brought each brother extraordinary professional success at an early age: less happy than their father but in other respects like him.

The sisters: Hermine, Margaret ('Gretl') and Helene

Their sisters had other functions, domestic, charitable and the care of their protégés – that is why it was so important later to avoid exile. Twice it could not be avoided for the most active of them, Margaret Stonborough, and she suffered enormously under it. Her place was in

---

[15] See *Young Ludwig*, p. 156.

[16] In one of his most confessional notebooks Ludwig says: 'I completely understand the mental state of my brother Kurt: it was yet more indolent, but only marginally so, than my own', 183, p. 125, 2 November 1931. Kurt also occurs significantly in a dream about faint-heartedness and Jewishness (MS 107, p. 220, 12.1.1930) which has been the subject of oneiromancy (see J. C. Nyíri, *Tradition and Individuality*, Dordrecht, Springer, 1992).

her jewel box of a house, built for her by Ludwig, where she could manage the outer and inner lives of those that depended on her. Her public life, pleading for Austria in the famine after the First World War, was a brief one: it showed what she was capable of, not what she wanted to do. Her studies of science and mathematics, much marvelled at in the family, were also indications of potential, but of a potential somehow designed not to be fulfilled. She said of herself that she would like to be known as the daughter of her father, the sister of her brothers and the mother of her sons.[17] For all her intelligence and culture she remained an amateur, a patroness, an inspiration (to Freud, for one) and, at her best, in Wordsworth's words, 'A perfect woman, nobly planned, / To warn, to comfort, and command.' The last of these functions appears to some extent in her management of the affairs of the others and can be seen in the correspondence, though we have had to omit her erratic steering of the tergiversations of Ludwig's intended and idealized bride. Her sisters certainly gave her credit for a good heart behind her 'strong language and low necklines'.[18]

The differing expectations for male and female make themselves apparent after 1918 in the private and public lives of the two surviving brothers and in the style of life of the sisters. Desmond Lee, a friend sent by Ludwig, found the hospitality on the Hochreith reminiscent of the Victorian age. Another friend Ludwig deliberately did not send, telling him that the sisters would be *too* kind and hospitable and obliging. A man of the family would be expected to have perfect manners, those of another age. Paul's nephew John Stonborough learnt much from him – the correctness of returning to hear the other

---

[17] See the report and judgement of Karl Menger in *Reminiscences of the Vienna Circle*, pp. 78ff.

[18] Unpublished letter from Hermine to Helene. There is an interesting account of Margaret in Ursula Prokop, *Margaret Stonborough Wittgenstein*, Vienna, Böhlau, 2003, though her perspective is a bit different from that adopted here. See especially p. 84.

*Margaret, 1920s © The Stonborough Portrait of Hermine © The Stonborough
Family.   Family.*

performers at a recital where he was the star. Pupils in New York and
Vienna also noticed it: if occasionally brusque in his reactions 'he
would apologize profusely when he discovered that he had offended'[19]
and this no doubt led John Barchilon to call his avowedly fictional
biography 'The Crown Prince'. In private a man was almost expected
to be someone for whose whims allowance had to be made. It can be
no accident that Margaret Stonborough's husband, Jerome, and elder
son, Thomas, were in the same tradition.

When Hermine shared the Alleegasse house with Paul, she had
difficulty in dealing with his aversion to some of her guests. Still, the
sisters felt it would have been even worse with Kurt: Ludwig (some of
his English friends would have been surprised to learn) was the easiest
to get on with. He had his own foibles, of course, and insisted on his

---

[19] Testimony of a colleague, recorded in E. Fred Flindell, 'Paul Wittgenstein (1887–1961):
Patron and Pianist', *Musical Review* xxxii (1971), 107, a fine account of Paul's teaching and
of many aspects of his life in music.

eccentricity – an army jacket and no tie at a formal dinner or in the Opera. But there was a deeper level – Ludwig had escaped: he would stay in lodgings or with friends. This was in the early twenties, but in fact his flight continued for the rest of his life. He had interiorized the values of the mother as well as those of the father but resented them. He found the loving graciousness stifling. He relinquished his inheritance in favour of the others and determined to make his living as a village school master. Other professions, alternating with humbler occupations, followed. Looking back in 1934 he says, 'If everything in a household is in order, then the members of the family sit down to breakfast together and have similar habits and so on. But if there's a terrible illness in the house, then everybody is in search of help and thinks of a different way out and totally contrasting tendencies can easily make their appearance. Paul and I, for example.'[20]

The surviving brothers: Paul and Ludwig

Paul lived on in the Alleegasse but his career and his emotional life were elsewhere and, except in an emergency, shut off from the others. With Ludwig he maintained a brotherly relation until the Second World War. Of course, each pair of siblings interacted according to what they had most in common – Ludwig discussed religious matters (Tolstoy and Dostoevsky) with Hermine, dreams and psychological questions with Margaret, while with Helene he exchanged the rather simple jokes that he favoured. Paul's own relations with his sisters we know little about and they may have been more strained. The relation between the two brothers had, it seems to me, spontaneity, without a shadow of dutifulness or formality.

---

[20] From MS 157a f.25v., notes written during a stay in Norway. The remark is no doubt intended as an echo of the opening of *Anna Karenina*.

Ludwig and Paul © Cambridge Archive.

Paul was the elder by two years and always the more practical and worldly wise. He would tell Ludwig how to deal with the High Command when he wanted to change his position during the war. He would explain how impossible it was for Ludwig, even in a mountain village of Lower Austria, to conceal his membership of their well-known family, just as he had told him when they were children that it was impossible to conceal their Jewish descent in order to get into a gymnastic club. All this without any condescension. Ludwig perhaps took the lead when it was a matter of personal relations within the family, explaining very rationally to Paul why he should not take offence at what seemed to him a grudging invitation to perform for the others.[21] But otherwise there was an exchange between equals. Ludwig would send Paul friends or old comrades for practical help, just as Paul would ask Ludwig for information on comrades when he

---

[21] See Letter 110. For another example of Ludwig's peace-making within the family see Prokop's *Margaret Stonborough Wittgenstein*, p. 199.

needed it. Paul showed especial kindness to Ludwig's friend and younger colleague Koder, offering piano lessons and introducing him to the world in other ways, even buying him a dinner jacket.

When, after his teacher training in Vienna, Ludwig went to live in the first of his villages, Paul provided support in an unobtrusive way, packages of food and the like. Paul seems to have been fairly sure of being welcome – he offers to come over and play a particular piece of music – whereas Hermine had great difficulty in obtaining an invitation. Paul sometimes walked across from the Hochreith with a book in his pocket, which he meant to read to Ludwig. During a later eremitical period in Ludwig's life Paul would send blankets, dried pea soup, chocolate – whatever was required – to Norway. Ludwig protested, but mildly, at this practical charity, which came wrapped in good-natured humour (see Letter 67).[22]

Ludwig as school master.

---

[22] See Letters 44 and 67.

Literature was one bond for these two. Paul loved to quote the German classics: it is an indication of common tastes that, to soften some advice to Ludwig, he said, 'It is physic not poison that I offer you', a quotation from *Nathan the Wise* – just when (though he can hardly have known this) Ludwig was reading the same play. That Paul read to Ludwig we know only from the letter quoted above, but it is of a piece with Ludwig's reading Johann Peter Hebbel to the young people when convalescing in Gretl's palatial rented apartment, and reading Wilhelm Busch or Rabindranath Tagore to the bemused philosophers of the Vienna Circle.[23]

Music

The brothers shared their reading as they shared their music, all in the family manner. A letter from the end of 1934 indicates the sort of conversations that they will have had. Paul refers to Hebbel's *The Nibelungs*, comparing it unfavourably with Wagner's treatment of the same subject. Ludwig, almost never a friend of Wagner's, takes the other side. His reasoning is in part wrong-headed and unfair to Wagner but in general perceptive and provocative and in the style that was brought out in him by conversations with valued friends – for instance Piero Sraffa, the Italian economist, in many ways his equal in originality and power of getting to the roots of any problem, or Engelmann. In his family it was his brother that could best elicit such talk. Paul had what Ludwig needed in an interlocutor, a brisk intelligence and a slashing style, the latter mirrored in an impetuous German cursive hand, a hand, by the way, such as none of his carefully

---

[23] Marguerite Sjögren (previously Respinger), *Granny et son temps*, in 'A la Baconnière', 1982, p. 100, writes of hearing '*la poésie de mon pays alémanique lue avec une compréhension profonde*'. *Galeotto fu il libro e chi lo scrisse*, for this was the beginning of an intense and tortured relationship. ('The book and its author were pandars to us' as Dante's Francesca says.)

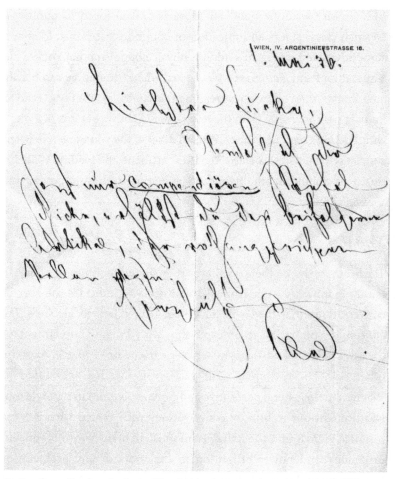

Letter from Paul to Ludwig, illustrating his use of Kurrentschrift [German cursive] © The Brenner-Archiv.

westernized brothers and sisters used. His literary style recalls that of his father, whose essays on economic matters and practical politics show contempt for amateur and professor alike.[24]

---

[24] Reprinted as Karl Wittgenstein, *Politico-Economic Writings*, ed. J. C. Nyíri, Amsterdam/ Philadelphia, John Benjamins, 1984.

Music was all of Paul's life and half (as Ludwig himself said) of Ludwig's. It dominated family life and hospitality in the Alleegasse and would bring Ludwig back there when little else could. We find Paul writing to ask what he should prepare to play – four-, actually of course three-handed – when Ludwig came. These were not meant to be concerts, but concerts were also organized, usually for the music of Josef Labor, their 'house composer'. Nearly all Labor's compositions after 1915 were commissioned by Paul, and the composer's frequent use of the clarinet surely either influenced or was influenced by Ludwig's choice of that instrument for both relaxation and schoolwork.[25] His taste for Labor is of a piece with Ludwig's remark that his cultural ideal was not one of his own time but perhaps of the time of Schumann.[26]

Paul's playing was not always appreciated in his family. 'Does he have to pound the piano like that!' his mother is reported to have said, and in a letter from New York printed here we find Margaret describing his playing as a kind of violation. Hermine, in a rare animadversion on the father she idolized, wrote: 'the restless side of Papa, his tendency to excess, comes out in [Paul's] playing'.[27] It is all the more interesting then to have Ludwig's judgement, 'you are unwilling to lose yourself in and behind the composition: on the contrary, it's yourself that you want to present'.[28] Ludwig's seems for once a more objective view than that of his sisters and mother. The romantic virtuoso, trained as such, would in that period feel free to treat the music as Paul indeed treated the scores composed for him by contemporaries. Still it contributed to a certain alienation from the family.

---

[25] Certificates, however, show that Ludwig offered the violin as his instrument at the Teacher Training College.

[26] *Culture and Value*, Chicago University Press, 1989, p. 2.

[27] Hermine to Ludwig, 11 July 1918.

[28] From a letter of the 1920s. He might have been describing himself.

The red drawing room at number 16 Alleegasse, an impressive nineteenth century town house, the centre of family activities and used for their musical recitals.

The nonsense collection

A third major impersonal theme in the correspondence between the brothers was the detection of nonsense which they found principally in the press, increasingly in the new illustrated weeklies. They seem always to have exchanged examples of absurdity that they came across in reading or everyday life. We find similar exchanges in Ludwig's correspondence with Engelmann, who had earlier collected items for Karl Kraus to pillory. Ludwig in fact saved up those sent him by Paul and by others, and no doubt some he had come across for himself. He inspired pupils to find instances – as we see from letters of W. H. Watson and C. E. Stevenson and of course from his collection itself. At the end of his life he wrote to Sraffa,

Rhine is one of those people who would make me feel sceptical about the law of gravitation if he told me about it. He isn't quite concentrated enough, however, to be amusing. If you meet him, please tell him that, if he wants to get into my collection of nonsense, he'll have to compress his rubbish a little more. Still – one mustn't be ungrateful.[29]

This form of amusement has the advantage, but also the defect, that practically anything, taken solemnly lends itself to mockery, especially when a particular sentence or phrase can be picked out and underlined in red (such was Paul's practice). Still, some of the brothers' targets seem justified ones – the theme of a wrong or trivial tone dealing with what should be serious or even sacred matters is a common one in Ludwig's collection. Perhaps akin to that is Paul's disdain for the application of modern methods of publicity to music, the confusion of levels of seriousness – a film, a Lehár museum (as if Lehar were of any importance!) and the like. That would not be today's reaction. Paul mocks the gullibility of professors who take seriously the machinations of spiritualists – all swindlers, the brothers thought, for Ludwig replied in kind and sent a similar cutting with similar comments (he asked for it back, so we still have it). The medium seemed very happy, says the report, but Ludwig comments, 'She must have been trying very hard not to laugh!'[30] Neither brother gives any credence to the thought that sometimes the very absurdity of the results reached is evidence that they are genuine, not the reverse.[31]

---

[29] Letter to Sraffa, 14 October 1950, *Wittgenstein in Cambridge*, p. 468. The Collection consists of some 127 items and is being worked on in the Brenner-Archiv, Innsbruck, where it is now housed. A provisional Digest was prepared by myself and Anna Coda Nunziante.

[30] Ludwig's comment on another piece of nonsense exchanged with his brother.

[31] A point made by Hans Hahn of the Vienna Circle, see Karl Menger, *Reminiscences of the Vienna Circle*, p. 59. Ludwig was informed of these discussions in the Circle.

This mixture of sardonic pleasure and intellectual concern appears particularly in relation to one of Ludwig's bugbears – Einstein (now sainted) – whose propensity for clowning they perhaps considered an affront to intellectual work. Is it part of the same phenomenon that Ludwig was particularly enraged or amused by pronouncements on general matters by scientists? They should have stuck to their last! Particularly bad was the thinking that led to a statue of Einstein's being included among those that surrounded the main portal of the Cathedral of St John the Divine in New York. 'As always, when I see the worst, I think of you' wrote Paul, who sent the cutting. No doubt it was to this that Ludwig replied, 'When I saw the picture with Einstein, I said out loud to myself, "It's not possible!" Unfortunately I have no one here who can really appreciate that and a joy unshared is only half a joy.'

The family split: 1938 to 1950

In 1938 Austria was annexed and Karl's children found themselves classified as Jewish under the Nuremberg laws since they had only one clearly non-Jewish grandparent.[32] Helene's children and the wider family of cousins were all relatively safe, since their Jewish ancestry had been diluted by marriage. From that period we have in Ludwig's Collection of Nonsense (which was far from being entirely comical) an issue of *Der Stürmer*, the Nazi anti-Semitic weekly, from April 1938. I suppose it to have been sent by Paul, a warning as well as an absurdity. The front-page article is 'Was Christ a Jew?', part of whose argument is that it was impossible for the Jewish race to have produced a spiritual hero, a giant in courage, devotion to truth, intelligence and knowledge of the world such as Christ had been. How could a Jew have instituted doctrines that would maintain their hold on the

---

[32] Their maternal grandmother, so that they would not have qualified as Jews from an Halachic point of view. The other grandparents were Protestant or Catholic converts.

Nordic peoples for two thousand years? It is a bitter irony that the wider Wittgenstein family were forced to use a similar logic, to argue that the Wittgenstein siblings of the nineteenth century were of such distinguished appearance that they could not possibly have been the offspring of full Jews, nor indeed could their father. This was part of the petition that Ludwig mentions in the letter to Paul of March that year: he is sure that it is right for those that are making it and he is content that they should refer also to his service and decorations in the First World War, but he does not want it to appear as if he were joining in the application on his own account.[33] The petition was eventually presented and approved, but only after considerable financial concessions had been made to the Reichsbank by the children of Karl and their trustees.

This brings us to an era and a chain of events that put under strain the personal relation between the brothers. The affection between them was usually implicit in their 'with love as ever' sign-offs or in some half-dissimulated act of kindness. Only once that we know of, when Ludwig was off in some village and all were concerned about his stability, did Paul permit himself some expression of concern, which led Ludwig to say 'from a *naiveté* that does you credit, you have no idea of how completely governed I am by the basest and commonest of motives. I am a lost being and quite unworthy of your love, unless some miracle should save me. Say no more!'[34] When a judgement

---

[33] Paul originally supported the idea of including an account of all the achievements of the family, including their war service (so says Hermine in her *Familienerinnerungen*, ed. Ilse Somavilla, Innsbruck/Vienna, Haymon, 2015), but the actual petition refers more specifically to appearance – '*arisches Aussehen*' – and to the fact that of the eleven siblings only one married a partner with Jewish ancestry (this is a reference to Karl's marrying Leopoldine, whose father (only) was from a Jewish family). One such inter-racial marriage was a small proportion in the Vienna of those days, or so the petition alleges.

[34] Undated letter from Ludwig to Paul, which goes on to ask a musical question and ends with the postscript: 'I'm extremely well!'

regarding Paul had to be made, Ludwig seems to have been (as in the case of Paul's piano playing) more understanding than the sisters.

A particular instance was the emergency mentioned above when Paul's private life impinged on the family. His lover was brought into the Alleegasse house and died there of cancer, cared for by all, but especially by Margaret. Hermine was doubtful whether he knew how much he had lost and sad that it had not brought him nearer to Margaret. Ludwig from England dismissed these ideas, rightly or wrongly, but it was an outburst of loyalty: 'I was well aware that dear Paul would lose much in Bassia. Why do you say that he and Gretl haven't drawn any closer to one another? Certainly they have!'[35] Later, when Ludwig was again in one of his black moods, the thought of Paul would often occur to him. Naturally enough he featured in a sketch for a confession or autobiography, because they had shared so much in their first years. Ludwig once dreamt that Paul and his sisters had admired his musical ability and woke up regretting his own vanity. Other times he would dream that Paul or one of the sisters had died. The passage, now in *Philosophical Investigations* Section 40, 'When Mr N.N. dies, one says that the bearer, not the meaning, of the name dies', originally read '*Wenn Paul stirbt . . .*' and was written about the time of the dream. 'Paul' is in fact the commonest Christian name used, for examples or otherwise, in the manuscript works.

The attempts of Paul and the others to avoid being classified as Jews had not matured when, in late June 1938, the Nazi authorities, by then in power in Austria, deprived most Jews – musicians, lawyers or teachers in particular – of the right to exercise a profession. Ludwig's letter to Paul of 7 July is a simple expression of solidarity, 'Just a line to say, what is obvious, that my thoughts are of you.' The measures were a body blow to Paul, who could not practice as a professor of the piano

---

[35] Letter 137.

or even go for his long walks. He emigrated shortly afterwards, settling in the United States. The negotiations to obtain a favourable racial status for the sisters, who wished to remain in Austria, led to bitter recriminations between Paul and them and especially one of Margaret's sons, John, who became involved. Margaret and her sons were American citizens and not directly affected by the decrees. Paul thought at first that the sisters too should emigrate, later that the financial demands of the Reichsbank (which were implicitly a necessary condition for the issue of the racial certificate required) should be held to a minimum – a tactic which, the others thought, risked the worst for them and which, while it may have been correct, was obviously in his own interest, always a fatal consideration where the Wittgensteins were concerned. Ludwig, once again the peacemaker, went to New York in July 1939 to try to reach an understanding, but this was viewed by Paul as a further attempt to put pressure on him. Ludwig was greeted, as his liner docked, by a letter from a lawyer, in whose hands Paul had left the whole matter and whom Ludwig must see before he could talk with Paul. His only comment on their eventual, fruitless and last meeting was, 'Paul is a poor devil!' Back in Europe the negotiations were concluded successfully a few days before the war broke out, so both sides could claim some justification. I will let other pens dwell on this story:[36] there is much that we do not know and much that was forced on the parties by a cruelly calculated system of blackmail. The almost predetermined ramification of a deep family disagreement renders ridiculous any attempt at a judicious account. We can perhaps do no more than record some of their reactions for the light they throw on the deeper dynamics of the group.

---

[36] It is succinctly told in Mrs Prokop's volume. I do not understand why she thinks that Paul and Ludwig were opposed to the application discussed above, but views may have changed over time. (pp. 231ff.).

Margaret, like Paul, remained throughout the war in New York but she had only indirect contact with him. Business arrangements were managed, if not amicably at least satisfactorily, by lawyers. Paul helped with the support of Jewish friends of the family brought out from Europe and seems to have made no difficulty about the sale of manuscripts and works of art necessary for present or future needs of the family in exile or in Austria. Inevitably the financial details now escape us, partly no doubt because they were at the time meant to escape the authorities. Ludwig played his part – keeping some valuable manuscripts in his Cambridge bank and offering Sraffa's advice on their sale. The family little knew what an adept of the rare books market Sraffa was. But there were no actual meetings. It astonished Margaret that Paul had broken with Ludwig and she seems to have permitted herself fewer gestures towards Paul on that account. Hermine, in her *Family Memoirs*, speaks with compunction of her own harsh feelings and expressions in relation to Paul and on her deathbed thought much of him.[37] No reconciliation between brother and sister took place, though Paul was in Vienna at least once during this period.

Ludwig did not see Paul again. On one occasion he sent greetings by a friend of Margaret's but when Paul's friend, Miss Deneke, a patroness of music in Oxford, tried to arrange a meeting there Ludwig indignantly refused.[38] Still, he told Koder in a letter (with how much self-knowledge is a matter for conjecture) 'as you know I do not feel the slightest trace of bitterness towards Paul nor do I share my sisters' judgement of him'.[39] He was critical not of Paul's actions but, rather typically, of his reactions – of his having broken with Hermine for no good reason.

---

[37] Ludwig to Rudolf Koder, 23 August 1949.
[38] Letter to Koder, 22 February 1949. Ludwig believed that Paul had permitted, but not planned, this invitation.
[39] This in his last letter to Koder, 20 March 1951.

And Paul? He went on living and indeed coming to Austria, where he would stay in Thumersbach with his cousin Lydia Oser. 'You are the band, carrying no fruit itself, that is needed to bind the sheaf' he told her, a quotation, significantly, from Grillparzer's *A Feud between Brothers in House Habsburg*.[40] He would meet there many members of the extended family. His son lives among them to this day. Paul treasured this bond and others too – he went on befriending Koder and found new objects in Austria for the kindnesses typical of the family; but the rupture with the sisters seemed a cleft in stone. The memoir written by Hermine needed, he wrote, a rectification. Margaret's sons had been overbearing with him and had treated him badly over saving the fortunes of the sisters in Austria. But, this apart, there is no hostility in his letters and he indeed acknowledges his own stubbornness and irreconcilability. Of his brother Ludwig he would speak kindly, but sometimes avoided in his abrupt way those who sought his acquaintance because of that relationship.[41]

Too much should not be made of this *Feud between Brothers in House Wittgenstein*. In part, it was one of the many examples of human relations damaged by the war. Sweetness and light did not simply return on 9 May 1945 with the immediacy of the light in Haydn's *Creation*. But we can use this closing episode to draw up a summary of the characteristics that the brothers shared but the sisters did not. The latter felt more severely the disagreement that had arisen but were if anything more inclined for reconciliation. The brothers could not withdraw from a position once taken up – *nescit vox missa reverti*.

---

[40] Their aunt Clara (whose heir Lydia was) had likewise been a central member of the family, though or because unmarried. The play's title means 'A Feud between Brothers in the House of Habsburg'. The phrase quoted is applied to himself by the Emperor Rudolf in Act Ill. I owe the knowledge of these circumstances and the sight of this letter to an old friend, now deceased, Mrs Mariela Kuhn Oser, another distant cousin.

[41] Personal communication from a pupil of his.

'What is once said cannot be unsaid'. This was of a piece with the uncompromisingness and insistence on correctness of tone seen in all the areas of the Wittgensteins' interaction and documented here in this collection of their family letters.

Kurt, Paul, Hermine, Max, Leopoldine, Helene, Ludwig – Neuwaldegg 1917
© The Brenner-Archiv.

1

LUDWIG'S EARLY LETTERS: THREE LETTERS FROM 1908

A nineteen-year-old Ludwig moved to Manchester in May 1908, after three semesters studying mechanical engineering at the Technical High School Charlottenburg (1906–1908). As a rather informal research student at the university, he was involved in experiments and research on aeronautics until 1911. In the autumn of 1912 Ludwig left Manchester prematurely. Still enrolled for the academic year, he moved to Cambridge to study logic and philosophy with Bertrand Russell.

In her *Family Memories*, Hermine speaks of 'the dual and conflicting inner vocation' under which he suffered. As early as 1909, as we know from Ph. E. Jourdain's diary, Wittgenstein presented his proposals for the solution of a leading problem of mathematical logic to the Russell circle, and most likely in the summer of 1911 he got in contact with the great logician Gottlob Frege. Encouraged by Frege and Russell, he decided to become a philosopher instead of an aeronaut. He spent the two years of 1911/12 and 1912/13 in Cambridge and the academic year 1913/14 in Norway, developing the logical basis of his early philosophy.

Young Ludwig © The Brenner-Archiv.

1 Ludwig to Hermine

[1908][1]

Dear Mining!

I think about you very often, and your painting comes to mind every time! Each and every time I revisit my conviction that the single most useful thing you can do is to procure simple geometric objects and study them from various perspectives until it's clear <u>why</u> a shadow falls precisely at such and such a place, etc., etc., and how that is connected with the position of the light source, and so on. Whenever you draw complicated objects, intentionally simplify them first and create a sketch of such and such an object so simplified; then you won't have any difficulties in adding further

---

[1] Ludwig's handwriting in this letter suggests that it dates either from his time in Berlin (1906–1908) or from his time in Manchester (1908–1912).

details to a second sketch, etc. Here, however, it is necessary that you draw the sketch so that it's <u>physically complete and entirely clear to you. The object can be as simplified as you want it to be</u>: e.g., a tree trunk drawn as a cylinder with branches emerging from it. But you shouldn't just draw the shadows as they truly fall with respect to the tree, but, <u>as they would fall, for instance, if the sun were illuminating the tree from a particular angle and if it were not overshadowed by other trees</u>. By doing it this way, you'll see what's essential about any given shadow, etc., etc.

Or you'll see that the crown of a tree is similar, say, to the form of a ball's surface. So draw it only as if it were a completely smooth ball and shade it accordingly, then add the details only in another sketch. What is more, if an object is shiny and others are reflected in it as, say, in any polished metal object, then draw it first as if it were matt and shade it from that point of view as well; only then should you add, in another sketch, the highlights the object'll have on account of its finish, etc. The main thing is always that, with each sketch, you draw a <u>completely concrete object</u> and that, consequently, you see an <u>object</u> in front of you whenever you look at each sketch, which you can compare with the <u>object</u> you intended to draw. That object may, as I've already said, be as simplified as it wants to be in your sketch. But it has to be an object, not something flat. Perhaps you'll now object that you can't, e.g., imagine how a shiny object would look if it <u>were</u> matt, but you will learn from your simple geometric models how certain forms of object look, and if you were to draw, say, an iridescent pyramid, then you'll always be able to first draw how your pyramid would have looked if it were painted white and to add the less essential tones only later. <u>But I have yet to recommend something of particular importance: in sketching objects, remember to draw the lines and edges which you can't actually see, but which more readily permit what's essential about the object to come to the fore</u>: for example, draw a prism like this

and not like this

that is, with the edges which are actually hidden, so that the physical connections are completely clear to you – or a cone like this

with its axis, etc., etc., or like this

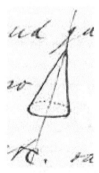

so that, e.g., the orientation of the base surface becomes clearer to you, and so on. I hope I have expressed myself clearly.

Your devoted brother,

Ludwig

2 Ludwig to Hermine

Ludwig arrived at the Glossop observatory during the summer of 1908. In a letter to Hermine of 29 May 1908 – the complete text of which seems to be lost – he reports how he and Mr Rimmer, a meteorologist and observer, were the only ones living in a secluded guesthouse. The food and toilet facilities were 'rustic', and Ludwig had difficulties in growing accustomed to it all. While his previous job consisted only in making observations, his current 'job was to provide kites, which had hitherto been ordered elsewhere'. What he missed, though, was a friend, and he was keeping a lookout among the students who visited the observatory on Sundays. He was sleeping well and reports that 'if my own ego weren't gnawing at me, then I would really have to find it agreeable here for the time being'.

3 Ludwig to Hermine

20 October 1908

Dear Mining!

I was with Lamb[2] a few days ago, and he is going to attempt to solve the equations[3] which I most recently came up with and which I showed him. He said he doesn't know for sure whether they are solvable with today's methods, and I am therefore very curious to hear how his attempt turns out. Incidentally, he was very gracious with me, which is quite a lot for a man some 70 years of age.[4] My evil spirits put me in the stupidest of moods imaginable. As I was

---

[2] Horace Lamb, later Sir Horace (1849–1934), a distinguished mathematician and professor at Manchester from 1885–1920, who solved a number of problems in hydrodynamics.

[3] Probably equations required for the construction of an aircraft propeller.

[4] Ludwig is mistaken here. Lamb was 59 at the time, not 70.

leaving the university after my talk with Lamb, my path led me past the machine engineers' draught room; I knew draught production was scheduled for that day and entered. I knew the assistant on duty, who is a friend of our observer's and a very dangerous person for me to be around. As you know, I can't stand the method by which engineering is taught; I was also down in the dumps after my talk with Lamb, though during it I had felt <u>very</u> happy, and when I saw the kind of things people were drawing and noticed that the assistant in question was quite content with it all, I became completely besides myself and went on to make a very excited speech to the good man, who was in no way to blame for the whole thing. I just kept getting more excited, as nothing made me angrier than seeing him so indifferent, and it was sheer luck that the assistant was called away all of a sudden, allowing me to come to my senses and leave post-haste. Coincidently, *Die Meistersinger von Nürnberg*[5] was being played that evening in Manchester, so I spent the evening in Manchester[6] and heard a very beautiful concert under Richter's direction, which restored my equanimity entirely. The Saturday before that, the observer invited me to spend Sunday with his family. I went and was treated with phenomenal kindness, so that I'm quite at a loss as to how I'm supposed to pay it back in kind. It's already very cold here, and I will soon have to give some serious thought to the question of heating. Mama wrote to me saying that Grandmama is living with you all; that'll probably disturb you quite a bit whenever you're painting. Now please tell everyone I said hello – with best wishes, your devoted brother,

Ludwig

---

[5] Ludwig's favourite Wagner opera during his Berlin years.
[6] Rather than returning to his research station in the moors near Glossop.

2

THE GREAT WAR: AUGUST 1914 TO APRIL 1918

Karl Wittgenstein, who died in January 1913, left a huge fortune to his children. In the summer of 1914, Ludwig returned to Vienna and made a donation of 100,000 crowns to Ludwig von Ficker, editor of *Der Brenner*, to be distributed to 'impecunious Austrian artists'. After the outbreak of the war, which he seems to have expected, he immediately reported for enlistment. On 7 August he was assigned to a fortified artillery regiment in Krakow.

His brother Paul was also immediately enlisted and engaged in combat. He lost his right arm in Russian captivity. Released in an exchange of prisoners of war, he was re-engaged, inevitably to play a less active role. Their other living brother Kurt was caught in America by the war and joined up only later. His sisters remained in and around Vienna. Hermine and Margarete (Gretl) and her husband Jerome engaged in varying degrees of war work, mostly medical in nature.

In the spring of 1916 Ludwig was transferred to Galicia. On 1 September, he was promoted to corporal and in October sent to Olmuetz/Olomouc, to the artillery officer training school. His family remained in their usual series of houses in and round Vienna.

On 26 January 1917, Ludwig returned to his regiment in Bukovina. In early June and then again in late November, he was on leave in Vienna. In autumn Gretl and her family, who were American citizens, had to leave Austria for Switzerland.

4 Margarete to Ludwig

Ludwig Wittgenstein
Festungs Artillerie Regiment n.°2
2. Cadre
Goplanaschiff
Kraków

20 August 1914

My Luckerl,
May this pinch on the chin find you well and in good spirits. I would give my life to know how you are. I fear your cards to Mama won't ever arrive because your handwriting, in its wind-scattered aloofness, will be taken as some kind of cipher. Willy Zitkovsky[1] is with the 6th Field Artillery Regiment somewhere near you. Maybe you'll see each other, then you two could play 'guess my thoughts'.

Regards, a thousand times over,
from all of us & kisses from
Gretl

---

[1] Family friend, especially of Margarete. She met with him and his brother – sometimes with her own brothers – for intellectual and cultural conversation.

5 Mariechen[2] to Ludwig

Mariechen Salzer
Vienna iv, Brahmsplatz 4

Ludwig Wittgenstein
k. u. k. Art. Werkstätte der Festung
Kraków, Feldpost 186

Vienna, 7 March 1915

Dear Uncle Ludwig!

Thank you very much for the card you sent me. It made me very happy; it's the first military correspondence card I've received. I am very glad that messages arrive from you so often and that you are well. Kind regards, from the boys too,

Your niece,
Mariechen

Mariechen 1915

Mariechen Salzer, the favourite niece 1916 [later von Stockert] © *The Brenner-Archiv.*

---

[2] A nickname for his niece, Maria Salzer, daughter of Helene.

6 Hermine to Ludwig

3 November 1915

My dear Lukas,

I really wanted to give the postman some news for you, but it's
going to be a very stupid card, I can sense that already, because I'm
in such a rush to get everything done today! I'm at the infirmary
again and didn't get around to doing anything I actually wanted to
do during my holiday. I had a lot to take care of and to think about
up at the Hochreit,[3] so there wasn't any time to do any reading, and
here too my free time is taken up with certain trivialities, which are
just <u>bound</u> to crop up. A strange life, what's unimportant is always
what's important at any given moment!

Will Paul be exchanged?[4] I really have little hope, and the
thought that he and Mama will be disappointed is just awful.—
Greti[5] has already moved back to Vienna and is living in a very
peculiar flat with almost a total absence of serviceable furniture,
but full of beautiful and eye-catching details.—Since your last
leave I've assimilated a word I didn't understand back then: i.e.,
'Weltanschauung'.[6] Since then, I've been catching wind of
Weltanschauungen everywhere and might almost have reason to
fear that I'm turning into you – because this is, I believe, the reason
you 'take everything so tragically', as I used to say. Or I am mistaken
here? But because I don't have a fixed Weltanschauung of my own,
those of other people aren't quite capable of irritating me all that

---

[3] The large family estate in Lower Austria, bought by Karl Wittgenstein in 1894 and later the
property of Hermine.
[4] Paul Wittgenstein, their brother, lost his right arm in the first year of the war and returned
to the Alleegasse in Vienna after a prisoner exchange.
[5] Their sister, Margaret.
[6] World-view.

much. How's your work going? If I could understand even a word of it!! Adieu my good Lukas, the <u>most heartfelt</u> regards, your

sister Mining

Margaret and (centre) Rudolf Wittgenstein with the brothers Zittkovsky ca. 1900.

7 Hermine to Ludwig

16 April 1916

My darling Lukas,

I think about you so much, but can't bring myself to write about it, I'm just convinced that you couldn't have done anything other than you did. But now Paul has drawn my attention to something <u>really important</u> and even though he has written to you already and wants to write to you about it again, it's not leaving me any peace – I just have to mention it: Paul said that, given your education, you have a claim to volunteer insignia and officer training: i.e., a volunteer training unit.[7] You shouldn't let anything at all mislead

[7] Numerous compatriots and officer friends had told Ludwig that he ought to file to be granted the status of a one-year volunteer. During his training course, he had – in a truly irregular way – enjoyed the benefits of such a position and was then assigned, but at his own wish, to a new regiment as a volunteer gunner on 21 March 1915. See *Young Ludwig*, pp. 237–8.

you into renouncing that even if you can tolerate being a common soldier in our army, there is a chance that you'll be taken prisoner, and Paul says that having to endure being treated like a common prisoner of war would have meant certain death for him. He just wouldn't have been able to take it. It's difficult enough as an officer. I don't know what's going on with you right now, so I'm taking a shot in the dark, but I <u>beg</u> you: if you have to take any steps in this matter, do not, stubborn and unworldly as you are, neglect them. If this matter were not so serious, I would say: there will be time for you to be a Jamesian type after the war is over.[8] But really I'm not joking! Perhaps I am simply doing you an injustice, and you are not at all as twisted as I think you are, but I am still afraid that you'll just see it as shying away from difficulties or the like and don't realise that your life can be at stake. I wish I could find out how you really are and what you've been getting up to without having to demand an answer from you! Mama was better, but is unfortunately in pain again, and we have scheduled an appointment for Bamberger[9] to come; I will write to you with what he says. Oddly enough, nothing's changed with Rosalie;[10] none of us knows whether we ought to be happy about that. She doesn't complain about anything, but is that any way to live? And yet we're glad to have this dear chap here with us! —I went to hear Bach's *Mass in B Minor* yesterday, I almost fell to my knees, it's just <u>that</u> powerful. It's so strange that something like that can be created only through the most intense belief in God. Perhaps faith, imagination and art are humbling in equal measure. How's your

---

[8] Wittgenstein was an avid reader of William James's *The Varieties of Religious Experience* in these years. See *Young Ludwig* p. 129. From a letter to Russell quoted there it is clear that he aspired to the 'saintly' rather than the 'healthy-minded' type, let alone the type with a 'divided soul'.

[9] The family doctor at the time and director of the Rudolfinum where Hermine was to work.

[10] Rosalie: housekeeper to grandmother Kalmus, spent her last years in the Alleegasse.

work going? I have relatively little to do now and even managed to paint a bit in the infirmary.

Warmest regards,

your sister,

Mining

Leopoldine Wittgenstein, Frau Mama, Alleegasse 1913 © The Brenner-Archiv.

8 Hermine to Ludwig

29 October 1916

My good Lukas,

We haven't seen a thing or heard a word from you, obviously because you've been studying very hard, but I wanted to ask: can't I visit you at all? Next Sunday perhaps? You can certainly spare a few hours, and I wouldn't ask for any more. If you agree, cable me and only then will I arrange the details. It would of course be better if you could come here, for Mama would be able to see you too, but you won't be able to do that and my proposal is a kind of wartime substitute. We missed you terribly yesterday when Paul and Menzel[11]

---

[11] Rosine Menzel (ca. 1863–1920): accompanist, friend of both Labor and the Wittgensteins.

were playing Labor's[12] new piano quartet (arranged by Menzel) for invited guests, truly an extraordinarily fine work, which everyone enjoyed immediately. Paul also played it very beautifully, with great warmth and fire. He also played two pieces by Mendelssohn, very beautifully and with passion, much to my delight; for the case of 'Paul' means a lot to me, and I enjoy confirming his right to play music for the sake of just <u>one</u> passionately played piece just as much as I want to deny him that right on account of any number of solecisms. It's charming to see the group of women Paul has gathered who truly and sincerely admire him; yesterday, to be sure, it was only the old crones, but he could have the young, beautiful ones too, nice and lovable as he is to women (just about as conciliatory as he can be gruff and arrogant to men at times). Labor was in the best of moods and apparently quite happy with the reception of his quartet. Adieu for today, my good Lukas, maybe I'll get to see you soon!

Warmest regards,

your sister,

Mining

Josef Labor, the composer
© *The Stonborough Family.*

---

[12] Josef Labor (1842–1924): Bohemian composer, organist and family friend of the Wittgensteins, who was blind from birth and lived in Vienna from 1868 until his death in 1924.

9 Hermine to Ludwig

Hochreit

Post Hohenberg

18 November 1916

My good Lukas,

I was told over the telephone today that you've received your commendation,[13] but nothing more, obviously because they didn't know anything else in Vienna. But I wholeheartedly hope for your sake (not for ours) that everything will be as you want it; you will, at any rate, be finished with that school. If only your leave does not fall through, then everything will be as right as houses. Thank you <u>very much</u> for recommending the Hölderlin poems,[14] which are something very special; unfortunately, the bookshop hasn't sent me a complete edition. Do you by any chance have a complete edition that you could lend me at some point? I'm very curious as to which are your favourites – certainly ones I can't understand, as I can understand only the ones containing simple thoughts such as 'Youth' or 'Evening Fantasy'. I took your Weininger[15] with me and am enjoying it very much; it replaces you a bit. The gelatine in head and heart that I'm always complaining of – that is, my absolute inability to think or feel – melts just a little whenever I read or hear someone else's thoughts; of course, it soon solidifies again!—I'll be returning to Vienna tomorrow, and Mama is supposed to get up and walk a bit once I'm there; Dr Bamberger, whom we have now since Dr Popper has been called

---

[13] Probably for Ludwig's promotion to Fähnrich in the Reserve on 1 December 1916 and not for the Valour 2nd Class, which he was awarded on 3 November 1915.

[14] The German poet, Johann Christian Friedrich Hölderlin (1770–1843).

[15] Otto Weininger: his most famous work was *Sex and Character* (1903) but 'your Weininger' may be Weininger's posthumously published *On Last Things*. Hermine quotes from this work in Letter 65 below and Ludwig echoes it in his wartime notes.

up, believes that her venitis is cured and that the pain is due to neuralgia, which can't be treated with bed rest; or rather he no longer believes that bed rest is appropriate because, in his opinion, the venitis is gone – and even another doctor, the one carrying out the electro-treatment for the neuralgia, is of that same opinion. Let's hope they're right! But I want to be in Vienna when Mama begins to walk again so I can see for myself whether there have been any changes in her leg and what kind of pain she might be having. How will Paul's concert turn out!!!

Adieu, my good Lukas, hugs from

your sister,

Mining

10 Hermine to Ludwig

[1917]

My darling Lukas,

Because I have no idea how much longer letters will be reaching you without impediment,[16] I want to send you my most heartfelt greetings before it's too late, as you should certainly receive these. I am writing to you from the Hochreit where we're not getting on so well; part of the time, I am supposed to inspect and put all sorts of things in order, but I have the feeling that I'm just trying to draw water with sieves, which is not very diverting; part of the time – when I had some peace and quiet – I even believed myself capable of having some kind of reasonable thought, but just became even more dull and stupid than I was before. Still I did take the *Karamazovs*[17] with me and do read bits of it every now and again.

---

[16] Ludwig was being transferred to the front.
[17] *The Brothers Karamazov* by Fyodor Dostoevsky (1880).

I'm finally beginning to understand the spirit in which this book has to be read, for you cannot believe that one will get very far with this book just by reading it. I really like that it constantly reminds me of you, so that it's often as though I can hear and speak with you. You were also in my thoughts during the final rehearsal of the Labor quintet, and I even enjoyed it at the time, despite the fact that it sounded terrible; unfortunately, it remained completely incomprehensible to the others because no one really heard it properly, and that was a great disappointment. But the concert seems to have made everything better again and, from what I've heard from Mama, turned out to be a delight for everyone.

I have also thought about what you said regarding Paul's living in the Alleegasse and am entirely convinced that, for both sides, the advantages will far outweigh their opposite (that you would have entirely different feelings here of course proves nothing). Mama would lose quite a bit if she couldn't take care of Paul any more, and such musical gregariousness is something stimulating and is certainly revitalizing for her. And besides, every now and again, someone comes to the house on account of Paul, whereas it would just be lifeless if I were the only one at home. There is no contact without friction between us and Mama, but should one abandon all contact just because of that?

How, my good Lukas, are things with you? With any luck, they'll remain bearable until some kind of change comes about; I have of course relayed your instructions to Trenkler.[18] Wishing you all the best and with the most heartfelt of embraces,

your devoted sister,

Mining

---

[18] Employee in the Wittgenstein family office. Wittgenstein's request to Trenkler is repeated in Hermine's letter of 7 June 1917 (Letter 17).

11 Hermine to Ludwig

vienna

iv. Alleegasse 16

1 March 1917

My good Lukas,

My warmest thanks for your kind letter. Well, I finally got the book[19] and, while the first shipment went missing, I am not being <u>so</u> hard on myself for not having tended to it better. With any luck, everything will arrive this time. The brief abridgements made by the translator are strange; I took a quick look just at the last few pages because I immediately noticed a few sentences were missing, which were in any event unimportant, but how does anyone come up with such an idea?

How's your work going? That you want to become better and wiser is a sign only that you are not content with yourself, but hopefully not to the point of actual depression, but rather only to the extent necessary to leaven your work? Can you imagine, I ended up staying on at my clinic; there's been more to do again lately, so I'm not as unhappy as I was before; breaking with the day-to-day there would have been quite difficult anyway and, besides, I would not have been working with Mitze,[20] but only in the same infirmary, as we found out later. Yet I don't know whether another wave of discontent won't strike at some point, which just might be strong enough to wash me out of the clinic; for this comes more from inside than from outside. At the moment, I'm all cheerful and childish.

---

[19] Dostoevsky's *The Brothers Karamazov*; Hermine forwards a book by him to Ludwig sometime between 1 March 1917 and 20 March 1917 (see Letter 12).

[20] Mitze Salzer: a relation of the Wittgensteins' brother-in-law Max Salzer and a close friend of Hermine's.

That Uncle Paul[21] is doing better is something to be very grateful for, and with any luck he'll make a <u>full</u> recovery. But it is more than hard that he had to fall so ill during the first year of living in his new house, which had made him so happy; I feel deeply sorry for him, because I'm convinced it will have an enormous effect on him. We can't visit him, he won't have it. If he did, I would of course gladly go to distract him a bit.

Wishing you, my good Lukas, all the best in every respect, especially on the inside,

your sister,

Mining

12 Hermine to Ludwig

vienna

iv. Alleegasse 16

20 March 1917

My good Lukas,

I would, from the bottom of my heart, very much like to write to you, but I find it impossible whenever I set out to do so; what's going on inside me is so thin that one cannot put it into words and what's going on around me is hardly of any interest to you, with everything being said in just two words. I would much rather <u>talk</u> with you, as I would certainly find topics enough, and you wouldn't believe how much I think of you and everything we've ever talked about; my head often spins like a mill wheel. You have given me much, without end! I have it so good; because of my compromising nature, I get something from the most heterogeneous of people,

---

[21] Karl Wittgenstein's brother.

from you and from Greti, from Mitze and Mima.[22] Each of you changes my inner being by pulling a kind of point out of it and expanding its surface, widening my interest. Today I spent the entire afternoon with Gretl. You won't believe what a good, kind person she is! For the time being, of course, no one can know for sure whether she'll be able to stay in Vienna – just how important that would be to her can't be said in just a few words! She still isn't well, and Jerome,[23] with his highly developed war psychosis, truly needs a counter-weight to make him bearable. We finally managed to get Paul to tell us that he was a huge success in Berlin – without any advertising; due to a bit of sloppiness, there was no mention whatsoever that the man has only one arm! He doesn't speak about it at all, but he is very pleased about the whole thing, for that is truly something; here anyone might say that, apart from his music, any number of groups are interested in him and his fate, but in Berlin he is just a musician. Incidentally, a lady recently told me all teary-eyed about how movingly he plays; who would ever have thought it! But we'll gladly admit we were mistaken on that point!

My good Lukas, I'm glad you've received the book by Dostoevsky; the abridgements don't mean a thing. Have you been able to work? Have you become more of a Jamesian type? You know what I mean and won't be upset at me for asking. I only want you to be happy and for me not to lose you. With the most heartfelt regards,

your sister,

Hermine

---

[22] Mima Bacher: friend of Hermine's, who became an important member of the family; her first son, Arvid Sjögren, married Helene's youngest daughter Clara Salzer; her second-oldest son, Talla, married Marguerite Respinger, previously regarded as his fiancée by Ludwig.

[23] Jerome, Gretl's husband, was an American citizen and Gretl a naturalized American. Once the United States entered the war, it became uncertain whether she could – and, as it turned out, impossible for her to – remain in Vienna.

13 Hermine to Ludwig

vienna
iv. Alleegasse 16
7 April 1917

My dearest Lukas,

In order to begin with what's especially close to my heart, I must say that I am terribly sorry (there's no adequate word for it anyway) that the break with America couldn't have been prevented.[24] It's a kind of sickness that has taken hold of mankind, a compulsion to destroy oneself and others; I am entirely certain that the reason every nation <u>must</u> have its war lies in that fact! There is a kind of lust in – at least for a time – tolerating hardships and causing destruction; if only everyone had begun at the same time, then they would've already had enough of it all by now. Can we really wait until America reaches that point?

Given the circumstances now, our dear Greterl will really have to go to Switzerland, barring a miracle, which she is still waiting for; yesterday, it seemed as if she would have to leave at some point over the next couple of days, but she learned today that we have to wait and see how America treats Austrians and that this could take 2–3 weeks. Each day is a gift she is grateful for. And now I'll still be able to go to her place a few more times to draw; maybe a small memento will come of it all. Since I tell you everything, I have to tell you something else I've been thinking about lately; I believe you'll be absolutely horrified: there is a plan to make Max and Lenka[25] co-owners of the Hochreit and for no other reason than that the two

---

[24] The United States declared war on the German Empire on 6 April 1917 and on Austria-Hungary on 7 December 1917.
[25] Their sister, Helene and her husband.

of them absolutely need to look for some property where they are not guests, where Max can hunt to his heart's content, Lenka can invite people over, decorate their house, etc. If they were to buy something somewhere else, then they won't go to the Hochreit anymore, which would be unbearably sad for Mama and a great loss for me as well; for the interest and love that, for instance, Mariechen[26] has for the Hochreit literally extends my life and my interest in the Hochreit by a generation. In principle, however, I'm pretty sure that some solution will have to be found, but how it should be done, so that both sides are satisfied and so that, in the end, perhaps Mama and I are not forced to give up because the situation is unbearable – I agonise over it just about day and night. This will certainly strike you as crazy, but the necessity existing here cannot be presented so clearly in writing. Of course, the Salzers would have to live in their own house, have their own vegetables, cows, etc., so that no friction comes about, and above all this needn't be arranged from one day to the next.

I visited Uncle Paul recently, but unfortunately found him still suffering from that terrible cough and frighteningly lively; he can't say the simplest of words without yelling and getting all excited, which really occurs to you only when you're anxiously listening and know that it's going to make him cough. It is also a shame that the weather just doesn't want to improve and that he can't go outside without making his condition worse. I needn't tell you how kind and warm-hearted he is and how much I wish he'd get better soon! It's a shame that old people are nicer than younger people! (With any luck, that can be said about us one day!)

Mama and her foot are coming along slowly, but they are coming along, she is in any event content. I am really happy to be on very

---

[26] Lenka and Max's daughter, Maria.

good terms with her at the moment, and even Paul has been a completely different person ever since Greti was kind enough to take him to task, which he himself thought was called for in the extreme. If need be, he'll be taken to task again and, as he himself has already requested, with even greater intensity. I wasn't there when it happened, but Greti told me that Paul was quite touching when he told her how he is suffering from his overall condition and his own irritableness.

My good Lukas, I say adieu. Of you and your life I know nothing and am therefore unable to pick up on any aspect of it. Taking a shot in the dark, and wishing you all the best with the most heartfelt of hugs,

your devoted sister,

Mining

14 Ludwig to Hermine

12 April 1917

Dear Mining!

Thank you for your kind letter of 7th April. I certainly do not believe that the reason the war has escalated is what you say it is. Here, we are dealing – I believe – with a complete victory of materialism, and the demise of any sense of good and evil. The idea that the Salzers ought to become co-owners of the Hochreit does not at all strike me as crazy, but as quite sane. For Helene is – I believe – the only one of us who is light-hearted in an utterly innocuous way and who has any mind for making social situations agreeable and pleasant.

Indeed, I believe that, if the Salzers can no longer go to the Hochreit, the entire Hochreit would be nothing more than a sad memory of good times past.

Mama wrote to me saying that Uncle Paul is being quite careless again! Terrible! Give him my <u>warmest</u> regards!

<u>Gretl</u> taking Paul to task is something I can't quite imagine. But there just are some things we are incapable of imagining. Of myself, I can say nothing. I'm still alive.

Warmest regards,

Ludwig

15 Hermine to Ludwig

vienna

iv. Alleegasse 16

28 April 1917

My darling Lukas,

Thanks a million for your kind letter, but I'm sorry to hear that you can't say anything <u>of yourself</u>, first because I see from this fact that all is not well and then because that is of no help to me whatsoever in getting clear about what's unsettling and allows me only vague suspicions of this or that. If I could only talk with you, I would no doubt still be shocked to see how the rift between you and everyone I know has grown, but at least I would know where I stand.

Unfortunately, we haven't had any letters from Greti, just unsatisfying cables; I am thoroughly convinced that she had been or still is ill. She was of course ailing here and was supposed to avoid any stress and anxiety, but the amount of stress and anxiety caused by the time leading up to the day of her departure is indescribable, and she is surely suffering from their effects. I hope a letter will arrive soon enough. The Salzers are all healthy, but I haven't seen anything of them since forever because I spend all my free time damned painting, which I curse daily because I don't feel up to the task, but that's where my heart is, all of it! <u>Yes,</u> I shouldn't have taken it up, but once I'm in for a penny, I'm in for a pound, and it is a long and heavy pounding! There's very little to do in the clinic at the moment, which suits me just fine for now, but if it goes on like this for too long I may just have another fit of despair. And I won't know what'll happen until it happens; I fear, however, since I don't want to go into the field (for various reasons), I shan't find what's right for me anywhere – jobs of this kind have all been hit hard here in Vienna.

Nothing has been decided in the Hochreit/Salzer affair yet because, as I told you already, I haven't spoken with anyone about it; I myself am infinitely curious to know what solution we'll come up with. For the time being, no one has any idea what'll happen this summer. Who will go to the Hochreit and when? Still, I hope it'll be possible to do it this year the way we did in peacetime: i.e., <u>Mama as lady of the house up top</u> and the Salzers as guests. When will you be on leave again? After that, I would like to arrange a holiday for myself; if it's at all possible, please write to let me know! Uncle Paul is feeling better, so much so that he's making his daily rounds up at Am Himmel and Cobenzl[27] again despite the dreadful weather; let's hope it doesn't do him any harm! Labor is well, but Frau David[28] unfortunately had a chest operation.

That is not a good way to end a letter, so I will mention that a small musical rendition will be put on at our place the day after tomorrow. A genius on the violin, la petite Morini,[29] will be playing; she's supposed to be fabulous.

With the most heartfelt of hugs,

your sister,

Mining

---

[27] Favourite Viennese excursion destinations.
[28] Labor's housekeeper.

16 Paul to Ludwig

Sr. Hochwohlgeborenen
Herrn k. u. k. Fähnrich
Ludwig Wittgenstein
Feldhaubitzen-Räg. No'6, 4 Batt.
<u>Feldpost 28d</u>

vienna

i. Albrechtgasse 3

27 May 1917

Dear Luki!

The following should be said regarding your request:[30]

That Herr Trenkler should go to His Excellency Löbl[31] is out of the question. In such a case as this one, we can't just send an employee, even if he is a friend of the family; rather, either I would have to go or you would have to write directly to His Excellency. But I do not believe Löbl to be the right man in this particular case anyway and, because of this, have turned to Field marshal Troll[32] who was an intimate friend of Uncle Josef;[33] moreover, he is a man of rare character and also very obliging, whom I personally hold in high regard and who, because he has been reactivated, presently holds a rather important position in the War Ministry. I initially wrote him a letter explaining the situation and asked only that he grant me an audience so that I might be able to obtain his advice in this matter. This meeting took

---

[29] The violinist Erica Morini (1904–1995).

[30] Wittgenstein sought a transfer from the artillery to the infantry.

[31] Presumably, Johann Löbl (1859–1917), artillerist, Field Marshal, director of the War Provident Office until his death on 17 October 1917.

[32] Most likely Field Marshal Ignaz von Trollmann.

[33] Josef von Siebert, General of Calvary who fought at Königgrätz and was married to Karl Wittgenstein's sister Lydia.

place yesterday; I placed the heaviest of emphasis on the fact that this matter does not involve a transfer from the front, that you are not interested in receiving a more comfortable assignment, but rather one that you could better carry out in the interest of the service. Field marshal Troll responded by telling me more or less the following.

Such a request cannot be handled completely outside the chain of command. What can happen is only that someone at the top clears the path for that request, so that it can be handled immediately once it has been filed. Any decision regarding such a request will be taken by the Artillery Inspector Archduke Leopold Salvator.[34] But he will not be easily persuaded to have anyone transferred from his corps to another. His Excellency Troll has, however, known him for quite some time and even has something to take care of with him either today or in the next couple of days. He then promised me that during his visit he would broach the topic of your request as well, and I hope he will be successful in propitiating the Archduke. Field marshal Troll also promised that he would advise immediately of how his meeting went: should it go unfavourably, then you should not file a request at all, as it would be pointless.

Warmest regards,

your brother,

Paul

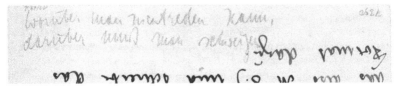

Letter from Hermine 7.6.1917 with an inscription (perforce later) by Ludwig: "Whereof one cannot talk, thereof one must be silent", which would become the last sentence of the Tractatus (final, printed version: "What one cannot speak about..." with sprechen for reden, wovon for worüber.) © The Brenner-Archiv.

---

[34] Archduke Leopold Salvator (1863–1931): General-Artillerie-Inspektor from 1907 on.

17 Hermine to Ludwig

7 June 1917

My good Lukas,

Today I wanted to copy your instructions concerning your writings onto better paper and attach them to my will and testament.[35] But I noticed that they might not be entirely clear and, now that I've copied them, I'm sending them to you with the following questions.

First, you write: '1) and 2) also exist in typescript in Olmütz with corrections'. This is obviously not identical to no. 5), as Russell is supposed to receive both. For this reason, please call this item no. 6) and add what format it's in.

Second, you write under no. 3) 'a portion of these already exist in the typewritten fascicle' – here, too, I would like to know what number that is, presumably no. 6), right?

Third: is no. 5) handwritten or typewritten?

One might call the typescript that Trenkler has no 7) so that everything has a number.

---

[35] Here Hermine is repeating Ludwig's lost January letter, already mentioned in Letter 10. It seems that only 2, 3 and 5 have survived. They are the two critical notebooks written during the war (Trinity College Library, Cambridge) and the so-called *Prototractatus* (Bodleian Library, Oxford), though it contains more than that. This evidence suggests two earlier versions of the *Tractatus*, a first *Prototractatus* through p. 70 (in the manuscript) of September 1915 and a second *ibid.* through p. 78 written between September 1916 and January 1917. One or both of these versions might be the two typescripts mentioned here. Neither of these versions will have contained the majority of propositions numbered 6.4 ... or 6.5 ... regarding ethics and the meaning of life. The Bodleian manuscript also contains the bulk of new or altered propositions that make up the final version of the *Tractatus*, which were added subsequent to the date of this letter. —This covering letter also contains – in Ludwig's hand – a variation on the final proposition of the *Tractatus*, which reads: 'What we cannot talk about we must pass over in silence'. It originally read 'speak', for which Ludwig ultimately opted.

My questions may perhaps be a bit surprising to you, but I think such instructions can never be clear enough.

It is all quiet on <u>our</u> front: Kurtl[36] is doing his infantry training at Stockerau, Paul is playing a new concert piece by Labor next Saturday. Warmest regards, my good Lukas,

your devoted sister,
Mining

Enclosure: Ludwig to Hermine

[January 1917]

1) Large ledger at offices with Trenkler
2) 2 quartos with Trenkler

handwritten, also exists in typescript in Olmütz with corrections

3) 1 quarto

(a portion of these already exist in the typewritten fascicle)

4) 1 octavo

literally every sentence in sequence without any corrections

5) A large ledger contains the reworked versions of 1) and 2) for publication. Russell is to receive 3), 4) and 5) and 1 and 2) in typescript and the gold watch

---

[36] Their brother

Pinsent[37] is to receive the manuscript of 1

Destroy typescript in Trenkler's possession

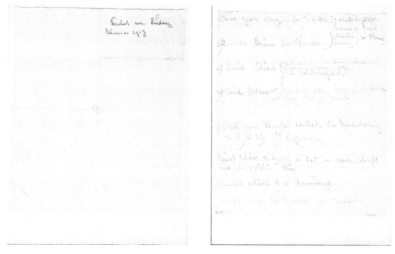

List of manuscripts and typescripts dictated to Hermine by Ludwig in January 1917 attached to her letter of 7 June 1917 © The Brenner-Archiv.

---

[37] David Pinsent: Ludwig's Cambridge friend, with whom he took trips to Iceland and Norway. He died in an accident on 8 May 1918 during a military test flight in England. Ludwig's *Tractatus logico-philosophicus* is dedicated to his memory.

18 Hermine to Ludwig

vienna

xvii Neuwaldeggerstrasse 38

10 June 1917[38]

My darling Lukas,

What I want to write to you about today, I really could have written to you about on Monday when you were still here with us, but that doesn't matter; I just wanted to tell you one thing: that you are, for me, inseparably connected with everything that's good and great and beautiful in this world, more than and in a manner different from any other human being. That and that alone is all I wanted to tell you.

Kurt is leaving on Sunday, but is first going to a six-week training course in the staging zone. Mama is not showing any anxiety at all; she talks only about her pain, she can't hide that. Anyway, she is playing a beautiful Schubert quartet for four hands with Kurt at the moment. Thank God that such things exist, it's a blessing whatever the circumstance of life!

Warmest regards, and wishing you only what you would wish for yourself,

your sister,

Mining

---

[38] The month in the date is not clearly legible. It was written in Roman numerals and has been read here as 'vi' (i.e., June), although it could be 'vii' (i.e., July). Because Wittgenstein was at the front at the beginning of July, the beginning of June is more likely, especially given that his leave is alluded to here.

19 Hermine to Ludwig

vienna

xvii Neuwaldeggerstrasse 38

30 August 1917

My good Lukas,

Not hearing anything from you is really hard for me, because I know that this isn't a good sign and that you're certainly not feeling well in your own skin. Nor has your situation taken a turn for the better;[39] everything was obviously for the birds and that hurts me quite a bit for you. Now that all the highest possible personalities have already 'been approached' ('set in motion' is not something one can really say) in your matter, I am at a loss as to what other path might be taken! But it's strange that you were unable to get anything decent despite your high patronage, especially when innumerable people are easily attaining or pushing things through which are really quite forbidden. Should one have started off differently?

Paul is supposed to come back from the Hochreit this evening, as he's finally been called up; I suspect he'll be leaving tomorrow – he has to report to Klagenfurt. I'm still hoping he won't be stationed too close to the front, as you yourself are assuming he won't be, and with this one condition I wholeheartedly hope for his sake that he finds something that makes him happy.

I wasn't able to finish writing recently, and Paul left yesterday for the army's high command at Villach; I believe he was somewhat disgruntled and upset that it's nothing more dangerous. Mama kept her composure again in grand fashion. Unfortunately, her foot's been acting up quite badly for some time now, and my hope that the Hochreit would do her some good – as it seemed it would

---

[39] The situation alluded to here is Ludwig's infantry transfer request.

at first – has not come to pass; it is a most treacherous illness which no one really understands. But if the Hochreit did not do any good for her foot in general, it <u>must</u> have done her some good, because it's been a very long time now since Mama's had such peace and homeliness with Lenka and the kids, and with Mima too, who is the nicest houseguest imaginable. Lenka was quite right in insisting on it; who knows whether such a stay at the Hochreit will be possible next year for all of us together! It'll certainly be more difficult than this year, when Frl Julie[40] had problems enough with the provisioning. But she managed the job brilliantly, in some matters there is no one like here. Louise Pollitzer[41] was recently at my place in Neuwaldegg for a few days and was thoroughly impressed with the almost motherly care with which Frl. Julie tended to her. I haven't that gift at all, and I excuse myself only by the fact that I could not look after myself in such a motherly fashion. The only thing I do is buy chocolate for my brothers whenever I can get my hands on it – could you use some? – otherwise it never occurs to me to do anything for anyone else. I went to the Invalid Craft Exhibition[42] with Louise and was filled not only with enthusiasm for what the invalids have achieved, but also with admiration for the beauty of an ordinary saddle or screw or wagon chassis, as made by any saddler or wagon maker, or the like. Then we went to the applied arts shop,[43] where we both bought something at some point, and these stupid things, which no one can use, which at most you can give to someone else as a gift, filled me with <u>horror</u>. This 'art' has no connection to life whatsoever, it's

---

[40] Julie von Paic, housekeeper.
[41] Family friend. Because of her Jewish ancestry, she went to America – with Gretl's help – during the Nazi period.
[42] This exhibition may have taken place at the Niederösterreicher Gewerbeverein, Vienna I., Eschenbachgasse 11.
[43] A local Wiener Werkstätte shop, I. Tegethoffstr. 7–9.

like the Cheshire Cat's grin, remaining behind when everything else has gone. I felt bad for Louise, who spends her life with such things, and who knows how much talent and work has ultimately been put into such nonsense. Keep well my good Lukas, warmest regards,

your devoted sister,

Mining

20 Hermine to Ludwig

vienna

xvii Neuwaldeggerstrasse 38

11 September 1917

My good Lukas,

You have no idea how glad I was to receive your letter, it did me so much good to receive a sign of life, to hear that my letters have arrived and were read and are even doing you some good; now I won't ask for anything more. If you ever have anything to write, you'll let me know, and I above all will continue to write because I am no longer writing into a void from which nothing echoes back – I'll be able to enjoy it again. I wanted to write to you anyway to ask for Engelmann's[44] address in Brünn; The reason is that I would like to have him as my architecture advisory board for the changes to Neuwaldegg.[45] What do you think? I hope that's all right with you? The issue is that I know exactly what I want, but it has to be done by an architect; but where am I going to find an architect

---

[44] Paul Engelmann: Wittgenstein met Engelmann, architect and student of Adolf Loos, in 1916 in Olmütz.

[45] A villa on the outskirts of Vienna where the family resided in spring and autumn, bought in the 1880s. Ludwig was born there. Some interior changes were effected at that time and Hermine was now planning further interventions.

who'll do what I want? Hoffmann[46] surely won't, I'd just get a Hoffmann room, and that's the very last thing I want; on the contrary, no one should know that the architect was there, save for the <u>absence</u> of the amateurish, botched – an absence that would be impossible in the stairwell and the new dining room without an architect. The music room is much easier to do; just for the fun of it, I recently moved 2 random sofas and tables to that room and was stunned by the beautiful effect and how well the pictures fit! If we can just get the interiors done for next year – I'm like a child the way I'm enjoying the preparations, and I'm spending way too much time and thought on it. It's my very favourite distraction.

There is nothing going on here at all. Paul writes that he still doesn't have an assignment he likes, but that he is hoping to see a change soon; I would like that to be true for his sake.

Greti is much better; she is planning on coming to Vienna in late autumn – her most ardent and greatest wish, which, with any luck, will be granted. She won't, it seems, have any difficulties from Austria, given her respectable patriotic reputation and that of her family, which makes me happy.

Fritz[47] recently spent a lot of time at my place, <u>so nice</u> and personable; he seems, I have to say, to have changed quite a bit. I'm very curious as to what will come of his <u>studies</u> this year; but his innermost being impinged on me deeply. I'd like to try it with him again some time soon to see whether random chance was a factor here. —Adieu, my good Lukas, warmest regards,

your sister,

Mining

---

[46] Josef Hoffman: the Jugendstil architect held in high regard by Karl Wittgenstein. One of the wooden houses on the Hochreit has 'Hoffmann rooms'.
[47] Fritz Salzer, son of Helene and Max Salzer.

21 Hermine to Ludwig

11 October 1917

My good Lukas,

Thanks a million for your kind lines, which made me <u>very</u> happy on account of what they say; of course, if my fingers being crossed would help you work, I would gladly have them tied together! Are the changes for the better internal or external? In either case, I say: may the spirit not leave you! Amen.

I was able to get Engelmann's address in the meantime, and he has been sitting at our place for about a week now and sketching for life or death and doing his thing superbly, as Mama says. He has already sketched the stairwell and the new dining room and, without any excessive changes, incorporated a highly pleasing system into the stupid gibberish; he's had the idea of a simple serving table with chair legs lengthened to serve as table legs. He's already sketched the sofas and a five-element glass case: in brief, everything works beyond reproach, and I'm especially glad that even Mama and Lenka are very much in agreement with everything and that Engelmann seems to be getting on very well with Mama, with whom he takes his meals every day. On account of this, she's been having some very pleasant, stimulating company and is looking forward to his staying just a bit longer. So, we are hoping to get his advice on the loggia and the old veranda too, and I believe other things will turn up, as he's artistic without affection and sensitive. How strange that he has come to us through your officer training! Tomorrow I'll go with him to the cemetery to show him the grave; maybe he can give us some advice on that as well.[48]

---

[48] Hermine is referring to the Wittgenstein family grave, which she did not like, at the Vienna *Zentralfriedhof.*

I am quite glad too that Mama has begun playing music with a singer[49] every week; I haven't heard her yet, but I do know that she is said to be highly musical (even if her voice is rather overtired), and that is the main thing by far. She is also said to be quite taken with Mama's accompaniment, which puts her in my good graces. Otherwise there is nothing new with us, or at least I know of nothing new. Wishing you well from the very bottom of my heart, and hugs, my dear Lukas,

your sister,

Mining

ps: I admit that I was very happy about The Great Silver Medal of Courage and that the Lt., as Mama tells me, spoke so kindly of you![50]

Copies of the medals won by Ludwig, Bronze and Silver class 2 for valour and Kaiser Karl Soldiers' cross. © Wittgenstein Initiative, with kind permission by Dr. Martin Pilch. Photo: Bea Laufersweiler.

---

[49] No doubt Elsa Stradal, a singer with whom Wittgenstein's mother played music.

[50] The Great Silver Medal of Courage, awarded on 25 August 1917. It is possible that Ludwig's mother was at the award ceremony and heard the reason for Ludwig's receiving it from a lieutenant. Wittgenstein's commanding officer at the time was Leutnant Scholz, who gives particular praise to Wittgenstein in his Report on Fitness for Promotion, not however without insight into 'his particular character traits', as Scholz wrote on 30 September 1917.

22 Ludwig to Hermine

28 October 1917

Dear Mining!

My warmest thanks for your letter of 11 October. That Engelmann is doing his thing well makes me <u>very</u> happy. Things are not going badly for me, and they could go better, if I were better.

May it come to pass.

Your brother,
Ludwig

23 Hermine to Ludwig

vienna
iv. Alleegasse 16
20 November 1917

My good Lukas,

My warmest thanks for your kind card of 13 November.[51] You were entirely right to suspect that I didn't receive your earlier card with the book order; I have just been out for the books, and a few Kierkegaards are already on their way. I hope they're what you want, for I selected a few volumes at random because I don't know anything about him or his writings. *The Seducer's Diary*, which I bought in another bookshop, will follow. Are these books something I'd like?

---

[51] On this same day, Wittgenstein wrote to Engelmann: 'I was pleased to hear that you are turning everything upside down at Neuwaldegg. My dear Mama, too, has a very soft spot for you – which, by the way, I perfectly understand. I work a fair amount but am restless all the same. May you remain as decent as would love to be / your L. Wittgenstein' (Engelmann, Letters from Ludwig, p. 9, translation by L. Furtmueller).

I of course do not have any time to do any reading now, but am happy that in other respects I can get a lot done and at any rate have no time to loaf about, which is just about the most disagreeable thing there is for me. Writing with Mama in the evenings is doing me some good; I can't, as I did in the past, just take any old book or drink a bit and then write well into the night; rather, I get all my work done in a regular fashion. I also fit in a bit of painting during the day, which is enormously refreshing. I had begun doing something very nice, which I was enjoying immensely; I was reading Schiller's plays to Lixi, and our enthusiasm knew no bounds. Unfortunately, however, he recently received a couple of 'unsatisfactory' marks, and now I'm not allowed to distract him – or myself either it seems – for a while. I am very sorry about this because I enjoy being with Lixi very much; he gives his undivided attention to everything (except to his studies, it seems, the scallywag).

We've had better news from Greti, and Mama, thank God, is relatively better at the moment; I don't dare draw any conclusions from that because there have been a few times in the past when she was better, but we can of course be glad about it while it lasts.

I believe Engelmann will be coming to Vienna again soon because the actual work at Neuwaldegg is set to begin then and because there are still a number of things to be discussed; I'm already looking forward to it, as he will surely be taking his meals with us again, which is very stimulating for me. If he were only in better health, it's such a pity that such a nice person is in such a pitiable state! Keep well, my good Lukas, wishing you all the best, and with warmest regards and affection,

your sister,

Mining

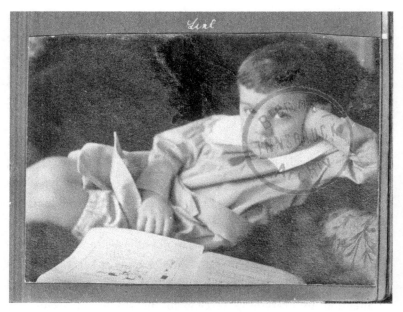

Felix Salzer 'Lixl', ca. 1911 © *The Brenner-Archiv.*

24 Helene to Ludwig

Vienna, Brahmsplatz 4

31 January 1918

Dearest Luckerl!

I had intended to go to the headmaster of the Th[52] right after you left in order to speak with him about Heinz.[53] But then it occurred to me that I won't be able to do anything without Elsa's and Heinz's permission; I, therefore, wrote to Elsa and asked her whether Heinz might go back to the Th if we were to get permission for him to do

---

[52] Th is probably the 'Theresianum', a traditional Viennese gymnasium not far from Brahmsplatz, attended by Helene's sons.

[53] Elsa Stradal's son (see the notes to Letter 21 above about the singer).

so. The response arrived just a few days ago and was not at all what I had expected. Elsa wrote saying that Heinz does not want to come back here, that he has completely settled in at Teplitz and is quite content at school. I can of course do nothing more in this matter; I am only afraid that you'll be quite disappointed with this outcome.

I miss you very much and am sending you the most heartfelt of hugs.

Your

Höllönö

Helene Salzer © The Brenner-Archiv.

25 Hermine to Ludwig

13 March 1918

My darling Lukas,

I spoke about you with Mama today, and out of the blue she said: 'Ludwig is interested in everything about everyone, one could ask him for advice about any and everything, and one would find a pillar of strength in him'. Hearing that made me so happy for you, and I just had to write to you with it right away. I always knew that you were the only one of the boys who listens whenever one tells him something and who takes a human interest in one, but only today did the significance of that become clear to me. It's funny that one sees only individual stones for such a long time, and then it suddenly occurs to one that they are a mosaic and have meaning.—Today, we played four-handed quite beautifully and thought of you the whole time, and tomorrow I'll be going to Neuwaldegg where you'll be in my thoughts again and then again and again.—

Continued. I have returned from Neuwaldegg, where I saw the second, more delicate profile which, I'm glad to say, I do not like at all; on the contrary, it only proved to me that the first is going to be absolutely right. Long live Engelmann! I have to tell you just one more thing, even if it isn't very pleasing to read such things; but my heart is brimming with it. I was talking with Lenka about you today, and she said something I liked very much: she said that you have what it takes to bring out the good in people, and that is entirely my feeling as well! Now I won't write with everything we said about you – that would be going too far; suffice it to say that we understood each another brilliantly and were happy to be with one another. That's everything that's happened since you left and, because I don't have anything more to report, I am ending this letter by assuring you that I love you very much.

Your devoted sister,

Mining

26 Hermine to Ludwig

Hochreit, 18 April 1918

and Vienna, 21 April 1918

My good Lukas,

I don't actually have any time or any right to write to you, for I should really be making an important decision, but I am feeling so absolutely uninspired and incapable of taking it that I'm playing the coward and looking for something easier to do. I am meant to decide whether my quasi-manager ought to be fired or not; it's indescribable how difficult such a decision is, because actually taking it requires a kind of painful operation, and just as your tooth doesn't hurt any more once you're at the dentist, so do his stupidities and transgressions seem, at this very moment, small to me. Oh, who will show me the light? Tomorrow I'll be leaving here again, and I can say that I have honestly tried to think of what's important and not to be interested in every flower more than in people and animals, as would be in my nature to do; now I hope that a day's distance will clear my mind. What a shame or how right it is that property comes with such stupid worries! I didn't even have time to think about beautification matters this time around, but I'm leaving everything for the time being anyway until Engelmann manages to get up here; for that will be a hard and tough nut to crack, I can see that already. In Neuwaldegg I did something stupid by ultimately allowing myself to be persuaded to choose the more delicate profile for the dining room, which no one can really see given the diffuse lighting, on the other hand, however, it'll surely work out very well due to the window's receiving the same arch as the doors and both being a very simplified and pretty picture. Engelmann was in Vienna again to take care of all the outstanding issues, and I was very glad I could talk with him about this and that. Unfortunately I don't have what it takes to get people to talk; on the contrary, I believe my innate reticence is contagious. It made me very happy that Paul was in agreement with everything; he was seeing the changes for the first time, and I was a bit afraid of what he'd say – it does seem, however, that there can really be only one opinion here. What ever would Papa say if we could show him! I've almost finished *Tristram Shandy*,[54] it's a strange book; sometimes I put it aside entirely frustrated and exhausted because I don't understand a thing, sometimes I wish it wouldn't end and I could read a few pages of it every day for the rest of my life. I left out the worst bits of *The House of the Dead*;[55] the rest, though, is great beyond all words. However, I did read the part where the convict threw that knife at the commanding officer, and I was glad that Dostoyevsky too shows the deed as an outburst of hopelessness and despair and not as something good in and of itself. I wanted to find that bit today so I could copy a bit of it verbatim for you, but I wasn't able to find it. My darling Lukas, God willing, you are meant for deeds other than those done out of hopelessness and despair! It would make me very happy if I were to hear from you again; of course it would make me even happier if I could see you, but that probably won't be happening any time soon!

The most heartfelt of hugs,
your devoted sister,
Mining

---

[54] *The Life and Times of Tristam Shandy, Gentleman* by Lawrence Sterne, 1759.
[55] Fyodor Dostoyevsky, 1862.

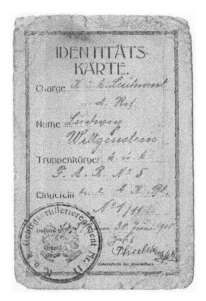

Wittgenstein's Military Identity Card.

Enclosure

I finally found the part and am copying it for you here. I'd like to take this opportunity to ask: don't you wish that Dostoevsky had just published *The House of the Dead* as if they were his own memoirs? I, for one, imagine the narrator to be quite different from the fictitious Aleksandr Petrovich – and surely he <u>was</u> completely different – so that I have to try to forget this bothersome A.P. I would like only to know whether anyone can be of a different opinion on this point?

... The convict who went mad, the one who used to read the Bible and went for the Major with a brick, was probably another of those who had given up every last hope; but since life without hope is impossible, he found a way out for himself through a voluntary, almost artificial martyrdom. ...

3

CAPTIVITY: NOVEMBER 1918 TO SEPTEMBER 1919

On 1 February 1918 Ludwig was promoted to lieutenant in the reserve. He took part in the battles south of Trento. After a long leave in the summer, which may have been allowed to him for health reasons, he returned to the front at the end of August. On 3 November 1918 he was made a prisoner of war.

In January 1919 he was transferred to Cassino, where he remained until 26 August, the official date of his release. In captivity Ludwig made friends particularly with two comrades who afterwards became friends of his family also. Ludwig Hänsel, later Director of a High School, and Michael Drobil the sculptor.

i 27 Mariechen to Ludwig

Salzer

Brahmspl. 4

Vienna 4

Leutnant Ludwig Wittgenstein

Prigioniere di Guerra

Bellagio

31 December 1918

Dear Uncle!

I want to write to you to show that I already have a good grasp of the Italian language!—We are all in good health and are glad that you too are well. We were given nice things for Christmas; I got the works of Gottfried Keller and other things, Fritz a camera, and Felix a bicycle. We had a nice tree here and another at grandmama's. All my family send you many greetings. We hope to see you soon. *Arrivederci*

Your niece,

Marietta

28 Hermine to Ludwig

iv Alleegasse 16

10 January 1919

My good Lukas,

Since I don't know whether you've received my card, I am writing to you again today with both the old and the new, in brief.

Mama had a cataract operation on one of her eyes yesterday, everything went <u>very well</u>, and she is not in any pain; she will, of course, not be able to write for a while.

Kurt fell on 27 September, it's very sad.[1]

Frege sends you his warmest regards and thanks for your work. A few sentences are missing from your work: between the sentence 'A proposition has essential and accidental features ...' of which there is only the beginning, and the sentence: 'A proposition can determine only one place in logical space'. The page numbers are right, but there must be a page missing. Can you write to us with what's missing?[2]

Kurt Wittgenstein ca. 1913. © The Brenner-Archiv.

---

[1] No agreed account of Kurt's death has come down to us. It was supposed to be an honorable suicide for an officer, who did not wish to surrender while his troops perhaps did.

[2] After Wittgenstein completed the final version of his *Logisch-philosophische Abhandlung* (later known as *Tractatus logico-philosophicus*) he made at least three typescript copies. He took one with him to the front and into captivity. Another went, as indicated here, to Frege. It is the very typescript now in the Austrian National Library (OeNB). A missing page was indeed replaced with a handwritten page, in the hand of Ludwig Hänsel (1886–1959), a gymnasium teacher, whom Wittgenstein had met while a prisoner of war, and who remained a lifelong friend. According to Frege, Hermine sent him the missing page on (or just before) 28 March 1919.

Labor is very well. Much to his delight, Paul will be playing his (very beautiful) clarinet trio everywhere.

Uncle Paul is very lively and sends you his warmest regards.

All our siblings and their children are healthy.

I think of you often and am sending you the most heartfelt of hugs.

Your devoted sister,

Mining

e 29 Margarete to Ludwig

Hotel National

Lucerne

Switzerland

Ludwig Wittgenstein

Kommandant der 8. Batterie

des Geb. Art. Regiment N. 11

de l'armee Austrichienne

Prisonnier de Guerre

a Bellagio

Italy

10 January 1919

Darling Lukerl,

I wonder wether my cards ever reach you. Everybody is well at home in V. We love you and are so happy to have heard from you at last after such a long and anxious time. I have sent you some money through the Red Cross and will do so every week or so. I kiss you and pinch your chin. Keep well and may I soon see you again! Love from Jerome and the boys.

Gretl

30 Margarete to Ludwig

Hotel National
Lucerne, Switzerland
S. Damiano

Ludwig Wittgenstein
Kommandant der 8. Batterie
des Geb. Art. Regiment n. 11
de l'armee Austrichienne
Prisonnier de Guerre
Campo di conentramento
Bellagio (Italy)

25 January 1919

My darling Lukerl,

Since I know you've been receiving cards from home, I'll write in German. I sent you 100 Francs three times – if only it's arrived!

Everyone is in good health both here and at home.

My heart is filled with love and affection for you, and I long to see you again. Who knows, perhaps we'll both be able to go home at the same time!

Thoughts and hugs from,
your Gretl

31 Margarete to Ludwig

> Margarete Stonborough
> Hotel National
> Lucerne, Switzerland

Ludwig Wittgenstein
Leutnant i. d. Reserve 2. Gruppe
San Pellegrino (Bergamo) Italy

> 4 February 1919

My darling Lukas,

I still haven't received any confirmation for the money I sent you. It was 400 Francs in 4 dispatches. I feel bad for you because you certainly need it desperately and unhappy for poor Mama too who would like to know that you're taken care of. But what can I do? I just hope that at least some of it has arrived already and that you're also receiving my cards and know that I am thinking of you with love and yearning.

> Your devoted sister,
> Gretl

Margaret with her sons Tommy and Ji in Swiss exile ca. 1918 © The Stonborough Family.

32 Margarete to Ludwig

Hotel National
Lucerne
Switzerland

Ludwig Wittgenstein
Leutnant i. d. Reserve
Luogo d'internamento: Cassino
Provincia Caserta
Italy

2 March 1919

Darling Lukerl,

Finally two cards from you!

I am overjoyed! A thousand hugs and worries. So glad that you've finally received some money; I will continue to send some regularly and from now on through the bank the Italian government has designated for these purposes.

The news from home is good. Mama is healthy, Minka is painting, and Lenka gave an afternoon of music for Paul and Labor. We are well, far too well materially, but exile is oppressive and difficult to bear. Ji[3] had a dream recently that somebody told him: 'The war should get lost in the woods'. Then he added: 'Unfortunately, the woods here just aren't big enough for that'.

My most loving thoughts are with you always and at all times. It seems now, though, as if you might not have to wait much longer for your return home. Love from Jerome and the boys, hugs and love from

your Gretl

---

[3] John Jerome Stonborough, Gretl's youngest son.

Margaret, 1920s © The Stonborough Family.

33 Margarete to Ludwig

Villa Schumacher
Tribschen,
Lucerne, Switzerland

Ludwig Wittgenstein
Lieutenant
Cassino
Provincia Caserta, Italy

24 March 1919

Darling Lukerl,

Mama's had some good news from you, the whole of creation is rejoicing. Everyone is healthy here and in Vienna. Busch[4] played here recently, the first time I've heard good music in over a year – it was a wonderful treat. In addition to the Kreutzer sonata and some Mozart, he played a sonata by Reger (in the Old Style), which went straight to my heart. Do you know it? Have you ever met D'Albert?[5] He lives in Lucerne and is a tiny manikin with a high-pitched voice. Busch told a story about the time D'Albert had to report the birth of his oldest son to the proper authority, and the clerk yelled: 'Nay, little man, your father has to come himself'.—I think the day of your salvation and my return home is nigh. Sometimes I fear I'll be struck by lightning first, it's been almost 2 years of waiting!—Keep well, my darling Luckerl, thinking of you and sending you the most heartfelt of hugs.

Love from Jerome and the boys.

Your Gretl

---

[4] Adolf Busch (1891–1952): violinist of international fame.
[5] Eugen D'Albert (1864–1932): pianist and composer.

34 Helene to Ludwig

Helene Salzer

Vienna iv

Brahmsplatz 4

Ludwig Wittgenstein

Leutnant i. d. Res.

Cassino

Prov. Caserta

Italy

24 March 1919

Dear Ludwig!

I would have written long ago if I had had something to tell you other than that I am very much looking forward to your return home and that I think about you a lot. We have already had a couple of beautiful concerts this year and heard and enjoyed immensely Brahms's fourth, among other things. I am working hard at playing with four hands in order to be able to do something when you get here.

Warmest,

Lenka

Leopoldine & Helene playing
four-handed in the Alleegasse
© *The Brenner-Archiv.*

35 Margarete to Ludwig

Villa Schumacher,
Tribschen,
Lucerne, Switzerland

Ludwig Wittgenstein
Leutnant
Cassino
Provincia Caserta, Italy

25 May 1919

My darling Lukerl,

I've been writing to you weekly, and Mama's been writing to you weekly, but it doesn't seem as though you're receiving any of our messages. The devil take it!

Everyone at home is extremely well, and we here are healthy too. Unfortunately, I'm still not allowed to go home yet. Perhaps we'll both get home at the same time? Oh, my darling Lukerl, it would be so nice! But I won't hold it against you, really and truly, if you get there first.—I bought a book by your friend Russell.[6] It's called *Roads to Freedom* and is keeping me quite occupied. The boys send you their love, I speak with them about you often. You'll find that they've changed quite a bit. I often believe that I see similarities between our Rudi[7] and Tommy. Perhaps the wish is father to the thought. With tender love and, hugs from

your devoted sister,
Gretl

---

[6] Bertrand Russell published a defence of Guild Socialism in America.
[7] Their brother Rudolf, who committed suicide in 1903.

36 Hermine to Ludwig

vienna

Alleegasse 16

27 May 1919

My good Lukas,

I have just learned of a new way to address letters to prisoners of war and am trying it out right away with a letter to you. It upsets me more than I can say that you're not receiving our messages, which we send you regularly, God knows who's to blame; in any event, the censor can't be finding anything objectionable about them because we write only with news of the family, nor were they too long, as we write open cards most of the time. It is just <u>too</u> sad! We of course think about you an awful lot; I in particular ask myself in any number of situations what you would say, and I often imagine what you are doing and thinking and what your plans are for the future. And of course I'm unable to come up with anything; I can only hope that things will finally settle down a bit – because no one can really call what's coming 'peace' – and that we will see each other again soon.—There is probably no such thing as peace amongst nations, there is only the time before war, during war and after war; that's how it seems to me now. We're in the city because the weather has been so bad this year and the rooms don't want to heat up at all. Our life hasn't changed one bit.

It's true that Mama does sometimes have a severe pain in her foot, and the eye that was operated on does not want to work with her healthy one, but no one notices any trace of that in the way she lives; she is either writing or darting about the house, and quite often plays diligently with Fillunger[8] and Röger.[9] I am painting a whole lot now and intend to carry out, bit by bit, my plan of capturing characteristic interiors. At the moment I'm painting Baumayer's room, which is very exciting, and I would like to go to Laxenburg[10] when I'm done! Paul is working very hard at the piano and is easy to get on with all the time now. Labor was here just a few days ago and played Bach and Chopin splendidly; he told me that he feels particularly well at our place and that that finds expression whenever he plays here. His only, but very enthusiastic, audience were Mama and I, and that's what set the tone so. Uncle Paul should be visiting us soon; he's very well, much better than he was last year. All my letters look alike, but what can I write other than news about your friends, which I repeat because I'm afraid you aren't receiving many letters. That is what makes writing so difficult! Engelmann was taking his lunch with us 1–2 times a week, and we were always glad to see him; but he has left for Olmütz with a theatre group, where he's working as a stage designer, and has been gone for a couple of weeks now. The food situation is said to be better there, and that's important for him. If he were only healthier, he is such a worthwhile human being.

Hoping, for you my dear Ludwig and for all of us, that we'll be happily reunited soon, with the most heartfelt of hugs,

your devoted sister,

Mining

---

[8] Marie Fillunger, a singer and friend of Poldi Wittgenstein's. She was often a guest at the Wittgenstein home.

[9] Marie Röger-Soldat and Marie Baumayer were musical friends of the house, a violinist and pianist respectively. Both were admired and counselled by Brahms and Clara Schumann.

[10] Where Karl Wittgenstein's sister, Aunt Clara (1850–1935), had a villa.

*Marie   Baumayer   and   Hermine   ©   The
Stonborough Family.*

37 Ludwig to Hermine

Cassino

Provincia Caserta

Italy

25 June 1919

Dear Mining!

Received three kind letters from you today, yesterday and the day
before yesterday! My warmest thanks! The post is the only ray of
hope here! My life here is perfectly monotonous. I'm not working,
and I'm constantly thinking about whether I'll ever be a decent

human being and how I am supposed to make that happen. My warmest regards, and tell everyone I said hello.

Ludwig

Cassino, the town in the 1920s © Collezione Mauro Lottici.

38 Hermine to Ludwig

Hochreit

Post Hohenberg

18 July 1919

My dear Ludwig,

My warmest thanks for your card where you confirmed receipt of 3 letters from me; it's just too stupid that they all arrived at the same time! Yesterday I sent you 2 copies of a letter Frege wrote to you, and I need to say the following about them: at the beginning of both copies I omitted some bits containing nothing more than excuses for not having read your treatise because, I believe, the shorter the letter, the easier it is for it to clear the censor – one copy is missing 2 sentences because there just wasn't enough room for them, as you will see in the second letter: namely, these 2 right at the beginning: 'is it the same when I say, Let A be the case, as when I say, Let A be a fact?'[11] And the last sentence 'I want to have an example for the claim that Vesuvius is a state of affairs, etc.'[12] But, because I still had room, I did add, as a postscript to the second copy, a sentence Frege wrote to me in his covering letter saying that he would very much like a visit from you so that the two of you could discuss this in person as soon as you've recovered from the hardships of captivity. If we were only there already! I don't want to put the original letter in the post; it's just so unreliable. I sent one copy via Innsbruck,[13] the other with a man who has forwarded you several letters for me, but I heard later that he just tossed it in the mailbox because, according to him, nothing further is necessary anymore. With any luck that copy, which is the complete one, will reach you.

That you are wearing yourself out and going to great pains to be a decent human being makes me happy and upset all at the same time; for I know that this's going to be an *idée fixe* with you (that only people with such an *idée* do extraordinary things) and that anyone with an *idée fixe*, which of course he will never be able to live up to, is usually unhappy and lost to his surroundings – unless they move in his direction. I ought to say only that 'I believe I know all that' instead of 'I know', but it all seems so particularly clear to me.

---

[11] Frege's text actually reads: 'Is it not the same when I say, Let A be a fact, as when I say, Let A be the case?' translation by Dreben and Floyd.

[12] Frege's text actually reads: 'I want to have an example for the claim that Vesuvius is a constituent of a state of affairs', translation by Dreben and Floyd, with the substitution of the Pears/McGuinness 'state of affairs' (followed in this volume) for the Ramsey/Ogden 'atomic fact'.

[13] In the hope, not fulfilled, that L. v. Ficker would publish it in *Der Brenner*.

I passed on your regards to Engelmann; he has written to you too. He is again coming to luncheon every week, and I'm always glad to see how much Paul likes him.[14]

Mama is coming up here next week; she is meant to stay by herself with Mariechen or Fritz and to get some peace and quiet. For her nerves are quite strained on account of everything she and you all have been through. She complains that she can't remember anything, and even if that isn't true, she's suffering from the idea all the same. The pain in her foot is excruciating, still and often. Otherwise everyone is in good health and everything all right.

Regards, a thousand times over,

my good Ludwig,

your devoted sister,

Mining

---

[14] See Ludwig's postcard to Engelmann of 24 May 1919 (translation by L. Furtmueller): 'Many thanks for your kind postcard of 3.4 and for the favourable review. I am going through hard times mentally! I, too, have a lot to say! Now a request: please send me, safely and quickly if you can, Frege's *Grundgesetze*. You will manage somehow, I am sure. May things go well with you' (Engelmann, Letters from Ludwig, p. 17). Wittgenstein had been studying Frege's *Grundgesetze der Arithmetik* since his Manchester years.

39 Ludwig to Hermine

Cassino
Provincia Caserta
Italy
19 July 1919

Dear Mining!

Thank you very much for your kind card of 1 July.[15] You're all certainly mistaken if you truly believe that my captivity can now only 'last for a short time'. Don't you know that prisoners will be transferred only after peace has been made? And then not all on one and the same day! I certainly hope to be with you all at Christmas. —I recently wrote to Engelmann and asked him to send me Frege's *Grundgesetze*.

Warmest regards,
Ludwig

40 Hermine to Ludwig

Vienna
xvii. Neuwaldeggerstrasse 38
6 August 1919

My dear Ludwig,

Thanks a million for your kind card of 19 July. I now regret that in each of my letters I expressed my hope of your returning home soon; I didn't consider how long negotiations and transportation might take. But maybe some auspicious coincidence will be of

---

[15] Hermine's card, which is lost, may have been sent in response to news of the Treaty of Versailles, which was signed on 28 July 1919.

some help in your case! The books Engelmann ordered arrived today; I had them sent straight away. But will you ever receive them? Have you received the copies of Frege's letter? Your friend David's mother[16] wrote to me an infinitely kind and truly touching letter. How such love and warmth do us good and how sad that they don't go on to set people on fire the way hate and other bad characteristics do! How strange that weeds are more fertile than good plants. —We are very happy that Mama is much better and that her stay at the Hochreit has been good for her in every way; she calls me on the telephone all the time, and I can hear an improvement in her voice alone. And it's about time too! —I'm going to see Labor on Saturday, who always plays beautifully for me, and we speak of you whenever the two of us are together. Playing Bach's *Toccata* recently, he said that it's your favourite piece. He gets a little upset with me every now and then because I just can't help myself and try to interpret a few passages and speak of moods in pieces of music, but overall we get on very well. I'm sorry that Engelmann is in Olmütz, but that is what's best for him, and Vienna is just poison at the moment.

Keep well, my good Lukas, longing to see you and warmest regards,

your devoted sister,

Mining

---

[16] Ellen Pinsent, mother of Ludwig's friend David Pinsent.

41 Ludwig to Hermine

[August 1919]

Dear Mining!

Received Frege's letter through you the day before yesterday. Admittedly, I never did think that he'd understand my work.[17] But I was somewhat depressed about his letter all the same. I've already written my response,[18] but haven't been able to send it yet. I've been able to work again lately. A great boon! The prospects of my coming home seem to be improving.[19]

Warmest regards,
Ludwig

Cassino, Police Barracks, used as Prisoner of War camp from 1916
© *Collezione Mauro Lottici.*

---

[17] Ludwig wrote to Russell on 19 August 1919 saying that Frege 'wrote to me a week ago and I gather that he doesn't understand a word of it all' (Wittgenstein in Cambridge, p. 63

[18] On 3 August 1919, according to Frege, who however does not give the content (Briefwechsel 267).

[18] Ludwig was officially released from captivity in Italy on 26 August 1919. He began his teacher training on 16 September and moved in – perhaps as early as the end of August, as suggested by this letter – with Frau Wanicek in the Untere Viaduktgasse, in Vienna's 3rd District.

42 Hermine to Ludwig

Vienna

1 September 1919

My good Lukas,

I was shocked not to find you here when I arrived at Neuwaldegg; I had got it into my head that the big changes would come about slowly over the next few months and of course would not have gone to the Hochreit with the boys, had I known that these were going to be my last few days with you.

Apart from the fact that I would have liked to have you to myself for a bit longer, I also now regret that I wasn't there when you spoke with our siblings about giving away your inheritance.

Of course I don't understand why you passed Gretl over. That is, I believe, an enormous slight – not because of the money, but because it's wounding to be 'disinherited'. If you're pursuing some purpose here, then that is something else entirely; one does what one believes is right, but perhaps you haven't yet looked at it from this perspective. If you didn't want to include her, you wouldn't have had to do anything more than write to her with a line or two saying that you're not trying to slight her here and that you're doing it because we shall lose a large part of our money, which won't happen with her. Won't you do that?

I'll be seeing you this afternoon at Max's, but I didn't want to say any of this to you in front of the men. Keep well my darling Lukas.

With kind regards,

your sister,

Mining

4

THE ELEMENTARY SCHOOL YEARS: OCTOBER 1920 TO MARCH 1926

Immediately on returning from captivity, Ludwig renounced his inherited fortune in favour of his siblings. Only Gretl was not included since it was thought she was already well provided for. When in Vienna he often chose to stay in rented accommodation, with friends the Hänsel's or with Hermine's friend Mime Sjögren, rather than in a house of his own family.

In July 1920 Ludwig finished his training as an elementary school teacher. In August he worked as assistant gardener at the Klosterneuburg Abbey outside of Vienna, and in September became teacher at the elementary school in Trattenbach in Lower Austria.

From autumn 1922 until summer 1924, Ludwig taught in a town called Puchberg am Schneeberg. Frank Ramsey, the brilliant young Cambridge scholar, came to visit him and also got to know Gretl in the town where Ramsey had come for psychoanalysis. It was here that Ludwig made friends with a younger colleague of some musical ability, Rudolf Koder, who became a close friend of the family. He spent the summer of 1924 in Vienna and on the Hochreit. In the autumn he moved to Otterthal as a teacher.

In 1925 Ludwig worked as an elementary school teacher in Otterthal, visiting Keynes in England in the summer. Then he went to Manchester, Cambridge and Sussex. Ramsey joined them in Sussex but managed to quarrel with Ludwig.

Ludwig found himself compelled to resign in 1926 from his post as teacher because of alleged ill-treatment of a pupil. He spent the summer as a gardener in the Hütteldorf monastery on the outskirts of Vienna. From autumn he worked with Paul Engelmann on the planning and construction of a house for his sister Margaret in the Kundmanngasse.

43 Paul to Ludwig

tel. 59102.

vienna, 27 March 1920.
iv. Alleegasse 16.

Dear Lucky!

Just learned Herr Nähr[1] was here & said that his landlady will not allow you to move in tomorrow – & this because she cannot answer for it to the housing police on hygienic grounds. The landlord himself is coming next week; perhaps something can be arranged with him.

---

[1] Moritz Nähr (1859–1945): family friend and family photographer, older than the Wittgenstein siblings.

Perhaps you could tell us your decision tomorrow; is it not possible for you to stay where you are at least for a couple of days?

In haste, but with affection,

your Paul

44 Paul to Ludwig

Neuwaldegg
September 1920

Dear Lucky!

Unfortunately, I arrived in Vienna just a day too late and was not able to see you before you left for Trattenbach. Well there is now the well-founded fear that you'll be overfed. Our country is choking on its riches & most of all its elementary school teachers!! They are swimming in luxury, wallowing in abundance & 'as well fed as an elementary school teacher in a mountain village' has become a proverb. Their income has climbed to the fantastical, their wastefulness knows no bounds, they're outdoing the Orient with their greed, the Romans during their decline and fall with their luxury, Lucullus is an orphan child compared to them, in a word: they are bags of tripe, as Aunt Luise[2] used to say, & most of them will have to be sent to Marienbad[3] because they are so fat.

Even though that is all true, I hope you won't be too very reluctant to accept the small package of forage sent to you contemporaneously with this letter.

I'll be organising a Labor evening at the beginning of winter. If I can only find people who will go to it & if, in their turn, at least no <u>more</u> than half of them fall asleep!

[2] Louise Pollitizer.
[3] The famous thermal station in Bohemia.

We'll miss you there, for a convinced claque is what'll be needed.

Warmest greetings,

your brother,

Paul

45 Ludwig to Paul

24 September 1920

Dear Paul!

The warmest of thanks for your kind letter. I haven't received the package yet, but will gladly devour it all, even though I do get enough to eat here. It's very nice of you to have thought of me!

If your Labor evening were to fall on a Saturday, then I might be able to come to Vienna to attend. For I'll be able to afford such an excursion only after I've learned the ropes a bit. Will you be playing the new *Phantasie*? I've heard only the beginning, and it is of course genuine Labor, but it seems a bit thin to me – which, however, means nothing because one ought to hear it several times. —I think the bassoon solo from the brass quartet is very beautiful, and the beginning and the end in particular are wonderful.

Again, my warmest thanks,

your devoted brother,

Ludwig

46 Paul to Ludwig

Vienna, Neuwaldegg
8 October 1920

Dear Lucky!

The Labor evening I mentioned will take place on Saturday, 27 November, in the small hall of the Musikverein.[4] So do come come, if it's halfway possible for you.

When I was at Heller's[5] place to discuss the preparations for the concert with him, one of the things I asked him was where he had spent the summer, and he said: 'In Bavaria with Johannes Müller'.[6] When I asked who that was: 'He's a true Christian, a utopian and a do-gooder. He lives in a kind of sanatorium, hot and cold water in every room, a concert hall has just been built, Hermann Bahr[7] discovered him. However you do get meat only twice a week there and are allowed to help with the haymaking'. His true Christianity really seems to consist of the latter two penitential practices.

I should have retorted that he's probably more of a true Jew and asked how much his true Christianity nets him a year?

The programme will most probably include: the two clarinet trios, the new *Phantasie*, a few Canons for Female Voices performed by the Mandyczendsky women's choir.

I agree with every word of your assessment regarding the introduction to then *Phantasie*: 'Genuine Labor, but a bit thin'. Of

---

[4] The Wiener Musikverein, a concert hall in the city centre of Vienna, Austria.

[5] Hugo Heller (1870–1923): book dealer, organized numerous readings and concerts.

[6] Johannes Müller (1864–1949): evangelical religious writer. The sanatorium is Schloss Elmau, his 'meeting place for searching souls'.

[7] Hermann Bahr (1863–1934): The leading critic and director from Vienna. Founder of Young Vienna.

course Labor's music needs the charm of diversity in timbres and diversity of voices, which is possible only with several instruments.

So, God willing, till November!

Paul

47 Ludwig to Paul

November 1920

Dear Paul!

Thank you very much for the tickets. But aren't they the wrong ones? They are dated for Wednesday instead of Saturday. I am returning them to you enclosed. Should they really be valid for Saturday, then please send them, or the right ones, to Dr Hänsel, Kriehubergasse 25, where I will be going before the concert.

I hope I'm not bothering you unnecessarily, but a mistake could have been made.

Regards,

your Ludwig

ps: I am very much looking forward to the concert!

48 Hermine to Ludwig

Hochreit, 11 October 1920

My good Lukas,

I see now that it's going to be a long time before I'll be able to visit you, everything is going so damned slowly with me; in the end, you'll probably come to Vienna first. You can imagine how great of a disappointment it was for me not to be able to visit you; I had been looking forward so much to having you all to myself and hearing everything about you and being able to see you, and now I have to forgo it all! At least allow me the joy of sending you something useful; I'll send this letter to Frl. Julie, who'll get started on that right away.

Thank you very much for your kind letter (I hope you received the one from me in which I cancelled!). Regarding Drobil:[8] he is out of harm's way for the moment, since I'm away, but I think, after all, if someone is going to sculpt a bust I'm meant to own, then he has to put up with my speaking with him about entirely trivial matters as well, even in the company of Mima. (Or is that just using him as a means to an end?)

In any event, I won't be inviting him. You needn't think that I don't understand what you're saying at least to a certain extent; I'm just saying that the domesticating influence wouldn't be all that great anyway. But as said, I'm certainly not going to be inviting him. I would certainly not want to humiliate anyone, believe you me!

Keep well, my good Lukas, I hope you're well, and that you think kindly

of your devoted sister,

Mining

---

[8] Michael Drobil (1877–1958), academic sculptor and member of the Wiener Secession. Like Hermann Hänsel, he was one of the friends that Wittgenstein made when a prisoner of war in Cassino.

49 Hermine to Ludwig

5 November 1920

My good Lukas,

You can imagine that it wasn't a matter of indifference to me to be stuck up here instead of being able to be with you; I cursed, and continue to curse, because the prospects of my being able to visit you in the foreseeable future are not good. I have to take it so pitiably easy in a way hitherto unimaginable to me, and whenever I start to think 'oh, what, the doctor's an ass; I'm going to do it differently this time' I learn right away that I'm the one who's the ass, and not the doctor. Of course it would be different, if I were alone in this world or if it were of any import to the world that I perform some definite activity at precisely this moment; but as things stand I have to see to it that I make a full recovery, though I shudder at the thought. I wonder how long it'll take. Mima wrote me an extremely kind letter yesterday and described Trattenbach and everything; I can picture it perfectly already. I was very sorry, however, that she was at Drobil's place and spoke to him the way she did; but everything she writes is precisely what I myself thought. From the heads in the Secession, I at once saw that Drobil's aim and ability consist in looking for and illustrating the multitude of minor forms in nature: i.e., in a certain sense, in exaggerating. This profusion of minor forms is characteristic of the heads of women and small children, and his search has been rewarded quite nicely. But whenever he looks for such profusion on a head that seems to have been worked over by a carpenter (of course they exist there too, but to such a negligible degree that their apparent absence is what's characteristic), whenever he exaggerates these minor forms – and he must exaggerate them, if he truly wants to express them – he acts against what's characteristic of this particular head and that exacts its revenge. For a portrait must be characteristic, if it's meant as a portrait. I'm just glad I wasn't there; I certainly wouldn't have been able to hold my tongue and this is exactly a case in which anything one says is really like trying to tell an apple tree that it ought to grow pears! It of course does not want to grow pears, and it is still an apple tree even if pears are ten times more what's required. I am writing to you in such detail about this because you're incapable of imagining that Drobil can be so far off the mark despite all his good qualities.

—At the moment I'm carrying out an experiment that puts me to shame: mathematics was always difficult for me as a child, though I later thought my teachers were mostly to blame for that because they never taught me how to do it properly. Now I've brought a 1st and 2nd grade maths book here with me because I would like to be able to do basic school maths for a certain purpose. And I often sit here for hours at a time with rules and exercises that a ten-year old is expected to understand before I really take them in. No one watching would be able to understand it at all; he'd be bound to think that I'm distracted and that my thoughts are wandering all over the place, when really I'm concentrating on proportions, calculating fractions, etc. The following proposition can be found in your book: 'The processes of calculating serve to bring about that intuition. Calculation is not an experiment': [Tractatus 6.2331]. That's not true when I do calculations; they're always experiments, and I'm always very anxious to find out what the result will be. I now understand that I was unable to understand it as a child; but I still don't understand how any child can understand it!

Keep well, my good Lukas,

warmest regards,

your sister,

Mining

Paul & Mariechen In Silhouette © The Stonborough Family.

50 Paul to Ludwig

Tel. 59102

iv Alleegasse 16.

Vienna, 17 November 1920

Dear Ludwig!

The inevitable has occurred: because it was inevitable.

When we heard in autumn that you turned down a position in Reichenau so you wouldn't be recognised, Hans Salzer,[9] who just

---

[9] Max Salzer's brother.

happened to be with us at the time, said: 'It'll just take 14 days longer somewhere else'. And that's what we all thought too.

Given the unbelievable degree to which our name is known and the fact that we're the sole bearers of it in Austria – this fact falls particularly heavy in the balance – given the enormous numbers of our father's, Uncle Louis's,[10] Aunt Clara's acquaintances, the properties we own spread across the whole of Austria, the various charitable causes we're involved in, etc., etc., it is impossible, truly perfectly impossible, that any person bearing our name, and whose distinguished and refined up-bringing anyone can see from a thousand feet off, will not be recognised as a member of our family.

Even changing your name as the last resort would be of no use to you. That is the one thing, hard as it may be, that you had better learn, and that, hard as it sounds, you will have to get used to.

As for me, I'm just happy that I'm in no way to blame. I saw Mrs. Mautner[11] just once this year, there was never any talk of you, and she probably doesn't even know – and at any rate not from me – that I have a brother.

But even if I had been the one who told her, I can assure you that it would have been like the case of two children where one catches the measles: you intentionally put the other one near the one with the measles so that the he'll get them sooner rather than later, for he is going to get them one way or the other. The truth is a person is more likely to die without ever having had the measles than to belong to our family and not be recognised as such. ''Tis medicine, not poison, that I give you'.[12]

---

[10] Louis Wittgenstein (1845–1925), Karl Wittgenstein's brother.

[11] Presumably a relative of the engineer Mautner, who routinely was involved in family projects. There were also mill-owners called Mautner in Trattenbach.

[12] From Act 1, Scene 2 of Lessing's *Nathan the Wise*; translation by Frothingham, 1868.

Enclosed I am sending you 2 tickets for the Labor evening. Perhaps you can make it, if only for Mama's and Mining's sake. As, I believe, you already know, there will be performances of: the two clarinet trios, the Canons for Female Voices, and the new *Phantasie*, a four-course vegetarian dinner.

Bon appetit!

With love,
your brother,
Paul

Herrn Ludwig Wittgenstein, elementary school teacher <u>Trattenbach bei Gloggnitz</u>
Lower Austria
<u>Registered</u>

51 Hermine to Ludwig

Wednesday,
17 November 1920

My good Lukas,

Now I'm doubly and triply sorry I wasn't here during your holiday because, from everything I've heard, it seems you weren't feeling very well. Perhaps I could have done something for you, be it in respect of accommodation, topics of conversation or something else. What do you think? I better not have such bad luck next time! I was released today, thank goodness, with a clean bill of health, but I am still supposed to be careful and that is the reason I can't tell you when I'd like to come; I really want to be as fit as a fiddle <u>for that</u>, with no limitations whatsoever. Let's hope that'll be the case soon. I am infinitely sorry to hear that, as Paul tells it, you weren't able to get on with Gretl at all. I really like her quite a lot, and I must admit that

I am awfully impressed by her as well. But there's nothing to be done about that! Oh, my good Lukas, already I have such a longing to see you! I wonder very much what my own life in the near future will be– whether I'll ever find a path to a fulfilling life. I just live day to day until I hit a dead-end and am obliged, very drudgingly, to live my way out of the day. Yet, I have so much that makes me happy and, since I've already written to you about my shameful experience with the maths book, I am also obliged to tell you that I was occupied with Pauli's[13] mathematical prowess during the last few days of my stay up at the Hochreit and, to my mind, not without success either. The tricks I've found for myself seem to be helping him a lot and to have earned his respect. But what a crying shame it is that I learned next to nothing in my youth; I feel the lack of it at every turn! — Unfortunately, you can't take pleasure in anything, because small gratifications of vanity are foreign to you and there's nothing on the outside that will really make you happy; you live only in your breast. If someone could make it a bit more friendly in there, I would gladly plant a few flowers there, and all your friends – and you have a lot of those – would gladly contribute something as well! Mima likes you a lot, the dear soul that she is. But no one can live on that. What can we live on? I'm still not clear about that in the least.

(Continuation) ii

My good Lukas,

Paul just told me you're quite upset that the people in Trattenbach know who you are; I cannot say just <u>how</u> sorry I am to hear that; for I can so clearly imagine how it all is! Of course, I know the discovery was <u>inevitable</u>, but that doesn't make it any easier for you! I can only think that what was new and unprecedented for the people there will

---

[13] Paul Mudigler, a Hochreit employee's son.

soon turn into something familiar and that you'll be less of a phenomenon for them once they have all the facts and stop suspecting everything under the sun; the reason is they must have found out soon enough, for goodness sake, that you belong to a different race, and you were surely a mystery to them because of that? That wouldn't exactly be something I would be embarrassed about; I have often been a mystery to people and have been able to talk about it without giving offence, because there was no secret about it. As soon as I wrote that, I saw how untrue it is, because of course I try to keep my wealth a secret when and wherever I can. But that is just <u>a half measure and cowardice</u>! Yet, you truly have nothing to hide, except for good things, and you needn't preach any morality you don't practise to the best of your ability. That people will not understand you is, of course, a fact that can't be changed, but, at least, they have to respect you – doesn't that mean anything to you? It would mean <u>very much</u> to me, I believe; my precious Lukas, if only you could come on the 27th, so that we could talk a bit, together, it's already been so long since I saw you last.

Warmest regards and best wishes,

your devoted sister,

Mining

52 Margarete to Ludwig

[November 1920][14]

Dear Lukerl,

Two things I said during our last conversation are weighing on me because they aren't true; they seemed true to me only whilst I was

---

[14] This letter is dated on the basis of a remark in Letter 51 where Hermine writes: 'according to Paul, you were not able to get on with Gretl at all'.

angry. To wit: 1) It is not true that you are not better than me. You are better. 2) It is not true that I would not like to be you. I would rather be you than me.

Your sister,

Gretl

53 Paul to Ludwig

Tel. 59102

iv. Alleegasse 16

Vienna, 20 November 1920

Dear Luki!

Just a follow-up to my recent letter. I already wrote to you about how it was inevitable that people would catch on to your parentage and family background – indeed, how it was astounding that it didn't happen much sooner than it did. If it weren't Mautner, then it would have been some forester's boy who used to work for us up at the Hochreit that had recognised you, or a teacher who was once employed at the Alleegasse or a waiter in some guesthouse who used to be a waiter at the works hotel in Kladno, or in the municipal restaurant in Wiesenbach, or a factory worker who used to work for Uncle Louis in Koritschan, or a peasant girl who used to be a milkmaid in the Trauch, and who knows how many more inevitabilities there might be. I need not tell you that no one is capable of simulating or dissimulating anything – and that includes a refined upbringing. For this reason alone, you would have been better off if you had just said from the start who and what you are; by doing that you would have taken the bite out of all the exaggerated rumours from the very outset.

I should have given you this advice myself, even though it probably wouldn't have done any good.

Now the abscess you didn't want lanced has burst of its own accord, and when the initial pain from the operation is over, you'll feel better than you did before. Because – and this is what I actually wanted to write to you today – the initial talk will soon come to an end, or at least will begin to come to an end: *cela séchera comme la rosée au soleil.*[15] Then there will be less gossip about you than before: for you were once a mystery to people which they attempted to solve the best way they know how; but now they have the key to the cipher, know what they are dealing with, and the gossip will stop when the mystery ends. The more I think about it, the more I believe in the likelihood that this prophecy will come to pass. (I want to add that our mother still doesn't know a thing about this whole ordeal.)

As for the Labor evening, the traditional adverse star is presiding over it: on the same evening, there is a grand concert by the conductor Furtwaengler and a concert by the violinist Busch, two great musicians who are quite in vogue at the moment, and are the big 'draw'.[16] As if, in the end, these works of ours could cause too much of a sensation!

Warmest,

your brother,

Paul

Herrn Ludwig Wittgenstein, elementary school teacher

<u>Trattenbach</u>

bei Gloggnitz

---

[15] It will all pass, like dew in the sunshine.
[16] Wilhelm Furtwaengler (1886–1954) and Adolf Busch (1891–1952).

54 Hermine to Ludwig

23 November 1920

My darling Lukas!

Your letter of the 17th, which I just received, upset me indescribably; I just don't understand how the whole thing can be so torturous to you? You aren't a millionaire anymore! I, half-nun that I am, am bound to be embarrassed whenever anyone finds me out. But you? You have made a choice and can stand your ground and say: 'what was is past, and my situation is different now'. How long will this wonder last? People will have long taken notice of you, for our facial features alone betray a good family, not to mention how we talk and think, etc. It's no wonder people made inquiries about you! Can't you speak openly with them about it? Or at least say: like it or lump it? At the front and in captivity you were certainly less inhibited and were, in every situation in life, one man amongst others; is that not possible in Trattenbach? Of course, I won't come until you want me to, but I do hope that you'll come here, so that we can finally have a word with each other. If I could only have some thicker skin made for you, I would gladly do it at whatever cost!

You're not made for this world!

With the most heartfelt of hugs,
my darling Lukas,
your devoted sister,
Mining

55 Hermine to Ludwig

28 November 1920

My good Lukas,

It was of course a great disappointment for me that you didn't come, but there's nothing one can do about that, as you well know. I only hope it's not because you're afraid to talk, for of course you need say nothing more than that you don't want to talk about this or that, and the topic just won't be broached. I now suspect that I won't be seeing you until Christmas; and I am sorry about that, because as much or as little heart as I have belongs to you, and being without contact in such a case is dreadful; I keep saying to myself: with any luck, it can't go so far as to become <u>real</u> estrangement?

The concert was, indeed, truly sad, <u>just</u> Labor, which is unbearable; he needs something bad to be set off against (like last year) or something good for variety. Even with the best of intentions and the best of help, it was anything but a pleasure; still I believe Labor enjoyed it immensely, and that is of course what counts.

There is, thank God, nothing going on with us, though that means there's nothing to report either.

Wishing you, from the very bottom of my heart, my good Lukas, all the best and a more tranquil inner life,

your sister,

Mining

56 Hermine to Ludwig

Vienna, 15 December 1920[17]

My good Lukas,

You have been gone for about a week now, but it actually seems longer to me; I, for my part, am living in quite a strange state of excitement and duteous egoism: i.e., I mean, thinking of oneself a lot whenever a duty looms ahead that one believes is beyond one's powers. Even the <u>smallest</u> of tasks is capable of exceeding one's strength, and difficulties are just as subjective as pain; whenever I feel them, they exist: even if someone else can prove that I'm just imagining it all. —We were really and truly sorry not to have been able to see you on Saturday, and I am even sorrier that you don't have the naïve feeling of joy at seeing each other again that I so intensely do. But that, of course, is related to our not understanding you; for nothing is as beautiful as being understood by another person, and affection alone can be dreadful. I cannot imagine anything more frustrating than the relationship between me and my Swiss patient, who is always inviting me to this and that; she is glad to see me, hugs me constantly, and I just stand there all the while like a stick, assuring her that I don't have a heart and that I'm entirely indifferent to everyone, including her. It reminds me, damn it, of how the two of us deal with each other, God forbid that that similarity should become greater still. Whilst my understanding of you may wane, if you move any further away from us, my love for

---

[17] The date reads 5 December 1920, but is given here as 15 December 1920. Wittgenstein was not in Vienna a week prior to 5 December, a Saturday, 27 November, when the Labor concert took place (see Letter 55 and letter to Hänsel of 30 November). The Feast of the Immaculate Conception, a school holiday, 8 December, may have been an occasion for Ludwig to visit.

you will not. Still, I'm grateful for just being able to write to you
with whatever comes into my head and to pour my heart out to
you. And I believe, in the final analysis, I have not been <u>entirely</u>
uncomprehending; I can imagine a miniature model of some
things even if I am incapable of imagining the grand design and
even though I've formed the stupid habit of wanting to talk things
out of existence, which is so tiresome for me in other people when
I myself am morally down and out. Oh, what a complicated and
disturbing world we live in!

My good Lukas, I wish you nothing but the best,

your sister,

Mining

57 Hermine to Ludwig

8 January 1921

My dear Ludwig,

I immediately sent your letter to Helene Lecher.[18] I am really <u>very</u>
sorry to hear that it wasn't especially agreeable in Laxenburg. Aunt
Clara can be so charming, and the whole atmosphere has something
magical about it. Surely she didn't understand the suggestive record
herself. How could she have? If she had, she wouldn't have been
able to play it in front of young people! There's an analogy here
with Tristram Shandy, God knows what she was thinking![19]

---

[18] A friend of Hermine's who directed a day-care refuge for malnourished and ailing
children.

[19] For Clara Wittgenstein see Menger, *Reminiscences of the Vienna Circle*, p. 77; she was in
fact well-informed and modern in her reading. What shocked Hermine may have been that
members of a younger generation were present. She also (conversely) seems to think Clara
incapable of understanding the masked suggestiveness of *Tristram Shandy*.

Engelmann was here yesterday, and I argued with him until noon about his social notions without our coming one step closer to a consensus. But I like his sketches and draughts very much; a unique personality is immanent in them. As regards actually building something: we still can't decide – I can't explain it with any brevity – but it's certain that neither Paul nor I will have something built by anyone but him. If only we had known him beforehand! How our family grave pains me every time I see it, and unfortunately it's a hopeless case, it can't even be repaired like the things in Frauenfeld's[20] work. *Mea culpa!*

My dear Ludwig, your being here passed like a breath, and I saw very little of you, but you give me so much. In French, the expression 'le peu' (the little) affects the subsequent verb in different ways, depending on whether it underscores the absence or the presence of something. Hence, after you leave, what remains is the underscored part – the little I did have of you. May you keep well!

Warmest regards,

your sister,

Mining

58 Helene to Ludwig

xii

Neuwaldeggerstrasse 38

[undated]

My darling Lukerl!
I can't help but take advantage of this reliable opportunity to send you some chocolate and ask that you eat it to my health. If I had

---

[20] Frauenfeld, leading interior architect, who first modernized the villa of the Wittgensteins at Neuwaldegg.

heard soon enough that Nähr was going to visit you, some other edible thing would have come with it. With affection and hugs, your,

Lenka

59 Hermine to Ludwig

Sunday, 21 January 1921

My good Lukas,

Nähr was just here, good and kind person that he is, and what he told us again awoke in me the very keen desire to visit you in Trattenbach. I would so like to come next Saturday, the 22nd; come, don't say no! I am of course going to visit you at some point and show those Trattenbachers the poor teaching assistant from Gutenstein;[21] hence, it makes no difference at all <u>when</u> you swallow the bitter pill, does it?

Nähr also told me today that I ought to visit you sometime; but I told him that you have expressly forbidden it and that I would go against your wishes only if there were extreme pressure to do so. I can only hope that I can do so <u>with</u> your permission before it comes to that, and I would like to come on the same train as Nähr and to stay for as long as he does. Come, write to me by return with what you think about this idea, just don't write me off! There's nothing new here and, thank God, nothing wrong with the old.

Warmest regards,
your devoted sister,
Mining

---

[21] Like Trattenbach, Gutenstein is a valley village in Lower Austria, but is somewhat nearer to the family property. The allusion, however, is probably to Hermine's tutoring one of the boys up at the Hochreit (see Letter 51).

60 Hermine to Ludwig

23 January 1921

My good Lukas,

I was of course very disappointed about your cable – the letter hasn't arrived yet – as I was very much looking forward to seeing you and hoping, given what Nähr said, that a more human attitude had come over you. So, everything is as it was at Christmas and, God knows where it's all going to end. I don't want to be a hypocrite and will certainly not say that it makes me unhappy; I'm far too occupied with myself for that, besides I always enjoy people most when I'm actually with them, and they fade for me once they've been away for a while. And yet thinking about the past saddens me greatly. How I enjoyed being with you, how much you've given me. How I always enjoy writing to you and telling you everything that pops into my head. Does that too have to come to an end? Not on <u>my</u> account: I need to write to you and to imagine how you'll judge this and that, although I have perhaps long been unable to keep step and you have become a different Ludwig from the one I have come to expect. If I could keep up just a bit, but no I don't want to; I don't see any good in it or it's not something I've been tasked with. My ideal lies elsewhere entirely. I can't write any more today, it seems to me that I have to know where I stand with you before I do; one can't talk into the telephone when there's no connection. Perhaps a better time will come for me yet.

Warmest regards,
my good Lukas,
your sister,
Mining

61 Ludwig to Hermine[22]

24 January 1921

Dear Mining!

I was unable to respond to your letter in any detail right away because I was in bed with the mumps. Your letter is actually quite incomprehensible to me. The devil only knows what Nähr could have babbled which would have made you want to visit.

With a bit of reason and understanding he might have known that I was and am now not at all disposed to be visited by you! (Please show Nähr this letter!) How could you not have known I was serious when I asked you not to visit me for the time being?! (It would, of course, make no difference whatsoever how you come, for people here already know that my sister is a millionaire and not a teaching assistant.) But I see from your letter that, under certain circumstances, under particular pressure, you would visit me even against my wishes. That is of course entirely incomprehensible. Not that you would do something against my wishes, but that one human being can ever visit another human being against his wishes. In my eyes such a visit would be the crassest disregard conceivable, a sign of an absence of any respect which one free human being owes to another. In our family, such absence wouldn't be anything new to me, given the numerous cases in which one of us has lovingly tyrannised another. —But I hope you believe me to have what it takes to resist such tyranny; in my case, it would have come to the wrong address.

---

[22] This letter is a draft, written on the back of Letter 59. In a letter of 24 January 1921, Ludwig tells Hänsel that he did not send the letter printed here, but a 'milder, more well-intentioned one', which had a disquieting effect all the same.

Now that I re-read your letter, I can believe only that you wrote it without thinking. Or did you too have a fever?

Farewell,

Ludwig

62 Paul to Ludwig

tel. 59102

iv. Alleegasse 16

vienna, 25 January 1921

Dear Luki!

Contemporaneously with this letter you are being sent a copy of the *Andante* from Weber's sonata:[23] I also copied the romance from Weber's Concerto in E-flat major. This piece is not exactly the most important – the last movement is incomparably richer – and is rather difficult too, as I conclude from the fact that even Behrends allowed himself a simplification: but there is no harm in it, and I wanted to show it to you anyway because I very much like the middle bit, the demisemiquaver passages and the subsequent recitative.

I am about to travel and can therefore only leave instructions for the copying and hope that no mess comes of it and, if everything is otherwise in order, that the copyist does not make too many transcription errors, which no one can correct in my absence. If the copy does contain mistakes that are too detrimental to the sense of the music, then perhaps you'll be so kind as to write to me at some

---

[23] Weber's clarinet concerto no. 2.

point in February, after I've returned, with the relevant bars, so that I can correct and send them back to you.

Warmest greetings,
your brother,
Paul

Herrn Ludwig Wittgenstein, elementary school teacher,
Trattenbach bei Gloggnitz.

63 Hermine to Ludwig

29 January 1921

My dear Ludwig,

Your letter was very hurtful, all the more so because I can't understand how I came to deserve it. I no longer recall what words I used in my letter, but I certainly did not seriously write that I would visit you against your wishes. At least, I can't imagine that at all now. I was in a good mood then and wrote more in jest. I know that, but I no longer remember what my exact words were. Could you not send me the letter?[24] I do remember that I intentionally wrote more in jest because I wanted to avoid sentimentality. In any

---

[24] In a letter of 6 February 1921 to Hänsel, Ludwig comments: 'Even the milder letter to Mining had quite a powerful effect – and not a good one. But there's nothing I can do. Perhaps though the end-effect will be a good one.' Two messages, lightly disguised in Latin, suggest that Hänsel in fact advised an invitation to Hermine, which did in fact result. The first, dated 22.2.1921, reads '*C. c. s. e. i.*' and has to be interpreted in the light of the second, dated 10.3.1921, '*Optime fecisti, bene facias (sororem invitatam esse novi*, worueber der alte Cato, der Mordsphilister freut,)', respectively, 'I persist in the view that your sister should be invited' ('*Ceterum censeo sororem esse invitandam*') and 'You have done an excellent thing, good for you! (I know your sister has been invited and old Cato hard-bitten curmudgeon though he is, rejoices.)' '*Ceterum censeo*' is the phrase with which Cato (the Censor in every sense) repeatedly prefaced his insistence that Carthage should be destroyed ('*Carthaginem delendam esse*').

event, it would never have occurred to me to come to Trattenbach unannounced or against your wishes. Also when we parted, I spoke the way I did only because I thought you would invite me yourself. I didn't suspect that a visit from me would be <u>so</u> disagreeable to you. The change in you is happening so rapidly that what seems possible today will be completely inconceivable tomorrow. With you, one needs constantly to aim ahead and indeed also allow for the acceleration, as when shooting at a falling object. If only you could be satisfied and happy! Do keep your friends at least. Maybe Nähr was talking without understanding because he is capable of reporting only on your external life, still he is such a nice, good and affectionate person and doesn't intrude any further because he is so sensitive and tactful – and precisely that, I think, is what's so beautiful about him.

If I can be of use to you at some point, then I will of course be very glad to come, because my love can't be affected by anything.

I am very sorry that you had the mumps; it must have been very uncomfortable and painful.

Farewell for now, my dear Ludwig, warmest regards, your devoted sister,

Mining

ps: Please send me my letter, if possible; I don't understand what I'm supposed to have written.

64 Hermine to Ludwig

1 March 1921

My dear Ludwig,

I recently wrote you a frightfully stupid letter because I was in a very unpleasant frame of mind;[25] that evening, however, I made the decision to tell the children that, whenever I get angry, they have my permission to smack me the way I do them (which, by the way, has never had much effect on them), and everything seems better to me since then. Or maybe it was just one of those recurring high points of agitation that occur in me, which are then followed by better times. However that may be, I am happy about the peace and quiet at the moment. I would really like to know how you are – I mean, on the inside – but, presumably, that wall will always be too high for me; I just won't be able to look in there anymore! I hope you enjoyed Hänsel's visit! —I was recently at Drobil's studio and was very glad to find that the bust is much better than I expected it to be. It is of course a 'Drobil bust' insofar as it displays his soft spot and love for hidden forms, but it also displays such a likeness that I was able to praise it <u>honestly and from the heart</u>; I hope he noticed. I dislike his other works so much, especially, e.g., his wife as a maenad with a body marred with traces of all the dismalness of the war and post-war years; it's just too much of a failure for my tastes and I wasn't able to find words for it. I believe portraits in the broad sense of the term, which can also be understood as portraits of a landscape or of a still life, are the only thing artists are still capable of doing today. Even a Drobil, it seems to me, can't muster up the <u>imagination to sublimate</u> elements of reality; rather, he stops short at <u>love</u> and

---

[25] The 'stupid' letter is presumed lost. It is highly improbable that Hermine is referring to Letter 63 above.

<u>loyalty</u>. But you can't turn your wife into a maenad with that! When I see what the best artists are doing today, I'm always happy that I gave up painting; it's just that I have to replace my art with something else of value, and that is damned difficult! But now I have to ask you something practical, which is: when will you be coming for Easter and for how long? It's just that I want to go up to the Hochreit and will have to do so around that time and want to plan accordingly so that I can be in Vienna on your free days. Or would you like to come to the Hochreit with me? But that would just be too disappointing for Mama! In any event, I ask only that you write to let me know when you're coming. I am infinitely looking forward to seeing you! Perhaps, you are still of this world, just a bit, so that I can have just a bit of you. Warmest regards, my good Ludwig, your devoted sister,

Mining

65 Hermine to Ludwig

Wednesday,
[16 March 1921]

My dear Ludwig,

I haven't managed to tell you how happy I was that I could visit you; it was so refreshing and uplifting![26] —My journey home was very nice despite or because of the fact that I once again took a big detour; taking the shortcut to Weissenbach, I ended up, obviously due to the symmetry, just about as far to the right as the Syhrntal is to the left of the proper route.[27] During it all I even lost my lovely

---

[26] We know from a letter of Hermine's to Hänsel (9 March 1921) that Ludwig sent Hermine an invitation via Arvid Sjögren.

[27] Hermine is describing the path – some 8 km long – from Trattenbach via Sattel von Wartenstein to Gloggnitz, which all of Ludwig's visitors had to travel by foot.

Loden cape and noticed only once I had made my way all the way down to the Landstrasse, far too late to do anything like look for it. I can only hope that my allotted task is something other than being practical, because I would fail miserably at that! I had to laugh at myself because I was so light-footed as I skipped down to the valley that I even noticed it myself. Of course I was light-footed, I didn't have that heavy cape on my back which I had lugged up to Wartenstein, but I didn't even think of that possibility! —I immediately sent you the new razor blades, I hope they're the right ones. —Much to my delight the *Homburg* performance[28] is said to have been very beautiful and to have met with general approval. I am really and sincerely happy about that! Lenka is still ecstatic about how beautiful her costume was and how everything had been admired, and both our sisters are said to have delivered a very good performance. Paul was particularly taken by Greti's acting, and he's not prejudiced towards her at all! I would like to know what you would've said about it! On Saturday, Tommy is going up to the Hochreit with the Sjögren boys[29] for 8 days; so, there must be some kind of contact there. By the way, I too will be going and staying for a few days and shall see what I see; I will also watch Tommy with an eye for your concerns, but I believe I am too blind to form any judgment;[30] I can only hope that you're wrong about him and that there may be different roads to happiness. —Please don't think, you can do without a real milk-road on what you call the "Milky Way" (at present, its a mere *lucus a non lucendo*[31]). If

---

[28] The family performed Heinrich Kleist's *Prinz Friedrich von Homburg* on 12 March 1921.

[29] Presumably Arvid and Talla Sjögren.

[30] Tommy no doubt suffered from their nomadic life: there are many references to his nervousess and depression in Prokop's life of Margaret. He also stammered: Freud, who prided himself on instant diagnosis, asked whether this began when a younger brother was born. (Information from the late John Stonborough.)

[31] Something which is the opposite of its name.

memory serves, Weininger thought milk to be the only innocent nourishment, because it doesn't destroy germs; hence you can drink it to his memory.[32] I would be very happy if you came, except that I know it doesn't make you happy! What a shame!!! I spoke with Zimmermann,[33] he too thinks it better that way. Regards, a thousand times over, my dear Ludwig, your devoted sister,

Mining

66 Ludwig to Paul

March 1921

Dear Paul!

My warmest thanks for the 'tropical fruits'! But chocolate, sausage & cheese aren't tropical fruits, and you ought to be more moderate anyway!

I'm very much looking forward to the music over Easter. But if you want to organise such a concert, why don't you just get them to play the clarinet quintet for us. Because: however beautiful the other one is, that quintet is the real hit. Of course I don't mean that I am not extremely grateful for the brass quintet. I heard Bruckner's 5th[34] when I was in Vienna over the semester break. It certainly left an impression on me. The beginning is especially great. I also heard Baumayer play and was quite delighted. Now: my warmest regards & and thanks again!

Your Luki

---

[32] Hermine appears to be quoting Otto Weininger's *On Last Things* (p. 70) from memory. Hermine may possibly be encouraging Ludwig to accept the milk offered to him by one of his students, see Letter 69.

[33] Ludwig lodged with Zimmermann (III. Rasumofskygasse 24 Vienna) from April to July 1920.

[34] Austrian composer, Anton Bruckner (1824–1896).

67 Paul to Ludwig

tel. 59102

iv. Alleegasse 16

vienna, 12 April 1921

Dear Ludwig!

Arvid told me that you'll be able to make it to Vienna on Saturday, the 23rd, to hear a rehearsal of the Labor quintet.[35] I immediately got in touch with Fräulein Baumayer so that she might call everyone for the afternoon of the 23rd. Over the next couple of days, I hope to learn something definite about whether and at what hour on said day the rehearsal will be held, which I will then write to you immediately.

Warmest regards,

your brother,

Paul

68 Hermine to Ludwig

Saturday, 1 May 1921

My dear Ludwig,

I've done something very bad and am reproaching myself for it in a big way, and you, too, are quite caught up in this mess and are going to be very upset at me. I have to explain everything to you from the beginning because you have to help me rectify the situation. As you know, Nähr once came to us from Trattenbach and, in response to his inept story, I wrote to you with an even more inept letter. In response, you wrote to me with a letter that

---

[35] Probably the brass quintet in D major played on 4 May with Marie Baumayer at the piano.

upset me very much. I was devastated the entire day, and by chance Lenka came over that evening and immediately saw that something was the matter with me; I told her about your letter and how sorry I was that we had completely fallen out with each other, because that was the conclusion I had drawn. Of course this thought bothered me to no end, and I felt compelled to go over the situation over and over again in my mind: what Nähr said and what I wrote, etc., etc., as these things go. By chance Nähr learned of your letter (but not about the bit concerning him) and asked me about it. I was far too perplexed to consider my reply properly, and quite wrapped up in your letter as well; otherwise, I would have just asked him what he knew and what he wanted to know? But I just said that you didn't really mean what you wrote, that you weren't feeling well, that the mistake was <u>mine</u> due to my stupid letter, etc. Only after I had sputtered this all out, reaffirmed and corroborated it all, as happens quickly with us, did it slowly emerge that Nähr had no idea of what you had written about him. But because I had excused and softened everything the way I did and also because the severity of your letter was addressed to <u>me</u>, I hadn't at all thought that it would upset him as much as it did. Nor did it occur to me that <u>I ought to tell you about it</u>, and appallingly I just forgot about poor Nähr. Today Mima told me that Nähr has been depressed and miserable ever since I told him about your letter, and this being all <u>my</u> fault has hit me very hard! I beg you, dear Ludwig, to just let him come and visit you; he is such a kind and caring person and is so devoted to you. I can't take any steps regarding Nähr because I don't know how well you are disposed towards him; I do hope, however, that you still like him. It would be horrible if I were to blame for something permanent. A chain of coincidences was at work that made my letter and everything I did as damaging as they've become, and the horrible thing is that I had completely forgotten about it; I thought only of myself and my relationship towards you and was glad that this had all improved; I didn't give Nähr a second thought. If I had only heard over Easter that he was upset, maybe you would have visited him! <u>He</u> didn't know what to make of your letter, because he's so sensitive!

Today, I can accuse myself only of not having sent Hänsel the copies of *Der Brenner* yet, though I did write to him. This is because a stupid accident led to the copies getting stained, and I immediately ordered new copies from Braumüller;[36] I was promised them right away, but have yet to receive anything. I've written to Hänsel asking only whether he wants the stained or the new copies and sent him my sincerest apologies.

The third thing I did wrong, and what I am very sorry about, is that I completely forgot your birthday![37] Don't be angry – it's the least of the three mistakes I've made, and you know how much I love you! The matter with Nähr is closest to my heart. It would mean a lot to me, if I could know that it will be taken care of before very long.

Regards, a thousand times over,

my dear Ludwig,

your sister,

Mining

---

[36] Not Weininger's publisher Braumüller, but the bookseller of the same name.
[37] Ludwig's 32nd birthday, 26 April 1921.

69 Hermine to Ludwig

[5 May 1921]

My dear Ludwig,

Are you coming to Vienna for Whitsun? I hope so for Mama's sake, but it would be a real pity for me because I <u>must</u> go to the Hochreit for Whitsun; I have to use the double holiday, which I can easily bridge with Saturday and then Tuesday as well, in order to tend to things there. The last time I was up there, I saw a lot of abuses that cried out for remedy, as if my eyes were suddenly opened and I saw clearly that it had long been my duty to pay more attention to the Hochreit than I had in the past. I believe, I wouldn't have started the Grinzing project, if I had seen that so clearly 4 months ago;[38] but it's been started, and I have to try, as best I can, to combine the two and get myself out of this affair with my honour still intact. The 13 boys, who were at my place yesterday and today, seem very nice, and I haven't been upset with them yet, but – as always – quite a bit with myself, due to my absentmindedness and fidgetiness. May this mind and character massage, as I've come to see the whole thing, be of some help yet in bringing about some small change in me. I believe, it can only do me some good! —I've already sent Hänsel the copies of *Der Brenner* because he told me they were your property. Is it not sad and Austrian that it's impossible to get a journal if it's published in Austria? I subscribed to it, but have yet to hear anything more, even though a month has passed already. There was a performance of Labor's quintet yesterday;[39] I really

---

[38] Hermine had founded a day home for at-risk school children in Grinzing, where they could go in the afternoon to receive help. Hermine managed the organization until the Anschluss in 1938, when she was forced to give it up.

[39] According to the *Neues Wiener Tagblatt*, this Labor evening took place on 4 May 1921, with Marie Baumayer, Paul Wittgenstein, and others.

enjoyed the third movement with the canon, but none of the other ones. But I was glad to hear the horn variations again which, I believe, the audience enjoyed. Paul played beautifully and delighted me and everyone else mainly on account of his affectionate commitment to Labor, lost cause though he is. I think it was very nice of him to take Labor home after the concert. Baumayer, who can never behave herself in a way befitting a concert, did something extremely sweet and naïve: after long applause, Labor, who was in the audience, went up and stood <u>in front</u> of the podium, which is of course not an option at all, and Baumayer reacted immediately by giving him both hands and pulling the old man up onto the table-high podium. You could see how much he enjoyed the applause. Do you know that he recently played in public at a concert of Machodka's? Of course it wasn't anything for the general public; but I enjoyed it with all my heart! —The flower books cost 500 Kronen, who's actually going to be paying for them? I could just donate them to your school? How are things with the boy from the dairy farm and his father? Just don't be too perverse in your dealings with people. Warmest regards, dear Ludwig,

your sister,

Mining

ps: To my horror, I've just noticed that the flower book still hasn't been sent to you, my apologies! But I did just receive *Der Brenner*!

70 Paul to Ludwig

TEL. 59102

iv. Alleegasse 16
vienna, 4 June 1921

Dear Luki!

We have a question: we would like to know whether you, at least for a time, intend to stay with us at Neuwaldegg. The issue is this: as a consequence of the housing shortage and the continuing demand for single rooms or entire apartments, it is desirable that, if possible, the house be used in its entirety. Should you want, which of course would be the most preferable solution for us, to stay with us for a longish period of time, then your room in the large house will of course be occupied, and we will be in the clear with the housing authority. However, should you not want to stay with us at least for a while, then we would offer the room to some acquaintance, probably to old Fräulein von Alt (the painter's daughter).[40] Otherwise, we run the risk of the housing authority placing some stranger in the house. Should you want to stay with us only for some shorter period of time, or for several shorter stays of a few days each, then it won't make much of a difference if your room has already been given to someone else. You can sleep in my room or we would put a bed in my drawing room, or find you some other accommodation. Naturally, you are somewhat spoiled on account of your bachelor's apartment outfitted with its wasteful luxury, but perhaps you can turn a blind eye, if it is just for a couple of days.

But you needn't make any commitment now, perhaps you still aren't sure what you will want to do in the summer; but just in case

---

[40] Daughter of Rudolf von Alt (1812–1905). She presented Hermine with a female head painted by her father, best known for town- and landscapes.

you do already know what you will be doing then, it would be very good for us to know.

I have already said it often enough, but I will repeat it here all the same: should you want me to visit, so that you might hear Labor's *Phantasie* or anything else, I am always ready to come. (Just not next Sunday, as I'll be away for a couple of days.)

Warmest,

your brother,

Paul

71 Ludwig to Hermine

Skjolden, 4 August 1921[41]

Dear Mining!

We arrived here a few hours ago, and I received your letter. How strangely everything has turned out. Of course how sadly too – not that Fritz has died, but that he had had such a <u>sad</u> life!![42] –

I would like to write to Helene, but can't. Tell her something for me that won't upset her. –

We've had <u>a good and comfortable journey</u> till now. We've been received all too warmly here. I hope to find some reasonable work here, because a life of nothing but eating and sleeping, such as we've had until now, is bound to become unbearable very soon.[43]

---

[41] Ludwig spent the summer with Arvid Sjögren in Skjolden, where Ludwig built his house.

[42] Helene's son died young, a natural death.

[43] Both Ludwig and Arvid found work at a fruit pressing company (see Hänsel letters in Somavilla et al. (eds), *Eine Fieundschaft*, p. 70.

Certainly, Mima is the right company for Helene at the moment, and that she needs company at the moment is something I understand all too well.

Till we meet again,

your brother,

Ludwig

Best wishes from your Arvid

72 Hermine to Ludwig

26 September 1921

My dear Ludwig,

One or other of your friends will be visiting you on Sunday, and I look forward to hearing then how you are; I hope you haven't had anything especially unpleasant and that you're healthy! I am also <u>very</u> sorry to have seen so little of you while you were in Vienna, but as it happens something important was going on up at the Hochreit, something to do with the estate workers, which as a matter of fact couldn't be postponed even for a day. I only wonder how I am going to address the problem of sitting on 10 chairs with <u>one</u> b . . . Sometimes . . . [44]

The Stonboroughs and Mariechen are coming on Sunday or Monday, and I have to make some free time for them; Engelmann was recently at our place and showed us his sketches, etc., which I liked very much. What a horrible shame that the tastelessness in our hearts is so complicated, and nailed down for eternity, that one is incapable of putting anything to rights by ordinary means and is

---

[44] The last line of this paragraph is missing.

forced just to tear everything down and start all over again. But if I were ever to have anything done, it would be by Engelmann – Lenka too was, I believe, delighted by his work. She herself even made the nicest papier-mâché model of a house, which is just amazing with its lovely details and handsome proportions, and so Engelmann was also able to admire something of hers, which made her very happy.

Your clarinet will be adjusted once Behrends[45] tells us where he means to take it.[46] He picked it up just moments ago. If I could just be a student at your school!

Keep well, my good Ludwig,

warmest regards,
your sister,
Mining

73 Ludwig to Hermine

September 1921

Dear Mining!

Please send me a book from 'my bookshelf' in the small guest room in the Alleegasse.[47] It's called *Die Erde* and is a geography textbook having a format of approximately 25 cm × 16 cm × 2 cm. It is bound and has a white dust cover. Second: if you have the time, be so good and get me the 4 hand *Fantasia* by Mozart (with the fugue) because I would like to send it and others to England. Enclosed a picture.

---

[45] Principal clarinettist of the Vienna Philharmonic.
[46] Ludwig began playing the clarinet during his time as a teacher.
[47] The Alleegasse was re-named Argentinierstraße at the beginning of 1921, but the family continued to use the old name.

It's strange how upstanding the criminals look when compared with the accuser.

Your Ludwig

74 Hermine to Ludwig

9 October 1921

My dear Ludwig,

I am very sorry to hear that you're having stomach problems, because the reason for it lies in your indigestible diet and, as you won't be changing that, I believe I can anticipate what's going to happen next. Let's hope the powder (Arvid requested <u>pills</u>, but that was presumably a misunderstanding) is doing at least some good.

Did your clarinet arrive all right? Behrends says that it ought to have a case. Does it have one or should I get you one or do you not want one?[48]

I was glad I was able to find the historical atlas on your bookshelf right away; something can easily go missing in those hundreds of bookshelves of ours.

Drobil was here on Sunday and started chipping away at the unsightly Adam's apple on that a bust of you. Every splinter that fell away was an act of charity, and it became clear that the base has to be <u>as small as possible,</u> but just big enough for the bust to stand on its own. Unfortunately, the tools were blunted rather quickly, so that we can only continue working on it next Sunday; I would have really liked to have seen it done already.

---

[48] Ludwig did not want a case; he carried his clarinet around in an old sock.

I have been thinking a lot about you lately, because Elsa Stradal[49] and her two daughters are here and much though you would have enjoyed her singing, the girls' chatter and their <u>abysmal</u> artificiality would have given you the cramps! What's more, the youngest girl is terrifyingly stupid by the look of her and poorly behaved to boot. A sad brood indeed, since she too is cross-eyed and can't see out of one eye any more. Poor Elsa!

Keep well my good Ludwig. Are you coming for All Saints' Day? It would of course be nice, and I would hope it for poor Mama's sake. She is in a lot of pain at the moment. I would also like to visit you at some point this winter, but I would arrange things more sensibly this time and above all bring something to read or study.

Warmest regards,

your sister,

Mining

75 Hermine to Ludwig

23 April 1922

My good Ludwig,

I'm sending you nothing but a shabby letter for your birthday.[50] But I also want you on Sunday to try on a pair of boots, which I wanted to show you at Easter and then forgot were there because of all the rushing about. The point is that they're boots specially made for the estate workers up at the Hochreit (and I think, would be something you could use. You already know that I wish you

---

[49] A singer with whom Wittgenstein's mother played music.
[50] Ludwig's 33rd birthday, 26 April.

everything that's good – much more than you already possess. Unfortunately, I see you so seldom that I haven't the slightest idea what that good might consist of; I guess I'm just wishing it generally!

Please do not forget the drawings; I believe they will be quite valuable to me.

Today Paul gave a very beautiful public performance of Labor's *Concertstück*. Unfortunately, Labor is in a bad way again and could of course not make the concert. 'Too late', he'll say!

I bought Drobil's *The Slumberer* today at the Secession[51] because I think it's really charming; I wonder where to put it and where it'll be seen at its best. Drobil is meant to get me a stand right away. With any luck, he'll be pleased too! He ought to switch completely to portraits of children; that, I believe, is his forte!

Keep well, my good Ludwig, I am <u>very much</u> looking forward to seeing you.

Your sister,

Mining

76 Ludwig to Hermine

[June 1922]

Dear Mining!

First, I wanted to tell you that Engelmann liked *The Sleeping Child* <u>very</u> much, I did too. I think it's very beautiful! Engelmann said it should be left in plaster, because he prefers plaster to stone, and I have to admit: the way he said it makes me thinks so too. You

---

[51] Secession. The exhibition building used by members of the Wiener Secession

should go to Drobil again and have a look at that funny looking portrait head. At some point this month, probably at the end of it, I would like to come to Vienna with about 15 children. Can we stay the night at your place, etc.?

—Please have the following items sent from my laundry: a few shirts, bedding, and 1 or 2 hand towels and a few handkerchiefs.

Auf Wiedersehen!

Your brother,
Ludwig

Ludwig with pupils in Lower Austria © The Stonborough Family.

77 Hermine to Ludwig

Neuwaldegg, 12 June 1922

Dear Ludwig,

I have just looked at the timetable and am assuming you'll arrive at 1:05 pm on Saturday and be in Grinzing at about 2:00 pm with the children.

Last year you came directly to my place, and lunch was at my place too; but I suggest, that, this time (although I will lose on account of it), you go directly to Lecher's at Hut 38. Last year you went to Lecher's only after we had eaten, the children also had to put their rucksacks away, and you all left Grinzing far too late. Apart from that, I now get my food from Lecher, so that it would actually be unfriendly, if I were to take your food over to my hut for you to eat with me, when she's the one offering you the hospitality.

My thought is: this time, you and the children will be at Lecher's place, and I will just go to her, both for your lunch and for supper. The visit will not be combined with one to <u>my</u> hut because that would take up too much time; if you really come and see <u>us</u> later on and engage a bit with my children, then that is a different matter entirely, and a truly valuable one, but one for which time is needed. Don't you think I'm right here? Lecher also wants me to tell you that you should certainly stay a bit longer, at least until Monday; but I think you'll have your reasons for doing it this way and not otherwise. At any rate, she would gladly keep you all for a bit longer. Please cable me either only with a 'yes', then everything regarding the scheduling will remain as I suggest, or cable 'Arriving at your hut at 2:15 for lunch', then I will arrange things accordingly. If I don't hear anything, I will assume the former – we can always change this or that. All this is for Lecher's sake, who must know what your exact schedule is. With any luck, it'll all work out and you can show your children a thing or two.

Warmest regards,
my good Ludwig,
your sister,
Mining

78 Ludwig to Helene

[1922][52]

Dear Helene!

Here are the measurements for the altar and the altar cloth:

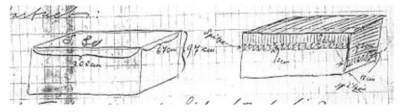

The sides of the cloth should almost touch the ground, and the front should hang down approximately 20 cm. The lace should – so the parish priest wishes– not be wider than 10 cm. Hence, the cloth and <u>lace</u> together must be 300 cm + 92 cm + 92 cm = 484 cm long (here I have worked out that the sides will hang just 92 cm: i.e., they won't quite touch the ground). and 67 cm + 20 cm = 87 cm wide. But the width needn't be so exact, let's say 90 cm then. The cloth without the lace should therefore be <u>464 cm</u> long and approximately <u>80 cm</u> wide with – as I said – the lace being as said 10 cm wide. Those are the measurements. Should you want to know the height of the priest himself, the age and the hour his cook was born, then I might be able to send you that information, and possibly even the cook's vaccination certificate, over the next couple of days. I will, however, be crediting the costs of this shipment to your account during the concurrent year at my own expense and risk per annum.

Now I'm going to bed.

Your brother,
Ludwig

---

[52] Ludwig probably wrote this letter from Trattenbach, where he was friendly with the pastor, Alois Neururer.

79 Paul to Ludwig

vienna, iv. alleegasse 16
Saturday, [24 June 1922]

Dearest Lucky!

Just received your kind letter, will go into the city immediately &
see what can be done for your friend Scholz[53] from our side. The
best thing to do here is that I just let him know what I find out
without telling you first.

Warmest greetings,
your brother,
Paul

80 Paul to Ludwig

TEL. 59102.

iv. alleegasse 16
vienna, 24 June 1922

Dearest Luki!

As a follow-up to the brief letter I sent you earlier this morning, I
am just letting you know that I was unable to do any anything for
your friend Scholz today: Herr Groller,[54] my factotum in such
matters, was not here, and I am not on such good terms with
Feilchenfeld and Kux at the moment that I could approach them
with such a request.[55] Groller will be back on Monday, he knows a

---

[53] Fritz Scholz (b. 1898), a fellow prisoner of war from Cassino. After he returned from
captivity he briefly resumed his gymnasium studies.

[54] Administrator for the family, especially valued during their 1938–9 troubles.

[55] Max Veilchenfeld and Wilhelm Kux – bank directors and former colleagues of Karl
Wittgenstein.

lot of people from various businesses, and perhaps we can get Herr Scholz a job via this channel.

But because that, in any case, will take some time, I have taken the liberty of sending the young man 60,000.00 Kronen. Don't be horrified that, asked for a recommendation, I am offering him some money, which

1 neither you nor he had asked for and
2 always has something cold, and therefore something offensive, about it.

I know that; but I believe I've wrapped up the offer of money in such a way, also leaving him the option of paying it back at some point in the future, that he can accept it without feeing humiliated.

We are very much looking forward to your visit; Mama has been practising her part for the Weber overtures arranged for four hands.

Warmest,
your brother,
Paul

81 Paul to Ludwig

tel. 59102.

iv., Alleegasse 16
vienna, 7 July 1922

Dearest Luki!

Herr Scholz was in our office today and told Herr Groller that he has found and accepted temporary work, so that he, at the moment at least, is in the clear. In the meantime, Herr Groller will be trying to get him a permanent position, and I wanted only to ask that you write to him when you get a chance in order to let him know that he can turn to us again once his current position is over or, alternatively, to let us know if he finds a permanent position himself.

This is necessary because he seems very modest and might not have the confidence to approach us a second time.

But now a request: when are you coming to Vienna? First, I want to be in Vienna, and second, Mama and I wanted to play Weber's overtures for you.

Warmest,

your brother,

Paul

Hochwohlgeboren

Herrn Ludwig Wittgenstein

Trattenbach bei Gloggnitz

82 Ludwig to Hermine

[End of August 1922]

Dear Mining!

You force me to write by all the presents you send. It was more agreeable at Uncle Paul's place than I had expected. Or rather: it was agreeable, but only <u>completely so</u> over the last few days. I believe, there's been another change for the better in him. I arrived here[56] a day after Engelmann and was therefore able to spend plenty of time with him. It was nice. Hänsel too was in Vienna for a few days; so on a couple of occasions I had all my acquaintances with me, and even regaled them with feasts.

---

[56] Ludwig is writing from the Alleegasse in Vienna to Hermine up at the Hochreit.

Engelmann and I were both delighted by Drobil's *Sleeping Child* – in its present form – and we therefore had it photographed by Nähr as it is now – at Helene's expense – and today I saw the pictures, and Drobil sent them to you. Each picture has merits of its own.

We'll see each other when you come to Vienna.

And thank you very much for everything,

your brother,

Ludwig

PS: I heard the *Eroica* yesterday (in the Burggarten). Yes, the second and the fourth movement! I no longer had them in my memory. There just aren't any words!

83 Ludwig to Paul

18 October 1922

My dear Paul!

Forgive me that I am replying to you only now. I have been very busy. Yes, Grodzinsky[57] was my superior in Kraków. Back then he was an *Akzessist* and was later an *Offizial* and no doubt an *Oberoffizial* too, although I don't know that for sure. He is competent, and I don't believe him to be anything other than decent. He wrote to me, but of course I can't do anything for him. It would be nice of you, if you were to do something. As I said already, I have been very busy lately because, among other things, I had to move again[58] – not to another village, but to other lodgings. I'm

---

[57] Ludwig Grodzinsky. See Leopoldine Wittgenstein's letter of 17 April [1915].

[58] See the commentary to Ludwig's letters to Ludwig Hänsel of 21 September 1922 and after 10 October 1922. Shortly prior to this letter, Wittgenstein did move from Hassbach or Neukirchen to Puchberg, but he is speaking here of a move within Puchberg.

now living with the widow Ehrbar, in a very large and really luxurious room with all the comforts of modern life. Electric lighting, service, etc., etc. I will, God willing, be coming to Vienna for All Saints' Day. Till then!

Warmest greetings regards,

your brother,

Ludwig

84 Paul to Ludwig

vienna, iv. alleegasse 16

13 December 1922

Dearest Lucky!

I just wanted to ask whether you have any requests concerning the 4-handed music-making at Christmas. The sooner I know what you want to hear, the better, so that I'll have time to look at it beforehand.

So far, I have received only the first 3 movements of Labor's quintet: Fräulein Staake[59] just doesn't write quite as fast as poor Menzel did. I would also like to play two trios by Bach for you at Christmas.

Warmest, your brother, who holds you in high regard,

Paul

---

[59] Fräulein Staake (d. 1945): pianist, who frequently came to the Wittgenstein family home to play duets with members of the family.

85 Ludwig to Paul

[undated]

Dear Paul!

I am writing to you in great haste. Thanks a million for your kind lines. Vienna will rejoice no matter what you play. You once had something by Schumann up your sleeve. Or do you want to play the quartet in A minor by Brahms? Everything would be a boon to my ears. Warmest regards, your devoted brother,

Luki

86 Paul to Ludwig

Neuwaldegg
Wednesday
[around Christmas 1922].

Dearest Lucky!

That was a disappointment! I was very much looking forward to being able to play for you with Fräulein Staake; bought & even looked at Brahms's *Haydn Variations* in Berlin – and I get here and find out that you're staying with the Hänsels! If only I am in Vienna when you get here!!

Paul

87 Paul to Ludwig

Vienna, 11 January 1923

Dearest Luky!

Contemporaneously with this letter I'm sending you Beethoven's clarinet trio and Schumann's *Fairy Tales* for piano, clarinet and viola. I don't know the latter, never heard it, but just now had a look at it. It is *Opus 132* and unfortunately has all the marks of belonging to Schumann's later works: confused in rhythm and feeble in invention.

Now of course there is an earlier composition by Schumann for that ensemble. Unfortunately, that wasn't in stock, I ordered it and will send it to you once I have it.

Warmest,

your brother,

Paul

88 Ludwig to Paul

26 January 1923

Dear Paul,

Received your enormous present the day before yesterday. Thank you very, very much! The reason the books arrived so long after your kind letter did is that in the meantime we've been snowed in with no train service. And my thanks are delayed because we just now had an inspection and a whole lot to do because of it.

Auf Wiedersehen and, again, my warmest thanks!

Your brother,

Ludwig

89 Hermine to Ludwig

3 February 1923

My dear Ludwig,

I had already begun a letter to you, but didn't get much further, and I believe this one is going to be a miscarriage as well; but I'll send it off one way or the other. There is nothing special going on here, and it's just so peculiarly dopey inside me that I have no idea what's stupid or reasonable, important or unimportant, to be changed and to be left unchanged; how is any one supposed to write a letter in such a condition?

Arvid told me that Koder[60] is losing his post in a downsizing, the only person you get on with; I was very sorry to hear that, but then he said that you too will be leaving Puchberg and that you will have to look for employment as a tenured teacher elsewhere, and now I have no idea what to make of it, since I don't know what your opinion is on the matter. Are you sorry or glad about it all? or indifferent? Always having to start over, with new people and in opposition to new people, would be frightful, more than frightful, for me – that's very wearing! In any event, the life you live is not relaxing, and maybe that's how you want it. I'm sorry you won't be coming to Vienna for so long; if it's really only for Easter, then we have to wait another 2 months, and I often want to speak with you. A shame that there are no mid-term holidays, or will something or other crop up at the last minute? —I haven't heard anything more from Engelmann, but I believe he will be in touch and return soon. I would be very glad if he were to stay for a while, and I would also like to spend more time with him, but unfortunately I completely lack the ability to seek and establish contact with others; I refuse to leave my convent, even when I'm surrounded by 100 people. I am often surprised, if I think about it, that Arvid and Talla take walks with me every day and that I haven't really spoken to them at all, save for asking them 'have you heard anything from Ludwig' or 'are you going to go skiing' – I can have some sort of conversation only if I really force and push

---

[60] Rudolf 'Koderl' Koder (1902–1977): elementary school teacher, and later school director, whom Ludwig met in Puchberg. Koder became a life-long friend of Ludwig's and indeed of the entire family.

myself to do so. Now I want to tell you that Mama, thank God, is having <u>much</u> better days; whether the radium is helping or whether better times in general have set in, no one can say yet. Lenka, too, is conspicuously better, which we are all very glad about. Keep well, my good Ludwig, warmest regards, your sister,

Mining

90 Ludwig to Paul

10 February 1923

Dear Paul!

My warmest thanks for your kind lines. I am coming to Vienna next Saturday, the 17th of February, at approximately 6:00 pm and returning on Sunday afternoon. I would, therefore, be very grateful if the rehearsal can take place during that time. There aren't any more holidays until Easter. —The latest news is that I am blowing into my clarinet, trying to play the first movement of Brahms's clarinet quintet. It's not enormously difficult. Of course, I'm playing it a semitone higher than it should be.

Auf Wiedersehen!

Your brother,
Ludwig

91 Ludwig to Hermine

[February 1923]

Dear Mining!

Thank you very much for the nibbles, the letter and the pictures. Koder probably won't leave; at least not this year, as the downsizing has been postponed. Have you ever tried to build furniture? I

haven't. But want to try it soon with the children. I think you'll see
what I mean from these scribbles.

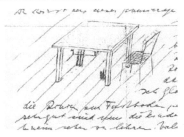

For instance, the back of the chair first shown perpendicular
and then tilted. I think the lines on the floor, the floorboards in fact,
are quite good for teaching the children to see into the space.
Perhaps your children are already too old for anything like that. It'll
be difficult enough for mine.

Tell Mariechen I wish her luck for her Leaving Examination. I'll
be coming to Vienna for Easter. *Auf Wiedersehen,*

your brother,
Ludwig

92 Paul to Ludwig

TEL. 59102

iv. Argentinierstraße 16
vienna, Thursday
[after 10 February 1923]

Dearest Lucky!
The rehearsal will take place at 9:00 am on Sunday. With any luck,
we'll play long enough for you to get an idea of the work, & hopefully
you'll like it. We are all very much looking forward to your visit!

Warmest,
your Paul

93 Paul to Ludwig

Tel. 59102

iv. Argentinierstraße 16

vienna, 15 May 1923

Dear Lucky!

1   I would like to know whether, if you are coming here for Whitsun,[61] you have any particular requests as regards music-making. I would still have time, if you would just let me know in good time, to have a look at any work you like.

2   Forgive me for not having yet sent you the top line from the 5th movement of Labor's quintet. I am having it copied today, & you will at least have it when you get here.

Looking forward to seeing you again soon!

Warmest,

your brother,

Paul

94 Hermine to Ludwig

25 August 1923

My dear Ludwig,

I am <u>very</u> sorry to hear that I won't be seeing you before the holidays![62] I hope everything will be set to rights as regards your flat in Puchberg, for it would be just too frustrating, if you didn't just <u>once</u> have the time you need to sow the seed and tend the fields

---

[61] Whitsunday was on 20 May in 1923.

[62] Ludwig is in the Alleegasse with Paul, and Hermine is up at the Hochreit.

and see what becomes of your students. If only I didn't in my head keep hearing you answer: 'that's piffle'! Ultimately, I myself don't know what's piffle and what's not! In your eyes, Hänsel's flat being painted and cleaned; surely I know it doesn't interest you, but it does interest me, and I am going to have the caretaker's wife tell me all about it. I wasn't able to do anything regarding the staircase photograph, because it is in Lenka's flat in the city; Mariechen is going to look for it; with any luck, she'll find the album.

I imagine you are with Paul very often and am happy for him. I haven't a clue as to why he doesn't come to the Hochreit; guests can't be what's keeping him away, as no one can ask more than to have his own house which he needs to leave only to come to meals. I'm finding it extremely cozy this year and good fun, and I'm glad I needn't hear everything with the ears you two have, which find evil character flaws in each and every word uttered. Here everyone is nice and good, and any flaws they may have are just small spots anyone can overlook. (I don't wish to say that you two are not right about certain things, but you are too demanding, and, in the friendly life here, one can be friendlier in one's judgments too.) — Now I want to ask you something: while here I read *Brand* by Ibsen, which I didn't know before; do you too think that God rejects Brand through those final words or does he mean: I'm accepting you, though not because of your ranting, but through my love?[63] I just <u>can't</u> believe it's the former. Didn't Ibsen say anything about that? —Keep well, my good, my dear Ludwig, warmest regards a thousand times over, your

sister Mining

---

[63] *Brand*, Henrik Ibsens' drama (1866). At the end when Brand, after many imprecations, is swallowed up in an avalanche, a voice is heard saying 'He is the God of Love'.

95 Ludwig to Hermine

[September 1923]

Dear Mining!

I wanted to write to you a few times already, and your letter finally gave me the prompt I needed. It's a shame that <u>you</u> did yourself in, but that can happen to anyone, and you need not try to find the cause in any particular stupidities of yours. I too was hardly able to talk for a few days because I recently had to talk all day long for days on end: mornings at school and afternoons with Ramsey[64] from Cambridge, who stayed here for approximately 14 days. I enjoyed it too, even though it was very exhausting – Ramsey will be sending me a copy of the treatise soon, and then you can have it. Engelmann's drama will certainly be good. I wonder why he didn't mention it. His idea regarding the antechamber is of course good, but I don't know if it'll turn out as good as it looks on your sketch, where one assumes there is high wainscoting but can't see clearly where the cabinets end. Once that's brought in I'm afraid everything will look cramped. —A few days ago, a colleague of mine told me that a Baroness Grimmburg, who is staying at a Red Cross nursing home, had asked about me and had asked him to ask me to visit her, as she doesn't have my address. I went, and it turned out that it was Frau von G., née Tschichek (or however you spell it) who at one time attended social gatherings at our place. She was bloody stupid and intrusive (but I wasn't having any of it). She told me, among other things, that she believes, for some reason or other, that she's most in tune with you and me. Rendel[65] has

---

[64] F. P. Ramsey, many-sided mathematician, logician, and philosopher was the original translator of Ludwig's <u>Tractatus</u>. Later, in September 1923, he visited Puchberg for two weeks to discuss the ideas of the book. He was also in Vienna from March to October 1924 and visited Ludwig in Puchberg on several occasions.

[65] Ludwig lived with a Rendel family in Puchberg for a time.

not yet made it to Marschik's place because he wasn't able to get away here. If you go to Marschik's, could you perhaps tell him that a certain Herr Rendel will be going to see him sometime soon, with whom he should deal.

With any luck, you'll get help soon.

With kind regards,
Ludwig

96 Ludwig to Helene

[October/November 1923]

Dear Helene!

Since my publisher wants to publish my correspondence with you and it would be desirable to put a handsome little volume together, I hereby want to resume our recently interrupted correspondence.

As you will remember, you once kindly leased an upright piano from Kohn[66] for my colleague Koder. The lease expired in September. Koder, who wanted to extend it for his younger brother, then turned to Kohn asking about the leasing terms, conditions and fees. Kohn replied, but his letter seems to have gone missing. Koder has since looked into the matter again, and finally received a reply, terms and conditions regarding the term of the lease, etc., and the notice that the rent has been paid through <u>October</u>. From that, he concluded, presumably correctly, that Kohn sent you an invoice, or at least enquired from you about the piano. This is all very embarrassing for him, and he has asked me to give you his thanks, his apologies, his regards, etc., etc. However I thought – but

---

[66] Klavierhaus Bernhard Kohn, founded in 1856, I. Himmelpfortgasse 20, Vienna.

of course said nothing about it to Koder – that it would certainly be in keeping with what you had in mind, if I were to ask you to pay the rent for him (as he's a poor devil). Of course I won't tell Koder; he'll hear of it from Kohn, if you should be so kind as to extend the piano for him. —Naturally, I do not mean that it would be desirable to extend the keyboard or the casing; rather, my expression 'extend' refers to the <u>time period</u> for which the instrument will be used, which period will always be capable of being extended for as long as time exists. Should anything from this letter not be entirely clear to you, then I will willing explain it in more detail.—

So that you can see that things are going well for me, I've left a few grease spots on the paper. You can therefore render the fat once you've read it.

Giving myself the warmest of thanks in your name for the good idea concerning the upright piano, I am

your unforgettable
(and yet so forgetful)
brother,
Ludwig

97 Ludwig to Paul

9 January 1924

Dear Paul!

Thank you very much for your kind lines. I have received both parcel & book. In response to the last remark of your letter I want only to say that, from a naivety which does you credit, you have no idea how I am governed by the basest & most vulgar of motives. You can even say that I am a lost soul, quite unworthy of your love, if I am not saved by some miracle. But enough of that.—

I enjoyed the cutting very much.[67] It is unbelievable that, in such matters, people always speak of an unmasked medium instead of an unmasked professor!

Now one more request: do you know an opera, or other piece of vocal called 'Axur'? In this piece – whatever it is – there is supposed to be a melody to the words 'Wie dort auf den Auen . . .' Would you, if you don't know the piece, be so kind as to look it up in your encyclopaedia and perhaps have the melody copied for me? Please forgive the imposition.

Warmest regards,
your Ludwig

ps: I'm extremely well.

98 Ludwig to Paul

11 January 1924

Dear Paul!

My warmest thanks for your letter. I'm now sorry that I asked you about that melody, as I had no idea that it would be so difficult to find, and the enormous effort you devoted to it was truly more than it merited! The point is this: there is a wonderful poem by Mörike[68] entitled 'For the New Year,' under whose title Mörike wrote 'Melodie an Axur: Wie dort auf den Auen'. Hence, the piece is certainly called 'Axur', and the remark sounds as if it were a well-known one. I wanted to sing the song with my children, especially because I've concluded that it'll be a remarkable melody given the remarkable rhythm of the

---

[67] Paul and Ludwig often sent one another what were in their opinion nonsensical newspaper clippings; the one here, for instance, concerns spiritualism.

[68] Eduard Friedrich Mörike (1804–1875), German Romantic poet.

poem. What is more, Mörike was very musical and, I thought, wouldn't have set the poem to a bad melody. So, it'll be Salieri's[69] music that he meant. Should you want to spend more time on this matter – which is not necessary in the least because I have enough songs to sing with the children, and perhaps the 'Neujahrslied' will prove unsuitable for them anyway. —That is, in the event that you do want to look into this matter further, I will copy the first verse of the poem here because its rhythm will give you a definite point of reference:

1 "Like angels descending

With soft silent steps

Alighting on earth

The rosy dawn came.

Sing greetings, good people.

With prayers and rejoicing!

With prayers and rejoicing,

Heart, do thou the same!

2 Let His be the New Year,

Who keeps suns and moons

In motion above

On high azure bands.

Give counsel! O Father,

Guide Thou and restrain us!

Place end and beginning,

Place all in His hands."

---

[69] Antonio Salieri (1750–1825), Italian classical composer and conductor.

I couldn't help myself and had to copy both verses, because they're so unbelievably beautiful. Please don't devote any more time to this matter, unless you are interested in it yourself. What I was hoping to do is not worth the effort. Once again, my warmest thanks!

Yours,

Ludwig

99 Paul to Ludwig

tel. 59102

iv. Argentinierstraße 16

vienna, 6 March 1924

Dearest Luki!

I have not forgotten about Mörike. I ordered a volume of commentary on Mörike's poems. While there is a chapter dedicated to Mörike's relationship to music and the *Neujahrslied* is even mentioned by name, there is nothing in it about an Axur melody.

A while back I spent a few days up at the Hochreit, wanted to visit you from there, and even had a small volume of Daudet[70] in my pocket, so that I might be able to read a bit of it to you. But I learned the path from Schwarzau to Puchberg is not yet passable, had therefore to give up my plan.

Warmest greetings, your

Paul

---

[70] Alphonse Daudet (1840–1897), French novelist.

100 Ludwig to Helene

[May 1924]

Dear Helene!

Thank you very much! It was disappointing to learn that Mariechen[71] had only <u>one</u> child, and, I believe, there hasn't been a thorough examination. There was probably another one in there somewhere, the way chestnuts often have a very small chestnut in some compartment somewhere. Maybe someone can give her another once-over. She must be checked from head to toe.

I'm enclosing a few stamps for her. Warmest regards,

your Ludwig

ps: Give Max my warmest regards.

101 Ludwig to Hermine

20 May 1924

Dear Mining!

Be so kind and buy a few flowers for Helene and Max with the money I've enclosed.[72] To be honest, I don't think the chorus from behind the curtain is a very attractive idea. Why behind the curtain. Just sing it openly and honestly yourself with a few others, because people won't think of their good fortune just because you want them to, and especially not when the whole thing has been arranged so artificially. For everyone, of course, knows that the chorus is being sung by completely normal human beings behind the

---

[71] Ludwig's niece Marie Salzer eventually had six children. This letter was written shortly after the birth of her first child, Johanna, on 9 May 1924.
[72] For their Silver Wedding anniversary.

curtain. And the mood will be ruined by such a sleight of hand. It certainly would be for me. People are more likely to be put in the right mood, if you just stand there like normal, upstanding human beings. But it doesn't matter a damn to me.

By the way, I have to reiterate that I liked Drobil's big head. You saw it only after the plaster was finished, when there was nothing to see. Take another look at it. Of course, it's possible that I liked it so much only with *The Sleeping Child* to set it off.

I want to come on an excursion to Vienna with a few of the children this year too. When, I don't know. At any rate, after Whitsun, and I'll be coming to Vienna for that. By the way, I was happy to finally hear about Mariechen's baby girl. And it's already been 8 days? With any luck, it'll be over soon.

Your brother,
Ludwig

102 Ludwig to Hermine

[Winter 1924/1925]

Dear Mining!

As a result of some incomprehensible stupidity, an invoice has been sent to Geiger's father from the boarding school where Geiger junior is a pupil.[73] Herr Postl,[74] to whom Geiger the elder – who of course can't pay it – turned, sent me the invoice, and now I am

---

[73] Ernst Geiger (1912–1970), student of Ludwig's in Puchberg through 1924. He remained a protégé of the Wittgenstein siblings for a long time and gave them more than just typical difficulties. In the end, he established himself as a pharmacist and remained devoted especially to Ludwig (see Letter [143]).

[74] Heinrich Postl from Puchberg am Schneeberg, where he played music with both Ludwig and Koder, was part of the Wittgenstein and Stonborough families' domestic staff from 1928 to 1971.

sending it to you. Please pay it and explain to the people at the institute whom they should approach in this matter. Thank you for the Kola.[75] And while I'm writing I want to ask you to send me 2 nightshirts as soon as possible. Mine is already in pretty bad shape. Tell Mama I said hello. Are you two still playing four-handed?

Your brother,

Ludwig

103 Ludwig to Paul

[1924/1925]

Dear Paul!

What were you thinking? Heaping on me all the treasures of the occident and the orient! My warmest thanks. The children here in Otterthal[76] are refusing to eat cabbage & dumplings and now want only Malacca grapes, oranges & dates. I'm looking forward to our seeing one another again at Christmas. A few weeks ago, Koder played a few organ pieces by Labor for me (from the *Organ Album*); much of it very beautiful & remarkable.

My warmest regards!

Your Ludwig

---

[75] Then taken medicinally.

[76] Ludwig taught in Otterthal from autumn 1924 to spring 1926. Perhaps both he and Koder visited Puchberg, where Ludwig at least was on good terms with the parish priest, as several letters about small donations for the church also indicate.

104 Ludwig to Hermine

18 December 1924

Dear Mining!

Thank you for your letter. I believe it would be better to cut the stone lengthwise: that is, like this:

because you can see its natural surface better. Of course, the school would be grateful for a rat. I haven't forgotten your birthday; I just didn't know what I should honour you with. It occurred to me recently, though, that you wouldn't be sorry to have the book signed by Loos: title in it hereby passes to you.[77] I knew nothing of Mama's illness. Tell her I hope she gets well soon, and give her my most heartfelt regards.

Auf Wiedersehen,
your Ludwig

ps: Will Hänsel's rack be ready by the 24th?

---

[77] The Adolf Loos book given to Hermine with this letter, on the occasion of her 50th birthday, was a copy of *Spoken into the Void* (1921) containing the following dedication by Loos:

> For Ludwig Wittgenstein, in gratitude and friendship, in gratitude for his ideas, in friendship in the hope that he reciprocates this feeling.

Ludwig met Loos in 1914 and looked him up after the First World War had ended, when however he gained an unfavourable impression – on 2 September 1919, he wrote to Engelmann that '[Loos] has become infected with the most virulent bogus intellectualism!' (Engelmann, Letters from Ludwig, p. 21) – but was still able to appreciate Loos as an architect. Loos's name also made it on a list of people who, Ludwig believed, had influenced him: 'That is how Boltzmann, Hertz[,] Schopenhauer[,] Frege, Russell, Kraus, Loos[,] Weininger[,] Spengler, Sraffa have influenced me' (<u>Culture and Value</u>, p. 16).

105 Ludwig to Hermine

14 January 1925

Dear Mining!

Thank you for your letter. As long as Drobil hasn't ruined anything by enlarging the breast!!! The pronounced concave breast was <u>necessary</u>. The reason is it's <u>very</u> possible that some <u>fundamental</u> nonsense has happened. Because the breasts musn't form four uniform hills together with the upper arms, which would give the overall impression of a corrugated inclined plane forming a background to the whole. Nor should the space between the right lower arm (the vertical one) and the breast be any smaller, as that space will otherwise become insignificant and – so to speak – accidental. Please convey my reservations to Drobil; he'll understand them (if he wants to!). That the breast wanted fixing is true, but that it wasn't to be fixed by enlarging the bosom is more than probable, and Drobil himself, as you will remember, told me in front of you that he was <u>not</u> going to take the breast out any farther than he already had. <u>The matter is – I believe – not at all so simple</u>. He ought to think about it for a few weeks rather than just cooking up something superficial that is basically nonsense!

One last request: be so kind and send Koder the 2nd volume of the *Brothers Karamazov*. You gave him the 1st some time ago, and he's finished it.

Auf Wiedersehen.

Your brother,
Ludwig

106 Ludwig to Paul

14 January 1925

Dear Paul!

Thank you for your kind letter and the candleholder. Funny as it sounds: if it had been a tasteful holder, it might have annoyed me somewhat, but I like this monstrosity! —I told the Trattenbach parish priest that you were planning to send him something for his poor, and he was delighted to hear it. I plan to come to Vienna on the 31st/1st. With any luck, I'll be able to see you then.

Your Ludwig

107 Ludwig

Song for Filu[78]
Lovesome the shrilling of the quail,
Lovesome the bulbul's sweet lament,
But by Filu's happy song
Your very heart with joy is rent.

Soft is moss on the forest floor,
Soft the rustling of the breeze
Softer yet is Filu's wool
As under your foot it curls and weaves.

Enduring is the oak-tree's trunk,
Long-lasting the bare mountainside,

---

[78] Marie Fillunger, singer, about the same age as Ludwig's mother. She was a frequent guest at the Wittgenstein's home. The verses are Ludwig's contribution to a party on the occasion of her 75th birthday.

Eternally will Filu's weft
Bear up as though on wings your stride.

Ludwig Wittgenstein
Otterthal, 21 January 1925

108 Ludwig to Helene

[1925]

Dearest Helenchen!

Please give the enclosed letter to Herr Nähr. I know neither his first name nor his house number. I do know the city he lives in, even the country, the continent, the planet, and the solar system. And yet it might still be possible for my letter not to reach him.

Accept the warmest regards from

your Ludwig

109 Ludwig to Hermine

[March 1926]

Dear Mining!

I wanted to write you a few days ago to thank you, among other things, for the various and all too abundant groceries. Now I've received your long letter and hasten to answer it. First: I am coming to Vienna next Friday, the 19th, and staying through Sunday afternoon (of course, I want to speak with Geiger). I too can't estimate how far-reaching his offence is. It can be terrible: that is, it may be the beginning of total vitiation. But it's also possible that it's nothing more than a tiresome escapade, and in that case it may even be a good thing that he tried it on and was found out before it was too late. (It depends on the lesson he learns from the whole affair: a good one, a bad one or none at all.) I can't take his cold-bloodedness – I mean his cold-bloodedness <u>after</u> the fact, not his deceitfulness – as a bad sign; indeed, I prefer it that way. —Of course, you must be severe with him, <u>but: I would let that severity be felt acutely, not chronically</u>. That is to say, I would be sharp with him and insist that he show me, for instance, his work, etc., but I would otherwise go on treating him normally, even speak with him cheerfully and <u>not</u> let him notice <u>any chronic depression</u>. (I say 'I would'; God knows what I would do, but I think, to the best of my knowledge and belief, that this is the right course of action.) I don't know what else I could write about this now.

Again, thank you very much for the groceries; but you've both gone mad, you and Paul; I had to give away ¾ of the stuff, it would have all gone bad on me otherwise! —Now the text of *Quem pastores*:[79]

Quem pastores laudavere, quibus angeli dixere 'absit vobis, jam timere, natus est rex gloriae'; ad quem magi ambulabant, aurum,

---

[79] A mediaeval Christmas carol, to be sung no doubt by Hermine's boys. The English translation of these quatrains by C. W. Douglas (1940) runs:

He whom joyous shepherds praised,
When the angel's song was raised
Bidding them be not amazed,
Heaven's all-glorious King is Born.

He whom sages, westward faring,
Myrrh and gold and incense bearing,
Worshipped, bowing low before him,
Reigns as King this happy morn.

Sing to Christ, the King who reigneth,
Yet of Mary manhood gaineth,
Born our God; let us adore him:
Glory be to God on high. Amen.

thus, myrrham portabant, immolabant haec sincere nato regi gloriae: Christo regi, deo nato, per Mariam nobis dato, merito resonet vere laus, honor et Gloria!

One more thing: please send me the third volume of *World History: The Modern Age* by Jäger. I need it.

I hope the Geiger matter turns out for the best and wish that you, too, can hope for the best. And I would like otherwise only to advise: storm whenever necessary, otherwise: sunshine, but <u>not steady rain</u>.

Please tell Mama I said hello.

Warmest regards,

your brother,

Ludwig

ps: Please tell Geiger that I was very sad to hear about his lack of decency.

5

A VIENNESE INTERMEZZO: A LETTER FROM LATE 1928?

From the summer of 1926 until the end of 1928, Ludwig lived in Vienna. A correspondence with the family is not available and would not be expected. During this time he was mainly busy with the construction of the house in the Kundmanngasse.

110 Ludwig to Paul[1]

Dear Paul!
Gretl tells me that there's been a serious rift in the lute between you and her and Hermine and that the difficulty consists in your belief

---

[1] Undated but clearly written when Ludwig was in Vienna, probably in 1928 when there will have been the interest of hearing music in the Kundmanngasse house.

that you're not being allowed to get at the truth. Gretl thought you would believe what I say if I were to speak with you. And I too believe that you'll take what I say at face value. I'm writing a letter instead of talking, perhaps primarily, because you can read the letter as often as you like (just as I would have to repeat myself whenever you interjected: 'of course, I thought, etc., etc.').

Gretl asked you to play the Labor at her place simply & solely because <u>she</u> would like it very much if <u>you</u> were to play something by <u>Labor at her place</u> – & for no other reason. She came to me when I was in the salon & said: 'Paul is said to have played that piece by Labor really beautifully. I so want to ask him to play it at my place'. I said: 'That'd be magnificent'. Her: 'Come with me, we're going to ask him!' Those are just about the exact words & certainly the <u>exact</u> spirit in which they were said. And you know the rest from then on. Now as to why she asked you: of course not, as you're supposed to have said, as a sort of treat to make up for not having been asked to play recently. Not a trace of that. Helene sang because *she* proposed *herself*. Baumayer played because she & she alone (perhaps as being held in high regard by me) was asked to play. If I had six siblings who were all artists on some instrument or with their vocal cords, not a single one of them would have been asked to play or sing on that occasion, for it wasn't meant to be a concert (and, just as an aside, it actually turned out to be too much something of the sort). But that was meant as an honour not as a treat to mollify you. —She wanted to hear <u>Labor</u>, first, because she has now for some time come to believe that his music is something truly important and, second, because she knows that I would really like to hear Labor, as I have often spoken with her about how beautiful instrumental music, & especially Labor, would sound in her house. As for me, I want to hear you play Labor at Gretl's place. And for no other reason than that I want to hear Labor at her place & that I would like to hear you play at her place, if you play Labor. (I have to add, even if you were to play Wagner or waltzes by Strauss). And even though my opinion of how you play is of no significance whatsoever in & of itself, I <u>do need</u> to say a few words about it now because it belongs here, as you're supposed to have said that you know that I wouldn't have asked to hear you play: I have already – in the Volksgartenkaffee – told you what I think, which is: the same thing distinguishes you from a <u>reproductive</u> artist that distinguishes an actor (and of course a good one) from a reader who wants no more than to give the poet's work, whereas the actor <u>can,</u> as it were, view the poetry only as a basis for his own & self-assertive activity. You – I believe – do not want to abandon yourself & step behind the composition; rather, you want to present yourself. Now I know something comes of that as well, which is worth hearing, & I don't mean just for someone who admires technique, but also for me & anyone else who knows how to appreciate an expression of personality. By contrast, I wouldn't turn to you if I wanted to hear a composer speak (which is usually the case with me). But there are a few exceptions here as well, such as Wagner (now I won't start philosophizing as to why you play Wagner in a different spirit from the way you do most other composers) & Labor too, whom you play (or seem to me to play) with a certain self-renunciation. I suppose it's not at all as simple as I've written here, but <u>on the whole it is.</u> — What's more is that you and I are connected, in the case of Labor's music, in our current interest in that music. Those are the reasons why I, in particular, want to hear you play. When Gretl suggested it to me, my pleasure and approval was <u>also</u> owed to the fact that I said to myself: it's good that he can have his say, even if it can't happen today. But that was not in the spirit of mollifying you, but in the spirit of veneration. —I believe that is all I wanted to write. Please don't reply to this letter, but take it as it's meant.

Your Ludwig

Ludwig, half-hidden, in drawing room of the Kundmanngasse with (left to right) Marguerite Respinger, Margarete, Head Physician Foltanek, Talla Sjögren (standing), Ludwig apparently asleep on the sofa, Georg Schönborn-Buchheim and Arvid Sjögren. © The Stonborough Family.

6

CAMBRIDGE: JANUARY 1929 TO FEBRUARY 1938

In January 1929 Ludwig went to Cambridge – allegedly on holiday, but soon decided to stay there in order to qualify for a doctorate and to pursue philosophy. In fact, he received the Ph.D. title in June. In the same month Trinity College awarded him a research grant of £100. He spent four weeks at Easter and two months of summer holidays in Austria. From 8 December he was again in Vienna for Christmas.

Ludwig commuted between Cambridge and Austria from 1930. In the summer, a further £100 was given him as a research grant. In September, on his return from Austria, he visited Marguerite Respinger in Switzerland. In October, he became faculty lecturer at the university and in December a Fellow of Trinity College. For five years, he was now assured of a salary and an apartment. The quarrel with Ramsey had been effortlessly overcome and the two did much work together. Tragically Ramsey had died suddenly in January 1930. Wittgenstein now saw the philosopher G.E. Moore more regularly, as well as the Italian economist Piero Sraffa.

Ludwig lived mostly in Trinity College in Cambridge, but at times also in Austria. In the summer he made a trip to Norway, accompanied by Marguerite Respinger. In Cambridge he acquired new friends, or disciples, as they were often called or 'all those Julian Bells' as he called them. One of his first students was Maurice O'Connor Drury, a life-long friend whom Ludwig launched on a doctor's life. In Vienna he remained in contact with Moritz Schlick and Friedrich Waismann.

From 1932 to 1934 Ludwig taught in Cambridge. He spent his holidays mostly in Austria. In 1935 Ludwig came to Vienna only for Easter and for Christmas. In the summer he remained in England until he set off on an alleged 'holiday trip' to the Soviet Union. The time of his Fellowship was coming to an end and he had thought of moving to Russia. His close friend Francis Skinner was to have accompanied him, and possibly also to have found work there (they had learnt Russian together), but his health prevented him.

Ludwig's Fellowship was extended the following year, exceptionally, until September 1936. In this year once again he came to Vienna only for Easter and for Christmas. In the middle of August, he retreated to solitude in Norway in order to complete his work and to 'come to terms with himself'. Towards the end of the year he wrote a 'confession' which he sent to his family and to some friends, as he occasionally did, a sort of confession of his sins.

In January 1937 Ludwig visited almost all his friends in England, possibly to read the confession to them. From February to April he was back in Norway and in May he travelled from Norway to Vienna (allegedly to avoid the tourists). In mid-August he returned, via Cambridge, to Norway, where he remained until Christmas. He spent the festal period in Vienna.

By January 1938 Ludwig was back in Cambridge and February until mid-March in Dublin, probably to work out a new life plan. Austria's annexation by the German Reich brought him back to Cambridge in mid-March, and he decided to apply for British citizenship and to seek a secure teaching position in England. His family were facing great difficulties in Austria, because of their partly Jewish descent. In April Ludwig met Gretl in Paris, in August and then in October Paul in Zurich, each time in order to find a solution to the problems of the sisters who remained in Austria. It was not advisable to go to Vienna himself, before obtaining British citizenship. His friend Piero Sraffa visited the family in Vienna at Easter. At the end of 1938, Wittgenstein submitted his application to succeed to Moore's Chair in Cambridge.

111 Hermine to Ludwig

21 January 1929

My dear Ludwig,

I was up at the Hochreit when your card arrived and sent word to Groller that <u>he</u> should write to you about the bank, as I myself knew nothing of the matter.

Your encouraging me to draw did me good, though I haven't been able to yet, nor shall be anytime soon; for I returned from the Hochreit yesterday and today am expecting Elsa Stradal for an 8-day stay. But after that I certainly want to try my hand at it again, and the nicest thing about it is its connection to you and Greti. In the past, I wouldn't have needed that, but now painting gets boring fast, if my siblings don't take an interest in it, because what I actually draw differs so much from what I wanted to draw, and the demands of everyday life sound off from all directions much more insistently. If I could manage them better – i.e., if they weren't just some unhappy love of mine – then they would not be so time-consuming and I could readily dedicate to drawing the time it needs without any pangs of conscience! I wonder whether a radiator and a window catch will be part of my next drawing, or the stairs?

I just left Lydia Oser,[1] to whom I'm reading Helene Lecher's memoirs. They are quite short and clumsy in part (over the summer I had arranged with H.L. that we'll eliminate the minor flaws together), but they are quite lively and convey something of her personality, and I really like being able to read them to Lydia Oser, who obviously enjoys it very much. Aunt Fine was very glad to receive your card; she told me several times that you had written to her. In fact, I found her sitting at her desk and writing (I don't know to whom); it seems like a miracle if you think about how it was back in autumn! I have been receiving very high-spirited letters from Fillu, who'll be turning 80 on 27 January, from Locarno (Hôtel Camelia, Switzerland) where she and Eugenie Sch[2] are staying; I'm very glad about it all, as her recent letters from Interlaken seemed to me to strike a very sour note and not to be indicative of any kind of harmonious life together.

But everything is obviously going smoothly now, and good Fillu is enjoying her life! How splendid! Perhaps you would send her a card for her birthday; that would make her very happy! I hope things are going as well as you'd like them to, with work and all! Warmest regards,

your sister,

Mining

---

[1] Lydia Oser, the slightly delicate daughter of Josefine (Aunt Fine, Karl Wittgenstein's sister married to a Professor Oser), became the heiress of Clara Wittgenstein. She contributed much to keeping the family in touch even after the break with Paul. Koder often stayed with her at Thumersbach, but whether on this occasion is not clear. The letters referred to have not been preserved.

[2] Eugenie Schumann (1851–1938), daughter of Robert and Clara Schumann.

112 Margarete to Ludwig

6 June 1929

Dear Luki,

There are only two important bits of news. The first is that, at the end of June, I will be going to America with Ji to see Tommy. Can I hope to see you before I go? It would make me very sad if that couldn't be managed. I'll be staying for two months and taking Ji and Arvid with me. I'll be travelling with an auspicious and a shitty eye. The auspicious one is meant for Tommy and the shitty one for you, because I've been looking forward to spending some time with you.

The second bit of news is that an *Als-Zauber* fountain is now being built in front of the *Hernalser Rathaus*.[3]—Now some minor news. Koder will be having dinner at my place this evening, the day before yesterday it was Hänsel and yesterday Wollheim.[4] And always we think of you.

Did you know that Schlick[5] will be staying on in Vienna? Old madame Lanckoronska told me so and added: 'Unfortunately, "she" too.'

The house and the garden are quite habitable now. But you know, the garden is just as demanding as the house and, as a result, I am unable to find any garden furniture suitable for the spot under the chestnut trees.

Please write with something about yourself.

Hugs,
your Gretl

---

[3] Dedicated to local musicians. It was first unveiled on 5 June 1932 and still exists today, with some restorations (17. Elterleinplatz).

[4] Oskar Wollheim, family friend and Max Salzer's successor as Section Head at the Ministry of Finance. Gretl brought him to New York during the Second World War.

[5] Moritz Schlick, the German philosopher, who refused a position in Germany and was the founding father of the Vienna Circle. To show its appreciation, the Vienna Circle dedicated to him their manifesto *The Vienna Circle: The Scientific Conception of the World*.

113 Hermine to Ludwig

Neuwaldegg, 1 July 1929

My good Ludwig,

I am ecstatic about the £200 Greti told us about and about your degree. I should still like to know <u>what</u> you now are, but she wasn't able to say. Greti has departed, and I only hope that she won't be doing too much during this journey, trying to be everything to those four young people.[6] She just isn't as well as one would want her to be, but she goes and sacrifices herself anyway. She always makes more friends doing so, but ends up having to give even more of herself; she would say 'that's how it ought to be!', but one just gets all worried and anxious watching it! I don't want her to burn herself out for Poppers,[7] Doblhoffs, etc., and, in the end, not be there for her family and me, who need her more than they do.

I was in Laxenburg yesterday and found Aunt Clara, thank God, very fresh and in the best of moods. Marie Baumayer was there as well, but she is still in pain, and it seems to me as if she were cheerier and more comfortable around us – she can just let herself go when she's with us! Even though it's very nice there, no one can 'let oneself go' at Aunt Clara's place, at least none of us can! The similarity with Papa!

Geiger got through without a promotion exam, which made me very happy. He was so pleased about the whole thing that he really and truly had a completely different face and voice, much more alive and normal (I gave him a piece of my mind a few times over the winter, because he would very quietly lisp something to himself after long

---

[6] Ji, Arvid, Tommy and Tommy's wife.
[7] Poppers: the family doctor and wife, see Letter 9; Doblhoffs: aristocratic friends of the Stonboroughs.

periods of hesitation in replying, even to the simplest of questions). I wonder what'll become of him, but I won't be assuming that kind of patronage from a distance ever again; I am the last person capable of that – I lose all points of contact and things get out of control.

Your card has just arrived. Thank you very much for it, and I am looking forward to seeing you. Warmest regards,

your sister,

Mining

Aunt Clara's apartments in Laxenburg castle © Wittgenstein Initiative.

Music room in Laxenburg © Wittgenstein Initiative.

114 Margarete to Ludwig

[October/November 1929]

Dear Luki,

I think about you a lot lately and have wanted a kind letter from you the whole time. What I would have liked even more is if you could have been here. I've been all sick and dopey, and once I was even close to sending a cable asking you to come and help me.

You see, Jerome seems to have lost the better part of my money in the present market crash, and just as I was at my most miserable it rained cables to the effect that I should muster up some cash, that I have to cut my expenses in half immediately, etc. Now that I am feeling much better I realise that, even if I had been healthy, I would not have been able to do much other than to let it rain. Losing the money doesn't mean much to me, there will still be enough for us to live a decent life. But I believe I will have to give up the Kundmanngasse and Gmunden. Renting the former and selling the latter. Renting a very small apartment seems to me to be the only way to radically cut my expenses. It's funny. You agonize over the solution to the chair problem and then the haemorrhoidal Gordian knot comes unravelled in an entirely different way. By the way, 2 weeks ago I had Wenzel the joiner come and asked him to make chairs in walnut based on both of your models. I thought we would be in a much better position to see just how far they are from being the right solution.

Mining is drawing in the hall. I hear her groans from my bed and sometimes she comes into my room with plenty of smuts around her nose. A consequence of rubbing her face all the time.

It is of course wonderful that Fine is so much better! This fact, then the one that your work is going well and that you are otherwise keeping well and the fact that everyone around me is being infinitely good to me are among the stuff my most pleasant thoughts are made of.

Hugs, but only with the right cheek.[8]

Your loving sister,
Gretl

115 Ludwig to Hermine

[November 1929]

Dear Mining!

Thank you for your letter and the page. I do not believe that this drawing expresses your <u>best</u> qualities as a painter – because here "line" is needed, as perhaps always when something is just indicated. Whenever Busch, for example, draws some dung on the ground, his lines expresses that dung and no one asks for long: is that straw or an old rag? But your flowers on the grave, if I'm not mistaken, are neither real flowers nor some symbol of such; they are just imprecisely drawn flowers, ribbons, etc., and the shadow, where it covers larger areas, comes across as dead on account of the even hatching; it too is, I believe, only an imprecise shadow that no one'll know what to make of. Still I like the page all the same, even despite the writing, which I find abominable. —Whose writing is that anyway, and why didn't you just use your own, which might well have been the only one that would fit the rest? I immediately cut the white from around the drawing and placed it on brown wrapping paper, and now it has a certain charm for me; and, for that reason, thanks again!

Please don't forget to give Aunt Fine my warmest regards, or to have someone else give them to her. It's wonderful that she's feeling

---

[8] Gretl was suffering from inflammation of the jaw.

better. Tell Baumayer too that I said hello, please, and Geiger. I would also like it very much if you were to paint something in the Kundmanngasse. I'm happy the statues look so good.

Your Ludwig

ps: By the way, my remarks regarding your drawing are superfluous because you of course know all that as well as I do.

116　Hermine to Ludwig

18 November 1929

My good Ludwig,

Thank you for your letter; you are completely right about the drawing. I myself know that line isn't my strength and that this weakness can only be overcome by refining to the uttermost; I'm not capable of indicating. In this particular case, it seems that a certain mood was struck, and everyone who has seen the grave appreciates the memory of it. The horrible writing fits well; it's the only one that would, I believe!

Greti is better (but those terrible days have left her quite agitated)

20 November

and you can see her progress from one day to the next. It's also evident from this letter, because I started it the day before yesterday and became more at ease regarding Greti in mid-sentence. Even with all that pain, she was still worried about Jerome, who was somehow involved in the market crash in New York, with his money and hers (I don't know the particulars), and I've just had to admire the way she's been handling the whole thing. Nothing but kindness and consideration for Jerome, who really . . .! It is hard to see into that marriage from the outside, but one thing seems certain to me, that Greti is visibly rising to a higher level and can't take her husband with her; who knows, perhaps a more aggressive, more energetic woman would have been better for him, he would have pulled himself together a bit more.

Aunt Fine is decidedly better. Baumayerl is indescribably high-energy; e.g., a philharmonic concert on Sunday – listened to Paul in the afternoon, who played one of Labor's concert pieces at a public concert – then to our place in the Alleegasse; she waited for me at the piano so she could play four-handed with me. She played 3 solo pieces before I could find the sheet music, then she played a sonata and variations by Mozart with me – after the buffet, she got Koder to perform (<u>very</u> beautiful and refined) and asked Paul to play the cadenza from the Labor piece again, which he played very beautifully and, I believe, if we had asked her to play something she would most certainly have done so. Isn't that unbelievably high-energy? Not to mention that she still has neuralgia! I started a drawing at the Kundmanngasse: of the doors from the hall into the salon with the discus thrower between door and window; it shows, I believe, something of the character of the space. Capturing the proportions is <u>difficult</u>, very <u>difficult</u>! Warmest regards, my good Ludwig,

your sister,

Mining

117 Ludwig to Hermine

[November 1929]

Dear Mining!

I can see that this is going to be a long letter. The reason is that I want to write to you about something I have been meaning to write for a long time and am earnestly asking you to take what I say into serious consideration and not just cast it to the wind. I want to ask you and

Paul something concerning our Christmas celebration (I mean the one in the Alleegasse). Surely you know that, since Mama's death, it has not been <u>entirely</u> satisfactory, and I believe that is very understandable; before I explain, however, I want to say straightaway what my request is, which is: to invite to that celebration a few friends whom we all like. (That would work only because we celebrate our Christmas on the 25th anyway.) Now the reason is that not even we 5 brothers and sisters (but even less so we and our nieces and nephews) are of such a disposition that we, <u>all of us together</u> and without the seasoning of friends, add up to good company: you can have a conversation with me or Gretl, but it is more difficult once all three of us get together. Even more so if it were with Paul and Gretl. Helene gets on well with each of us, but it would never occur to us that the three of us, you, Helene and I, should get together.

We are, all of us, rather hard and prickly elements able to be fitted together only with difficulty. —Nevertheless, things go splendidly whenever friends are present who bring into our company a lighter tone and other things we lack. We have our friends to thank for its being possible that we brothers and sisters can all gather in the Alleegasse on Sundays. <u>Of course I do not</u> mean that each of us comes only to meet his or her own friends and not to see only his or her brothers and sisters, but whenever too many of us get together it is pleasant only if we are diluted by friends. If the two of you think about it, you'll come to the same conclusion, if you aren't aware of it already. Now, I don't believe at all that one can say: how sad that we're incapable of making the time we spend together pleasant if there's no one else around. There's nothing sad about it; rather, it's in our nature, and our most valuable qualities are part and parcel with that. —Among ourselves, we're good for a conversation: that is, for being sociable in pairs – but not for playing games and the like. And whenever people get together they have to do <u>something</u>. It's impossible for people to enjoy being together without having something that connects them – (and being together isn't an activity unto itself). Nor will looking at the tree and gifts be enough. Of course you can retort: then we'll just keep our Christmas very short, made up of nothing but exchanging gifts, dinner and spending a bit of time together. But there couldn't be a worse principle! For doing it that way would turn the whole thing into a vacuous formality. Cutting time spent together short just so it won't become unpleasant can't itself be pleasant. For what do exchanging gifts and having dinner come to unless there's something *else* behind them that makes the time spent together enjoyable – because all of us can get good food elsewhere, and admire *objets d'art*, and have plenty of them. But it is an entirely different matter when friends are with us, because they share in our pleasure at the gifts we receive, and we in theirs (I mean at those that they receive), and we have a real reason to spend time together. —Again: it is impossible to see how we can be expected to do something we <u>are incapable of doing</u> and <u>do not want to do</u> the whole year through – i.e., all five of us spending time together without the company of friends – how we're supposed to spend time together on this particular evening to good effect. You might retort: we don't all have the same friends. Then we will just invite the ones everyone will get along with (I'll get along with everyone). Most of us like Koder, but should someone have anything against him, then I would gladly do without him, although he is my friend. Mima and Arvid might be agreeable to everyone, the same is true of König.[9] And you can all exchange gifts with them, as you do every year anyway, but to do so at our place, which

[9] Friedrich König, member of the Secession, who painted not all too modern works for Karl Wittgenstein (see Cecilia Sjörgren, 'Die Familie', p. 110).

is surely much nicer for them than receiving a gift in the mail. And should any one of you invite someone with some less agreeable character traits – such as Luise[10] – then that will be very nice because we'll know we've done something <u>very</u> nice for someone else. (I know, for example, that Mima and Arvid will have a very sad Christmas celebration – if you can call it that – and will be glad to spend it with all of you.) I once had a conversation with Helene up at the Hochreit about this matter which I tell you about now only so it doesn't seem like a secret. —Please, dear Mining, give this letter to Paul, <u>without any commentary</u>, as it is addressed to him as much as it is to you. I have written to you only because it's more natural for me to state my case to you. —Please take it into consideration, warmest regards, your

Ludwig

ps: Dear Paul, thank you very much for the invitation to the Alszauber concert. Unfortunately, I shan't be able to make it.

118 Hermine to Ludwig

22 November 1929

My good Ludwig,

When I wrote to you the day before yesterday, I didn't know to what extent Greti believes her money matters to be a settled matter and talks to others about them; but now she tells me that she has already written to you about it and as seems to be the case, that she absolutely means to give up the Kundmanngasse. I can't tell you how sad that makes me, or how sad it would, if I could really imagine it. Of course it's true that having such a house means you

---

[10] Louise Pollitzer. She was thought to be too 'German' and too talkative.

can't limit yourself; it demands a staff (I don't even want to speak of the <u>style</u> of staff, but merely of cleaning such and such a number of rooms, hallways, stairs, adjoining rooms, etc.). The house itself is such a princely gesture that you can't do anything but live in it like a prince – I mean on a large scale. But then I can't imagine Greti on any scale but a large one; of course, she can, when she pleases, live in just 3 rooms in New York, but moving into a small flat for good – no, that just won't do! Greti isn't making a big deal of it; she's just wonderful!!! Of course, I can't give Greti any money, though it is strange that this shouldn't be an option now when we're on such good terms with each other! What is it about money that prescribes such laws? But there is one thing, I believe, that I do have the right to do, i.e., it would be an injustice if I were not to do it: you divided your money among 3 siblings back then, because you weren't on good terms with Greti; you wouldn't have done that today, and the part (of what I received) that would have fallen to Greti belongs – so I believe – to her. I won't let anyone take that from me, and I'll find a way to do it for Tommy and Ji's sake. You'll be wondering why I'm writing to you and you'll be thinking: 'Mining can do what she wants with her money'. But it may happen that Greti calls on <u>you</u> for a decision whether this is a legitimate cause or a disguised form of support; I say this because she recently said 'Ludwig would understand exactly what to do in the case of losing one's fortune'. But don't write to Greti about any of this – the matter is not yet ready to be broached – but do write <u>to me</u> whether you are, on the whole, of my view. Of course, I can do it only if I have the feeling that this is a completely legitimate cause and the money legitimately belongs to Greti, which you completely failed to see back then, as I said time and time again and whenever I had the chance. Also: I wouldn't give the money away just so Greti could have a better life, but because I believe it to be the right thing to do, nor would it save the Kundmanngasse, alas! If only Greti were better, but she hasn't been so well for a couple of days now; she's in more pain, and Pichler says that it's neuritis and that there's nothing anyone can do. Of course, Greti won't admit that she hasn't taken care of herself from the first; she says that Pichler is allowing her to talk, but he can't imagine that she <u>always</u> talks, be it with Hedwig, her children, her favourites, friends, about trivial and non-trivial matters, serious and exciting matters, and the silliest of jokes! I tell you, the sight of it alone is painful! Plus, Jerome is expected, and she is unable and unwilling to tell him what needs to be said, but she will certainly talk for hours and work herself up dreadfully! Oh, my good Ludwig, I wish that he had already left and that those 14 days had already come and gone. I'm going to stop writing now, otherwise I'll just keep on railing; with any luck, I'll be able to write you with something better before very long!

Warmest regards,

your sister,

Mining

25 November 1929

119 Hermine to Ludwig

27 November 1929

My good Ludwig,

First, thank you very much for your letter, which I received today. I can say only that I welcome the idea wholeheartedly, and the same is true of Paul, and that we think your reasoning is quite right; I hope it'll work well in practice! Things have gone miserably for Greti since I last wrote, because some infection has exacerbated her condition, causing intense swelling and pain. To me, she seems somewhat better since earlier this evening, God grant it may finally be the definitive improvement and put her on the road to recovery. Jerome is expected over the next couple of days, and we all know – and are afraid of – what kind of emotional and physical demands it will place on Greti, who is physically and emotionally down-and-out at the moment. What on earth is he going to say? What's to become of us? Greti is splendid, as usual, and a role model for me, but often incomprehensible at the same time. I'm finishing this letter this morning, the 28 November, and have just heard that she's had a good night for the first time in many days and is feeling better.

Warmest regards, my dear Ludwig,

your sister,

Mining

120 Ludwig to Hermine

[End of November 1929]

Dear Mining!

Thank you for your letter. The thought that Gretl means to give up her house makes me very sad too. Now to your question: first of all, you are mistaken if you believe that I did not include Gretl in the division of my inheritance <u>because</u> I was on bad terms with her. I was on bad terms with her, but that of course had nothing to do with it.

Because Gretl was an American, her situation seemed to be secure at the time, and my other 3 siblings' financial situation to be precarious on account of the war – and that <u>alone</u> was the pivotal factor. If, at the time, Gretl had been an Austrian and you an American, I would have divided up my money amongst <u>Gretl,</u>

Helene and Paul, despite the little sympathy I felt for Gretl's character at the time. Yes – I believe that giving Gretl the portion of the money that she would then have received from your share if she had occupied the same position as you three had is the right and decent thing to do, <u>and I believe Gretl should unconditionally accept that</u>.

You will have received my very long letter by now. If you want, you can discuss it with Gretl as well.

Your Ludwig

121 Margarete to Ludwig

[End of November,
beginning of December
1929]

Dear Luki,

Of course my letter had hardly left my mouth! . . . But that's how it always is. —Your letter made me <u>very</u> happy. And I am even happier about your lecture. Something to look forward to. A great joy. I am quite all right. Shot through the mouth yesterday, on proud steeds today[11] with Marguerite[12] by car to the Kobenzl. By the way, I wouldn't want Marguerite to look after me in the least. Your feelings for her make her presence so refreshing for you. I know that all too

---

[11] Plays on well-known lines from Wilhelm Hauff's poem 'Reiters Morgengesang', which read: 'Gestern noch auf stolzen Rossen/Heute durch die Brust geschossen' (literally, 'On proud steeds yesterday, shot through the chest today').

[12] Marguerite Respinger: daughter of a Swiss business man; she was first invited to Vienna by Thomas Stonborough, who made friends with her in Cambridge. She came under the protection of Gretl and was a constant companion of Ludwig's, who spoke of her in Cambridge as his fiancée. She actually married Talla Sjögren, not without the ultimate encouragement of Gretl.

well from another case! Whenever I'm sick, I need a helper who quietly and carefully does all the necessary lifting, but also someone whom I love and who loves me, and the latter ought to come to light in a rather special way. That reminds me of a joke in *Le Rire*,[13] where the gramophone shop assistant says to a lady: "C'est convenue Madame, 'Un baisir voluptueux' 'Une nuit d'amour' vous aurez tout cela ce soir." I see I'm getting bawdy and will give my letter a different turn. —Jerome is leaving New York on Saturday and coming directly here. Believe me, I am shit-scared, I can't say how much. —And thank you very much for the manuscript, I could hardly imagine a greater joy. Hugs from

your Gretl

Christmas in the Alleegasse © The Stonborough Family.

---

[13] A French humour magazine.

122 Hermine to Ludwig

14 March [1930]

My good Ludwig,

I am very much looking forward to seeing you and hope to spend some time with you. I need my siblings very much, as a matter of necessity, and this year has been a bad one for me; to add to it all, I had the flu and was sent up to Semmering, and so have hardly seen anything of Greti, for instance. Unfortunately, she too hasn't been feeling very well and still needs to take care of herself better than she does. I, for my part, am very well and need only avoid going straight to Meidling, where colds are ten a penny. The day before I left, I was at Baumayerl's place; she doesn't seem to have changed all that much, but her heart is obviously getting weaker now. Popper has prescribed *Strofantus*[14] to her; I'm glad she has him as her doctor now. He recently forbade her to play any music at all, but he just might allow her to play a little by the time you get here! Baumayerl showed me your card as soon as I arrived; she was obviously very glad to have received it! The card reminds me of that day in Cambridge with Russell. Hearing what Russell said about you just made it into something very special for me;[15] it transfigured the building and the river and everything about that beautiful day, or more accurately it made everything meaningful to me.

How strange it is in your life that you always need people, find them and then grow further or beyond them: Frege, Russell, Engelmann occur to me at the moment. But I think it's quite understandable.

---

[14] Used to treat a weak heart.

[15] In her *Familienerinnerungen* (p.), Hermine tells of Russell's invitation to tea in 1912, where he told her: 'We expect the next big step in philosophy to be taken by your brother.'

I hope that this is a good time for you and that you're content to the extent one can and should be. I can only say that I hope you have what you want, because no one can know that but the person himself.

Into my idleness here, I brought pencil and paper and thought I might attempt a self-portrait, which Tommy wanted me to do; but nothing is coming of it, despite all the work I've been putting into it; between that and other things, I do finger exercises so we can play a little four-hands for you. But I just remembered that I'll be sending Staake – because she's been looking so awful lately – to Gmunden for 14 days, and over Easter at that! What a damned nuisance! Staake was ideal because she is always so gladly at one's disposal. Where can one get such a willing piano enthusiast? Koder will have to help out a bit over the holidays. A shame that I don't know what you like to hear at the moment? —Was it Moore who played Bach so beautifully, and do you listen to him play often? Warmest regards, my good Ludwig, and looking forward to seeing you again, your

sister Mining

Semmering, 14th of March
ps: It's stupid of me, but I haven't got your address up here with me.

123 Hermine to Ludwig

4 May 1930
Ended on Sunday

My good Ludwig,
The letter will be kept for Tommy; I believe he's coming at the beginning of July. —When I saw your handwriting, I hoped there'd be something in your letter about you and your business, which I

am very curious about. Let's hope it'll turn out well both for Cambridge and for you. Will you be advised of the phases or only of the final decision?[16] It is no joke when I say: I believe a decision would have to be made on the basis of your photograph alone, because, if you believe in your work at all, you should also allow for the possibility that its value will be brought out somehow, but of course I know no college can give money based on such subtleties!

I am up at the Hochreit and have to attend to a bunch of things I know nothing about, but when I'm not doing that, I do get to enjoy the flowers, birds and the crescent moon more than I can say! What do you think: will this coming summer be as nice as last year's? You at the Permanns',[17] we up at the Hochreit and you up at the Hochreit sometimes too? That would be just fine with me! Just to avoid any misunderstandings and the opprobrious 'con', I'm going to say straight out that your journey here must be set against your birthday. Because: if I recently gave Mariechen, who is only my niece, the 300 Schillings she wanted for her birthday, then it is only fair that I be allowed to donate two journeys to my brother, my next of kin (not to mention my love for you!)! I enjoyed accompanying you on the leg to St. Pölten, that hour in the cathedral and the spring-time landscape on my journey back. I don't think you're as much of a spring fanatic as I am; I get giddy over every petal! Paul should return on the 10th and – if Felix, who just told me, is well-informed – Greti is also expected around that time. I take that as a good sign regarding Jerome's condition; I hope it's

---

[16] Ludwig filed an application seeking a position as a probationary lecturer, and, on 21 May 1930, the university's General Board of the Faculties approved his application and granted him an annual salary of £250, effective as of 1 October 1930. A small allowance in addition to his salary for the concurrent year had also been retroactively approved. He also received a new research grant in June from Trinity College.

[17] The family of a gamekeeper who lived on the estate some distance from the main ('stone') house. Ludwig preferred to stay there.

true. I must say, I <u>very, very much</u> hope for Greti's sake that permanently living under the same roof with Jerome, which certainly has to come about at some point, can be postponed for a very long time to come!

I didn't quite finish this letter up at the Hochreit and brought it back to Vienna with me; Mariechen Baumayer is sitting next to me and wants to add a little something! Warmest regards and the very best wishes,

your sister,

Mining

Warmest regards and affection, thinking of you with many thanks for the beautiful card.

Marie Baumayer

4 April 1930

124 Ludwig to Hermine

[May 1930]

Dear Mining!

Thank you very much for your most recent letter. I enclose a letter which I received today and from which you will see that I am gradually becoming a rich man. The college still hasn't taken a decision, but it will probably give me something all the same, and it would therefore be improper of me to let you pay for my journey home. I'll be exploiting you over the summer anyway. So much for the con, for con it is. —I assume Gretl is back in Vienna. If so, please give her the letter to Tommy and tell her she can open it and possibly communicate its contents to him, as she is in a better position to know whether a letter and which points in it might still affect him. I hope to leave here in approximately 3 weeks and will probably then come directly to Vienna – but I don't know anything definite yet. Give Baumayer my warmest regards.

Your Ludwig

Whewell's Court, Trinity College Cambridge: Ludwig's room were in the top storey © The Stonborough Family.

125 Ludwig to Paul

11 January [year missing]

Dear Paul,

First, I want to give you my warmest thanks for the copious amounts of chocolate. We're going to have to put you under guardianship before very long. And second, I believe there is nothing more to decent and indecent words than what I said recently: using a word expresses a certain attitude vis-à-vis the meaning of the word. Take, for example, the three words: 'shithouse', 'lavatory' and 'restroom'. Using the first indicates that you are not in the least embarrassed to think of the very unsavoury use of this room. The second word is purely objective. Using it shows that you are speaking about the matter quite abstractly, purely scientifically as it were. And the third expression is a pure circumlocution and shows that the person using it would rather not talk about the matter at all. In short, we associate, as a matter of fact, various groups of ideas with the three expressions. It's the same with 'mouth' & 'gob'. If you use 'gob' to refer to a human mouth except in deliberately vulgar speech, you can only mean something very ugly, which shows that 'gob' does after all mean something different from 'mouth'. But enough of that. Again, the warmest thanks and regards,

your brother,

Ludwig

126 Helene to Ludwig

16 October 1931

Vienna iv Brahmsplatz 4

Dearest Ludwig,

I am happy to be able to write and tell you that I will indeed be allowed to work in the Volksbildungsverein library and will most likely be employed there for 3 times 3 hours. On the day you left, Fräulein Steiger, (the librarian) called to let me know that she will be keeping her job until further notice and that she can take me on as her assistant. You can imagine how happy I was to get this news. At the moment, my work consists in creating a foreign-language catalogue and reading all sorts of horrible German books, of which I have to prepare brief summaries. This coerced reading is the only unpleasant thing about the work, which I otherwise enjoy <u>very much</u>. Frl. Steiger, the person I share an office with, is quiet and pleasant, and even the two typists with whom I have to work every now and again are very nice. I haven't had anything to do with any of the men yet.

I was recently at the Hochreit for a Sunday and spoke with Ludwig about the girl. He still hasn't had the time to go, but will drive to Ägyd[18] as soon as he can to speak with her himself, as you wanted, and then report back to me with what she says.

I am looking forward to your visit in December and, in the meantime, send you my regards 1,000 times over.

Your devoted sister,

Helene

ps: Max sends his warmest regards.

127　Ludwig to Hermine

[October 1931]

Dear Mining!

My warmest thanks for the laundry and the books. Should you think of it, please tell Bazi[19] in the office that my address (for about a year now) is no longer 'Grantchester Road', but Trinity College. I'm well and working a lot. I keep thinking about what we once discussed up at the Hochreit (confessions, etc.), and, swine though I am, I have to be glad that I am nonetheless <u>at times</u> capable of being uneasy about it. If that unease weren't so superficial, an improvement would come about.

---

[18] St Ägyd, a small town near the Hochreit, where Karl Wittgenstein once owned a factory. He also built the Evangelical church there.

[19] Employee in the Wittgenstein family office.

Do you see Koder occasionally? —Please tell him to write to me. Play the scherzo from Bruckner's 3rd Symphony with him at some point. It often goes through my head, and I find it magnificent. Give my warmest regards to everyone.

Your Brother,

Ludwig

ps: Have you heard from Gretl?

128 Hermine to Ludwig

Started on 1 November 1931

My dear Ludwig,

Tomorrow I'll be playing with Koder, and of course we'll get out the scherzo from the third. I've already attempted it with Staake; it's so damned difficult, so peculiarly tricky, especially the trio. I like the scherzo <u>very much,</u> but the trio seems much too primitive to me; I wonder whether I'll ever acquire a taste for it? To my mind, it seems to be connected with the weird and primitive anecdotes that are told about Bruckner and which I always find too detailed! I do see, however, that in the scherzos they are connected with the devil and, I believe, also with the primitive sequencing of themes.

I play the adagio from the 1st every time I play with Staake and have already discovered a lot, but the first theme remains almost a complete mystery to me; I'm looking forward to our playing it for you – I usually understand it much better then.

(<u>Tuesday</u>) I played with Koder yesterday, and we enjoyed the scherzo immensely. He likes the trio too, and it indeed has some charm when he plays it.

Your letter also arrived in the meantime, for which you have my warmest thanks. I can't respond in writing to what you wrote about confession, etc., although I believe that I understand you very well. It is difficult enough to say what one means, but to write it all out is impossible. But you are certainly right that a feeling of unease is the only good thing anyone has. —

Marguerite was at my place recently, and she told me about Norway, very fondly and naturally; I was able to understand it much better than from what you said about it at the Hochreit. She has certainly changed very much since you and Greti came into her life, but in a way completely in keeping with who she is; in your version, I was able to hear only you or see only you before me, as when a large object conceals a smaller one in such a way that one can no longer reconstruct the latter at all.

ended on Thursday

Greti arrived the day before yesterday and was at my place yesterday, filled with interests and plans. She has started composing a kind of dramatic sketch for Mima's sixtieth birthday, which is so beautiful and touching that tears came to my eyes as she partly read it to me, partly told me about it. She is truly the most unbelievably multifaceted person there is! (Of course the playlet is a big secret; there isn't any chance you'll tell Mima about it, but I have to insist on that all the same.) Here, there is nothing but talk of saving at the moment, and I am now training to become the model housewife; I am glad that last year – that is, in the summer – I was able to paint at Greti's place, the time for that has, I believe, long since passed. Being a housewife is a time-consuming business.

Keep well, my good Lukas, wishing you all the best and looking forward to hearing from you,

your sister,

Mining

129 Ludwig to Hermine

[Beginning of November 1931]

Dear Mining!

Thank you for your letter. I only want to write that, in the scherzo of the third, only the <u>scherzo</u> made a great impression on me, especially the first – say – 16 or so bars of the theme after some 8 bars of introduction: these bars (of the theme) are indeed <u>primitive</u>, but magnificent. — Yes, you're certainly right this same primitiveness is also reflected in the sequencing of themes; even in the total absence of any transition from the first subject to the second in the first movements (as in Schubert and in diametrical opposition to Brahms's method).

I knew that Gretl was thinking of putting something on for Mima, and I thought it would turn into a sort of dramatic sketch. But, to be honest, I was and am almost afraid of it. Will that be able to melt the ice in Mima, no matter how nice it eventually turns out to be? And if not … Is a *playlet* what Mima really needs? Isn't it not like arranging a *playlet* for some poor devil longing for a bite to eat? You'll retort: it'll be done with such overwhelmingly good intentions that Mima can't but be overjoyed. Sure, but the real difficulty will not be resolved at by those means. And if you reply: but that difficulty can't be resolved at all. Then I'll retort: unfortunately, I almost believe so myself; but this only means that, consequently, Gretl will <u>never</u> be able to arrange a dramatic sketch for Mima. I believe you'll understand me: you can certainly embrace someone with whom you are not entirely on good terms, but you should do so only if the embrace is capable of melting the ice in that other person (that is, of bringing about a reconciliation), for if the embrace can't do that, then it'll just be a new misunderstanding; in such a case, it is better to be unobtrusively good to the other person without the least importunacy and <u>give up</u> the embrace, nice as it might be. (All this is written on the assumption that this playlet is not/does not contain a fire purging all animosity.)

When is Mima's birthday? I would really like to send her a present. Should it be so soon that there's no time to reply to me or to fulfil an order from me, then please buy her a nice bunch of flowers for me – unless you have a better idea. I would like to spend about 40 Shillings.

By the way, you wrote about having to save: has something happened to your money? It's strange, but that has unsettled me considerably.

Warmest regards,
Ludwig

ps: On the flower arrangement, you can hang a few pieces of aluminium ware (pots and pans of various, but practical, sizes). <u>Arvid</u> should buy them in the kitchen shop in the Rauensteingasse, but you must <u>arrange</u> them.

Hermine © The Stonborough Family.

130 Hermine to Ludwig

11 November 1931

My good Ludwig,

A thousand thanks for your kind letter; I read and discussed it with Greti, and a lot became clear to me when we did. I had similar reservations, even if they weren't so clearly formulated, and Greti was aware of them as well; but now we've clarified the following: Mima's character has two floes of ice. One that is very complicated in nature, a mixture of feelings of guilt (not acknowledged) and any number of other things; this general ice floe cannot be remedied by means of a dramatic sketch, but every act of warmth and kindness thaws the edges a bit.

Then there was a special ice floe in respect of Greti, and Greti herself was rather irritable and seemed to me not always or not completely to understand. Greti says that this special floe of ice has got much better over the last few years – that it hardly exists any more. And as evidence for that she cited, among other things, the warmth for Mima in her now that makes it possible for her to do and to write something nice for Mima. And that is the crucial point: the so-called dramatic sketch is a concentration of warmth, affectionate and truly felt, not something to be half swallowed, but to be expressed freely and openly at the right moment – no matter how things then go. Good can only issue in good, says Greti, and I now believe she is right.

The birthday is on the 29th, and I will take care of everything for you with Arvid; it is a very nice idea. I no longer know what I wrote about saving; the word is in the air at the moment, but I haven't the slightest idea what exactly it's supposed to mean – nor how much our means will still permit? Thank God I won't have to take any decisions about it; Paul and Max will massage everything into shape, and for the time being there is primarily the anxiety about the future, not about any immediate financial loss, and the anxiety primarily about how far it will affect everyone else, friends, family relations, and those in our charge! Keep well, dear Ludwig, with love from

your sister,
Hermine

131 Hermine to Ludwig

29 November [1931]

My good Ludwig,

I have been meaning to write to you for a while now, but I haven't got around to it, and finally I thought it would be best, if I were just to wait until after the 28th because I would be able to tell you about the celebration. It went off without a hitch (beginning with being a complete surprise) and was very nice and pleasant, and Mima enjoyed it immensely! A shame you weren't there and couldn't see it all; I'm sure you would have, I believe, approved of everything, especially the atmosphere!

The birthday table looked wonderful and picturesque with all the different gifts (picture in porcelain from Paul, lace from Lenka, etc.), and your present especially stood out because Arvid bought 4 aluminium pans of various sizes, and I put an azalea in flower in each and made a pyramid out of them. The piece went very well, much better than at the rehearsals where no one can give his or her best because there is no occasion to. We were all excited and to the right degree, and the audience was all taken in and quiet as a mouse. The flaring up of the candle flames was such an unbelievable culmination or, rather, climax to the beautiful speech to friendship that I was speechless the first time I heard it; you'd have to see it for yourself. It has just occurred to me: I am very upset that, in my absent-mindedness, I didn't send a few invitations, including one for Hänsel, which I can't forgive myself for – maybe we could perform it again for Tommy and Ji at Christmas, and you and the few people I forgot would be able to see it as well ...

Of course you can stay at Neuwaldegg <u>any time you want</u>, and I am <u>very much</u> looking forward to seeing you, even if I shan't be able to spend much time with you. With much of what's happened, I think of you and discuss it with you in my thoughts. I hope you're well!

With love, your sister,

Mining

The family villa in Neuwaldegg © The Stonborough Family.

132 Hermine to Ludwig

18 January 1932

My dearest Ludwig,

I am sending you the photographs of the Drobil figure; I think they are very good; of course, they show what's lacking in the figure, which I now see so clearly in those photographs, perhaps because I was with Drobil yesterday in the sculpture section of the Academy. I know he can't be a Praxiteles or a Michaelangelo, but I truly believed that not much more could be done with the figure, though I see now that, if it is truly destined for the tiniest of 'eternities', it still needs a lot of work. With any luck, Drobil will be able to manage it.

I received a letter from Engelmann yesterday, a bit of which I just have to copy for you because I find it truly wonderful. At his request, I sent Engelmann the photographs of the Kundmanngasse drawings, and he liked them very much and praised them as quite an accomplishment. And he went on:

In all of this, your sister's and your brother's accomplishments are also evident. Despite my not having any part in these images, the thought that I had something to do with the creation of something so beautiful is a satisfying one. More negatively than positively, I'm afraid. Back then I wanted something different, something of my own. Only now that your brother's work can be seen here in its final form has it become evident how far these of ideas of my own would have fallen short of his better solution – which I misunderstood at the time. Unfortunately, one is always wiser after the fact, and so, I acted more as a hindrance than a catalyst back then. But I was there, if that counts for something.

I can't tell you what kind of an impression these words make on me; they are truly beautiful and great. It's not easy to say something like that, and if it is really said truthfully, then the words become great and beautiful from the inside out. Even if he never will build anything that's so demanding, so targeted at perfection, as the Kundmanngasse, there has to be something about his buildings all the same. His talent has to find expression in some form or other!

I have now had a long conversation with Marguerite R.; the two of us were infinitely embarrassed, but I believe it went well on the whole, and it will go better still because we have the good will to do so.

I hope all's well with you, my dear Ludwig! With love!

Your sister,
Mining

133 Paul to Ludwig

19 January 1932

Dear Lucky,

Please enjoy the enclosed bit of writing and send it back to me once you're done with it, as Mining wants to incorporate it in her collection. The writer, Frau v. Oberleithner[20] is the wife of a bad composer,[21] who is related to the Chiaris.[22]

Just think: 90% of the recipients – and that's a low estimate – would be vain enough to fall for that. And all of them would of course buy at least one copy! She's creating an autograph album

---

[20] Vilma Oberleithner.

[21] Max von Oberleithner.

[22] The Chiaris family was a family of doctors in Vienna, the most well-known of whom was Ottokar von Chiari (1853–1918), a throat specialist.

with all those replies. And such promotional material for the musician in question: "Omelette à la Mayer"![23] Readers of this cookery book will probably believe that the meal was named after him, when really he has named it after himself!

Warmest greetings Yrs —

Paul

134 Ludwig to Paul

24 January 1932

My dear Paul!

Thank you very much for the various treats. Upon receiving the letter from Frau v.Oberleitner, I drafted a letter asking her to include my name in her cookery book, even though I'm not a musician. But I didn't send it because I thought that, in the end, I might be confused with you. My letter was composed very well & would probably have been published under the humorous responses. As such, it's a shame I'm not sending it. (I even wrote her a philosophical motto for a meal.) Please give Bassia my warmest regards. —Anyway, I'm sending you the draft of my letter to this Oberleitner lady. Don't you think my contribution would have been included?

Your Ludwig

Honourable Lady!

Your idea of a musical cookery book is delicious. As delicious, no doubt, as the meals, which any number of women will one day prepare by using your recipes. But what a shame that only musicians should enter the sacred space of this book. Oh, if

---

[23] Not clear whether a real or a notional composer.

only I were a musician. Unfortunately, I am nothing but a philosophising curmudgeon. And yet: is not philosophy music & music philosophy?! Now excuse this bit of sophistry. Aren't your husband's compositions, at least, philosophy turned into sound? That's why I, a philosopher, want to try to hustle my way into this musicians' symposium.

My favourite food is tomatoes in mayonnaise and, for that, I want to compose a proper philosophical motto for you:

The globe is to the creative theos

as the idea to the creative human mind.

Accept these greetings in admiration and amazement

from your

Dr Ludwig Wittgenstein

If you decide to honour me by including me in your book, then I kindly request that you provide my full name, as I would not wish to be confused with the pianist Paul Wittgenstein, who of course may also find his way into your book and to whom I am not related in the least.

135 Ludwig to Paul

[undated]

Dear Paul!

Thank you very much! When I saw the picture of Einstein, I said out loud: that's not possible![24] Unfortunately, I don't have anyone here who really knows how to appreciate that impossibility & an unshared joy is really only half a joy. And thanks a million for the

---

[24] The photograph in question is of an Einstein statue on the portal of St John the Divine Cathedral in New York. Paul sent this photograph to Ludwig for his Nonsense Collection.

plaster, etc.; presumably, I have Mining to thank for that. Please give her my thanks. (Deeply felt, because felt right at the bottom.)

Warmest greetings,

your brother,

Ludwig

Cutting from the Hamburger Illustrierte with statue of Einstein as a saint sent by Paul to Ludwig for his Nonsense collection © The Brenner-Archiv.

136 Hermine to Ludwig

26 April [1932]

My dearest Ludwig,

Today is your birthday and, instead of your receiving a letter saying happy birthday, I am writing it only today! Don't be angry, and do know that the blame really lies with a great turbulence surrounding me and in Meidling and up at the Hochreit! I wish you a very happy birthday and am very sorry that it really sounds like wishing a machine – about whose inner-workings one knows next to nothing – a very happy gearing and grinding! But what should one do? One can't give more than one has! And the intention is good!

Sometimes, I look back on our conversations, and have profited from doing so! What a deliverance to be out of the Geiger affair, it seems to me that he too has clearly taken the right path; he is now – metaphorically speaking – moving forward more steadily and something will come of him yet, he's actually making suggestions! —Marguerite will be at my place this evening. On Sunday, she told me you have bought a variety of things as presents for me, and just for a moment, despite the joy and despite having asked you to do so myself, I was horrified, because I just haven't any way of sending Pounds outside the country! But Marguerite will be helping me, inasmuch as she can take Schillings from me and send you money from Switzerland. I will be arranging precisely how with Max later today, for he knows his way about such matters, and I may write an extra note describing the best way to do so. For I would like to send this letter as quickly as possible! You'll have heard by now that Bassia has died;[25] it happened while I was up at the Hochreit, but I saw her laid out on Sunday, it was so strange to hear her mother

---

[25] Paul's lover died of cancer in the Kundmanngasse. She was cared for, at the end, by Gretl.

speaking to the deceased! She lovingly told her how beautiful she is, as she was recently worried she wasn't beautiful anymore. It was terrifyingly touching and yet so strange; I've spoken only very little about it with Paul. He's lost so much and even admits as much, although I am not entirely certain that he thinks the same thing I do when he admits it! Greti has overexerted herself again, a shame really! But I don't say anything about it; you're entirely right about its being her way of doing things, and her motivation in doing so is admirable! I am <u>very sorry</u> that all she has done hasn't brought Paul and Greti closer to one another. I would have thought that completely inevitable, but they really are as estranged from each other as never before!

With love,
my good Ludwig,
your sister,
Mining

137 Ludwig to Hermine

Thursday [May 1932]

Dear Mining!

Thank you for your letter! Of course, you shouldn't send me any money for the presents I bought! I have <u>plenty</u> here, and you'll give it back to me in the summer in Austrian Shillings, which will be much more useful to me then than English ones will be now. So, don't send me any money! By the way, I like the things I bought you very much and am curious as to what you'll say about them.

Of course I knew that our dear Paul would lose a lot in losing Bassia. Why do you say that he and Gretl haven't got any closer? <u>Of course</u>, they have got closer.

Please give Helene and Max my regards and tell them that I want to thank them for their kind card. Give Paul my best wishes.

Your Brother,

Ludwig

138　Hermine to Ludwig

[October 1932]

Dear Ludwig,

I just have to send you this quick note about a coincidence, as a footnote to my last letter: right after I sent it, Lenka came to my place to talk about something. All of a sudden, the vitrine with your presents caught her eye, and she was so astounded at this strange and serious sight that she pulled up a chair and studied them for quite some time. Completely of her own accord, she said, they're not knick-knacks or tasteful ornaments, rather there's something religious or mystical lying within; it has become a shrine, and not a vitrine. Isn't it peculiar that something like that would occur to Lenka – and on a day like today? For instance, that small glass in the wooden box strikes her as mystical, but only since the figure has taken pride of place in the middle on a throne. Do you have any idea what the figure means and where it comes from? Is it a sage, teaching? And what is the point of such a teeny figure? Perhaps you could ask Murakami[26] about it?

Warmest regards, my dear Ludwig,

your sister,

Mining

---

[26] The gifts came from Murakami, who was a retailer of Japanese *objets d'art* in London and whose taste Ludwig much respected.

139 Ludwig to Hermine

Sunday [15 October 1933]

Dear Mining!

Thank you very much for your letter. When I arrived here, I was rather worn down mentally and have found that I can't really work. Hence, after a long period of doubt, I decided to take an 8-day holiday, which I want to use for a walking tour intended to wear me down physically and so mechanically prevent me from thinking. I believe it will help me. Therefore, I am leaving Cambridge today and returning next Monday, the 23rd. I am not having any letters forwarded. —If there is anything <u>urgent</u>, cable me at the college. I will telephone from time to time to ask whether there is a cable for me and will have it relayed to me by telephone.

I believe I'll be able to work again in about a week.

Warmest regards,

your brother,

Ludwig

140 Hermine to Ludwig

Began on God knows when,

ended on 11 November

[1933]

My dearest Ludwig,

When I received your most recent letter with the news of your feeling tired and wanting to fit in a walking tour – of course, I <u>didn't like hearing that one bit</u>, because I know in your case that sort of thing means something very serious and that you are certainly suffering. There'd have been no point in replying straight away, since you weren't in Cambridge, and writing became more and more difficult for me as time went on, since I knew nothing about how you were, on the inside or out, and it would only have resulted in a questionnaire, or in the general wish that you get better. Now I think I'll just write to you about us and about things here – and you know how much I would like to hear about you! I often think about our conversations standing by the saw-mill up at the Hochreit when I would accompany you there; I did not understand much of what you were saying at the time, and believe that I understand it better now, but maybe I'm mistaken? Presumably, I won't be hearing much more about you before Christmas, or so I think!

Everyone is healthy here, I have to tell you that first, as it is something splendid. Then I should say there is a particularly agreeable atmosphere at our place, but I say that only hesitantly, as I know a threat to such an atmosphere can come out of the blue. I will say, however, that Paul is in a good mood; I'll be putting him to the test soon by talking about music – in my way, not in jest, but in earnest – about how I feel in my heart, and I'm almost sure he'll now be able to accept that.

Imagine – we had another theft, one that was solved very tragically, since it was the son of our porter Pöcker who stole the jewellery and money from me. Now it's also come to light that, before the burglary last summer, this particular son was the last to come home, that the porter himself didn't lock up and that he didn't sleep in his lodge either, because he wasn't feeling very well: in other words, there's no wonder any more as to how the burglars got in and were able to work as easily as they did. This is all quite horrible for the family, especially for his wife and daughter, and the whole affair was disagreeable and upsetting in the extreme.

I haven't seen Geiger since his studies began; he'll be coming to my place over the next couple of days. I did speak with Hänsel, who has a good impression of it all, and I myself have the feeling that, with study and living on his own, which requires especially frugal budgeting, something good and right will happen for Geiger. It just wasn't 'bracing' enough for him till now.

Keep well, my dear Ludwig, warmest regards,

your sister,
Mining

141 Hermine to Ludwig

[December 1933]

My dearest Ludwig,

First, I want to tell you that I am very much looking forward to seeing you and that I hope you are now more or less all right!! Second, I am extremely curious to hear about Marguerite, how she is and what you thought about her; she will have been very glad about your visit and, with any luck, she got the right thing from those two days! Things don't always work out the way one imagines, especially not when one's really looking forward to something! But it is all the nicer when everything goes really well!

Let's hope everything here will be really nice at Christmas too! I recently wrote to you saying how I believed that Greti didn't get anywhere with Paul, but I take it back: something has changed, and the relationship between the two of them has indeed improved. Now the only thing left to be fixed is the relationship with Tommy; I do think, however, that Tommy doesn't make it easy given his monstrous self-confidence: to be sure, as a woman that doesn't bother me, but it is not so easy for a man such as Paul, all the more so since the <u>great affection</u> Tommy shows me is absent from his dealings with Paul. Let's hope for the best; Paul will certainly do his best this year! It could be <u>entirely good</u> only if the two of them could just straightforwardly and quietly talk about their mutual failings, but it'll be some time before that happens!

With any luck, I'll get to see you soon, my dear Ludwig,

Warmest regards

your sister,

Mining

142 Hermine to Ludwig

10 February [1934]

My dearest Ludwig,

Very many thanks for your kind letter; I couldn't help laughing out loud about the knife comparison, it's strikingly apt! —Koder and I really enjoyed trying the movement from Bruckner's Third. We also really liked the fact that we now understand much faster and don't lose the thread every time there's a phrase that looks different, and even know in advance how the form will be and so don't experience any big surprises or misunderstandings. The first theme is truly magnificent.

Koder really liked your drawings[27] (that is, I showed him only the proofs, as I was able to order the copies only after I received your response.*

*The size of the head was not altered.)

---

[27] The drawings in questions are Ludwig's Drobil drawings, two of which are reproduced below (p. 193).

Because I liked them so much this time around too, I felt I wanted to go and see Drobil and there I much enjoyed the standing figure, which I found very appealing. Let's hope it'll survive the sad metamorphosis into plaster and continue to have something of its current beauty after it's been put into that awful material. Not but what clay is a splendid material and if an invention were made enabling its matt lustre to be maintained, then that would be something magnificent. Drobil, for his part, was charming when I expressed my admiration to him.

Tuesday, the 13th. Unfortunately, I now have to write about something entirely different; since I began this letter, a number of things have happened that I wouldn't have believed possible: there is fighting (as in war) between government troops and the social democrats in parts of the outer districts.[28] Everything is entirely quiet where we are; the city centre is blocked off, and the inner districts, Wieden Landstrasse, etc., are entirely quiet as well – only around the council-housing blocks in the outer sections of the city such as Heiligenstadt and Ottakring have there been skirmishes since yesterday evening. If only it were all over, we hear constant gunfire and don't understand how the reds were able to stockpile enough weapons to fight for days on end. But, as I said, these are isolated incidents, in the outer districts; I dare say it will sound different in the foreign newspapers, but it won't be true. At least not as of this evening.

Greti just called me saying that she joined the volunteer rescue society – and I am glad to hear that! I also found it moving the way Wollheim went to the *Verein* because he knew that it would have a

---

[28] Here Hermine is describing Austria's civil war, fought between 12 February and 15 February 1934, which led to the authoritarian regime under Engelbert Dollfuß.

huge calming effect on Frau Glaser.[29] A lot of people would have stayed at home today.

Warmest regards, my dear Ludwig,

your sister,

Mining

Michael Drobil, Sketch of Ludwig   *Michael Drobil, Sketch of Ludwig*
© *The Stonborough Family.*   © *The Stonborough Family.*

---

[29] Emilie Glaser, widow of Arthur G., an editor of the *New Free Press*, found intense support from the Wittgenstein family during the final stages of her husband's illness and the period of confusion after his death. At the time of this letter, she was employed at the Association Against Poverty and Mendicancy, which was also heavily dependent upon the Wittgensteins. Oskar Wollheim was the director of the Association. The Wittgensteins' cousin, Lydia Oser, Aunt Clara's heir, also worked there. Both during and after the war, Lydia and Emilie lived together in Thumersbach. Frau Glaser was the aunt who introduced the young Karl Menger to the Wittgenstein family circle (see his Viennese Autobiography' in Unexplored Dimensions (ed. G. Becchio, Advances in Austrian Economics Vol 12).

143 Hermine to Ludwig

[February/March 1934]

My dearest Ludwig,

I am very sad because I realize it was an injustice not to have written to you with further news! One does not allow for the fact that authentic, objective news is not to be obtained abroad, and especially not that, once things improve, not everybody everywhere gets to hear about it!

Everything was over on Friday, the 16th, and the schools were open on Monday as per usual.

Koder wasn't affected at all (except that he had a few days off); on the 13th, for instance, while there was shooting at certain points in Vienna, he was even able to come to our place without any problem and to take care of something with Paul in the city – indeed, everything was localised. Drobil had a number of unsettling days, but he and his family were not in any real danger. Of course, in the outer districts where all the upheaval was, there was the very real possibility of a grave misfortune being brought on by the reckless act of a single person with further consequences. Once civilians are equipped with weapons by their own party, you can imagine the consequences, and now everyone is free to give the greater blame to whom they choose: the Government Party or the Social Democratic Party? The government provided street-level protection, partly by elements equipped ad hoc with weapons, and this led to clashes with a greater portion of the general public. Meanwhile the armed social democrats fired on police and military personnel from their fortresses with machine guns and didn't really lose an ounce of popularity on account of it all! (That is a strange part of the story!)

Outwardly peace has been completely restored: cinemas, theatres and everything are open for business, but no one really knows what the future holds. We have, to be sure, driven one of the warring parties to <u>silence</u>, but not more than that: the other party – the national socialists – are more acrimonious and hostile than ever. How are we going to deal with them? Can one duel it out with knives and expect all to end well? Can reconciliation and any kind of *modus vivendi* be found now that the hostilities have gone so far?

I am of course the person least qualified to write about such things, as I know less than others who, at least, have a radio or contact with the lower orders (though who can separate rumour from truth?) None of <u>us</u> had any inkling of anything that black Monday, whereas my Meidling boys came to the home saying: today the government'll fall and Dollfuss'll hang!

Unfortunately, I don't have any reliable figures regarding the Social Democrats' losses in Vienna.[30] The police and army had 49 dead. I can't imagine that the others, who were shooting from cover, had greater losses?

It is a terribly tragic situation, and I am amazed how quickly this can all be forgotten by those who weren't directly involved! Everything is back to normal, Koder is coming over to play some music, Drobil was over for tea and, because no one knows what's to come, no one can sense what's brewing under the surface.

As soon as I know more, I'll be sure to write!

That's all today, my dear Ludwig, except for the warmest regards,

your sister,

Mining

---

[30] The exact number of victims has remained difficult to determine. Official figures estimate 118 dead respectively on the Government and Schutzbund side and between 250 and 270 among the non-participant civil population, but Steven Beller places the Schutzbund losses at over 1,000.

144　Ludwig to Helene

Thursday [3 May 1934]

Helenchen!

For my birthday (a week ago), I received from Gutruf i. Vienna, Milchgasse, a package of chocolate truffles. I was <u>very</u> happy, but didn't say thank you because I didn't know to whom I should say it. I was hoping to find out who the giver is by letter. This letter never came; instead, I received another such package today. 'Is it a god?', I've asked myself over and over again, but – after thinking about it for some time – I realized that it had to be an act of man because the packages didn't have enough postage. —So I'm left guessing: could you be the giver? If so, then accept my warmest thanks! If not, then please take a survey amongst my friends and let me know what your findings are, so that I'll know whom to thank. (By the way, after that second package, I have a supply of truffles for the next year of my life and kindly request that you rescind any and all additional packages until 26 April 1935.)

I am awaiting your esteemed response.

Warmest,

your brother,

Ludwig

145　Ludwig to Helene

Saturday [1934]

Dear Helene!

In your last letter, you write that I am a great philosopher. Certainly, I am, but I do not want to hear that from you. Call me a truth-seeker, and I'll be content with that. Certainly, you're right that all vanity is foreign to me and that even my students' idolatrous veneration is nothing compared to the relentlessness of my own self-criticism. Of course, I must admit that I am often astonished by my own greatness, unable to fathom it despite the enormity of my intellect. But enough words for now, when words are but vacuity compared to the fullness of things.

May you in all eternity ...

Your Ludwig

ps: My warmest thanks for the recipe, as my <u>body</u> also needs to be taken care of.

146 Paul to Ludwig

30 December 1934

Dear Lucky,

I wanted to write to you anyway because unfortunately I was unable to see you at Christmas. I would like to take this opportunity to tell you of 2 disappointments I suffered while reading on my travels.

The first disappointment was Hebbel's *The Nibelungs:*[31] I think this work is entirely off the mark. It begins as early as the dedication to his wife ... "So take this picture that thou filledest with life, For it is thine, & if it can endure, Then be it to thy fame alone ..." If a poet wants to write a dramatic trilogy, he has to have higher aims than this.

---

[31] Hebbel's *Nibelungen* (1862) was known to Ludwig (and will have been known to Paul) from schooldays. It is dedicated to Hebbel's wife, Christine Enghaus, a famous actress, who alternated the parts of Brunnhild and Kriemhild when it was first performed. It shows the self-destructiveness of the old Germanic ideals, so that their supersession by Christianity is not as surprising as Paul finds it.

Then this mix of classical antiquity & modern history (a mistake that Wagner does not make): Kriemhild is supposed, as Siegfried sets out on his journey, to pack his armour on top of everything!!! Siegfr. death, Act 4, Scene 6. Kriemhild: ... "old people,/Are strangely wont to be so fond of animals" (Kriemh. Revenge, Act 1, Scene 3). This alongside the thoroughly prehistoric, fairy-tale figure of Brunhild from Iceland.

Hagen & Gunter, whose behaviour is base & mean in Parts 1 & 2, become heroes in the last bit. (Even if that is the case in the epic poem that is not an excuse for the playwright.)

Why does Kriemhild's revenge take 5 acts anyway? The story has been pulled and stretched as if it were strudel dough; if she wants to kill Hagen, why doesn't she just do it right away?

The whole time she talks of wanting to avenge Siegfried; in the very last scene, where she kills Hagen, she suddenly begins to talk about the Nibelung treasure, which had hitherto been touched upon only in passing. So, she was only out for the gold?

At the end, Dietrich von Bern begins to rule "In His great name, who suffered on the cross". Here another new motif, to which we have at most heard only allusions. No sense at all!

Not to mention that Brunhild just falls by the wayside after she received such a significant introduction. (Even Wagner is more logical here.)

I dare say, these faults are outweighed by merits, which are not evident to me. But there they are, the faults.

The second disappointment was a book by Herbert Spencer: *Education*.[32] Lafcadio Hearn[33] says somewhere that he is the world's

---

[32] *Education: Intellectual, Moral, and Physical*, London, Williams and Norgate, 1861.

[33] Writer on many subjects, especially Japan. He curiously equated Buddhism, which he eventually professed, with the philosophy (much criticized by professional philosophers) of Herbert Spencer.

greatest philosopher. I would have said: quite a sympathetic character, perhaps more of a good institutional [. . .], but thoroughly unscientific.

If I have a piece of music copied, & I immediately find an error of transcription when I open it at random, then I can be sure that the entire copy is full of such errors. And if I discover a *quaternio terminorum*[34] on the 1st page of any philosophical work, then I am justified in drawing the same conclusion. To the extent I was hoping for some philosophical lesson, I could have turned back right after page one.

Do not respond to my scribbles unless you are particularly inclined to, and then address it to the Alleegasse, as I will probably be leaving here on 25 January. We shall see each other in April, God willing, at Easter or in the summer. Warmest greetings, your brother

Paul

147 Ludwig to Paul

26 January 1935

Dear Paul!

My warmest thanks for your long letter. I'll be able to respond to you only in outline & in an entirely unsatisfactory fashion. All the more so given that I don't have the Hebbel with me and haven't read it for quite some time now.

I believe, none of the traits you disapprove of is truly a flaw; though I am in no doubt that it can be said: the poet's abilities were far from sufficient to present the conflicts that demand to be presented here. Which only means that, in the end, the enterprise

---

[34] A gross logical fallacy.

hasn't been successful. —It is, I believe, as if we were reading a book about aesthetics, say, & were to find it flawed on the whole, as a system, but peppered throughout with excellent remarks regarding its subject matter. So here too one finds time and again deep insights & beautiful discoveries, many more, I'm sure, than I can even imagine. I believe, Hebbel & Wagner can't be compared any more than a blind man & a cripple, save to the extent that both are incapable of walking properly. In Wagner there is not the least bit of tragedy from beginning to end – just as there is none in a fairy tale or myth. That is to say, at no point are there collisions of forces that we feel to be on a par. Where collisions exist, they are between light & darkness. What is essential for Hebbel is precisely that everyone is in the right. That is to say: with Wagner, there is no problem, whereas Hebbel is teeming with problems. And, as such, the collisions in Hebbel are always between archetypes: cultures, peoples, races, eras (compare *Herodes & Mariamne, Gyges, Genoveva*). —You could even put it this way: the second half of the 19th century had, time and again, to deal with the problem of race: that is, with the comparison, the valuation, the claims of races. It's for that reason too that we find the *Jüdin*, the *Argonauten*, the *Makabäer* among Hebbel's dramas at the time. A confrontation takes place in each of these. (In *Nathan*, in contrast, there is no confrontation in this sense.)[35] The problem is solved for Wagner, however, with the division between light and darkness. (That's why the others are so much more in tune with their subject.)

In Wagner, the intention is to dramatize myth; in Hebbel, the collision between different worlds is meant to be on full display –

---

[35] *Herodes & Mariamne* and other tragedies by Hebbel; *Nathan* by contrast is by Lessing.

among other things, the collision so to speak between an arcane world & an ordinary one. This addresses your first criticism.

Regarding no. 2: this is, I believe, not a flaw at all. Is the figure of the King in the *Jüdin* heroic or base? Both!—

You can really call something a flaw only if the flawed thing would be improved upon the removal or correction of the flaw.

Kriemhild does not simply avenge herself on two people, but on an entire culture. (This is the same as Daisy Nagy's not allowing her children to learn German.) She allies herself with a foreign culture against that of her family. The difference between the two cultures is spendidly brought out in the dialogue between Etzl & Dietrich just prior to the Nibelungs' arrival.

The hoard & Siegfried are, in a certain sense, one and the same for Kriemhild. Committing the hoard to water was like disfiguring the corpse of a murder victim – and the reason that's so painful isn't that the dead body means so much to us. For Kriemhild, Siegfried was strength & power, & the hoard was a symbol of such power in more than one sense.

That a new theme is introduced as a sort of epilogue is, I believe, not a flaw in and of itself, though I would not say that it produces here the effect it ought to. The meaning is, of course, that the totality of the old epoch, together with all its conflictuality, is submerged & a new one emerges. And here endeth the second lesson!!

Forgive this scribble.

Your Brother,
Ludwig

148 Hermine to Ludwig

26 April [1935]

My dear Ludwig,

Today is really your birthday, and I am sending you at least a hello and the best wishes for your health. I hope you've been able to bring everything to rights with a proper diet and aren't suffering! And I hope everything else is going as well as you'd like! Nothing at all has happened today that would be remotely worth telling and 1 May: The letter has been on my desk the whole time, and I couldn't bring myself to continue writing. Nor would I have really known how to. In the meantime, Clärchen has married, and I thought of you and would have liked to talk with you about why it hadn't bothered me that in Tommy's case there was only a dinner at the Kundmanngasse and why it was such a dismal affair for Clärchen. There's no love, no interest and not the slightest emotional involvement. I don't know whether Arvid is just hiding his emotions; Clärchen seemed to me to be as dry as straw, with all the wedding guests the same. But, in the church, there is organ and festivity and a festive mood from the outside which can be taken for an inner one. —Now we'll see whether Arvid will dry up or whether he'll succeed at in moistening Clärchen! Let's hope it won't be the former!

There were the strangest scenes imaginable in the streets today;[36] wire entanglements were set up around the entire Ringstraße – that is, around the entire belt concentric with the Ringstraße where

---

[36] In 1935, 1 May became 'Constitution Day' under the Corporate State. Since the Labour Day ban in 1933, the government had militarily closed off Vienna's Inner City as a matter of routine. The Social Democracy – dissolved by the date of this letter – celebrated this day by organizing demonstrative 'walks'.

the suburbs begin – with military personnel carrying machine guns posted behind them (you could get into the inner city only with a permit), and curious, apparently harmless and cheerful spectators, etc., were promenading in front of the wire entanglements. There were reports that there had been a bit of tension in the morning, but everything was unthinkingly cheerful by the time USIUS was out and about. How funny people are – the 'spectacle' from *Wallenstein* always springs to mind. —Keep well, my dear Ludwig, warmest regards, your sister

Mining

149 Hermine to Ludwig

9 May 1935

My dearest Ludwig,

I'm a cow – that's all I can say. After receiving your card today, I was furious at myself because it didn't occur to me while I was writing my last letter that you couldn't imagine the situation in its entirety. There were, I must make clear, no disturbances, and all the dispositions, machine guns, etc., were there only to ensure that nothing of the sort happened: in other words, a very reasonable measure was taken to very good effect. No demonstration marches were able to form or move along the Ringstraße; neither the socialists nor the Nazis were able to demonstrate or set off any kind of ferment in the crowds looking on, for the Ringstraße was truly hermetically sealed. But there were plenty of people come to look at the street closures, and these curious, apparently cheerful spectators struck us all as typically Austrian. Had there been any trouble, I would have thought twice about writing to you, or would have written more extensively, but because it was entirely innocuous, I wanted to give you only an humorous indication of the whole thing, and that was stupid! Forgive me!

Yesterday, Arvid and Clärchen were at our place for Sunday lunch now that they've returned from their honeymoon, and I found Arvid's face has taken on an especially lovely aspect and with what a beautiful expression he looks at his wife. I almost believed I could see a change in Clärchen too; in any event, however, I am very glad that Arvid doesn't seem to me in any danger now, to the contrary!

Lenka too seems more approachable and Mima more cheerful; the former would be especially important, for Lenka is sometimes sadly lacking in this respect, and I was afraid of how it would be for her after the wedding. Now: keep well, my dear Ludwig, warmest regards from your sister who is quite upset with herself,

Mining

150 Ludwig to Paul

4 September 1935

Dear Paul!

Thank you for your kind letter. In 3 days I will be traveling to Russia for 3 weeks. Hence, we shall be able to see each other only at Christmas. I am not indeed excessively busy, but quite preoccupied with various matters, & we should, for this reason, have little of each other if we were to meet in the hotel.

Thank you for relaying Koder's greetings & the card that you two sent me; I wrote to him today. With best wishes and

warmest regards,
your brother,
Ludwig

151 Ludwig to Helene

Thursday

[April/May 1936]

Helenchen!

Was the Gugelhupf from you? If so, my warmest thanks! It arrived early yesterday and is almost gone today! As that shows, it's magnificent; but the form is not the one this sort of Gugelhupf typically has. The Gugelhupf you sent me, has (or had) <u>precisely</u> the form of a Germkugelhupf, & my thesis is that the Biscuitkugelhupf had a different form from the Germkugelhupf.[37]

The latter has more or less this form

and the former this one

The next time I'm in Vienna I will be sure to investigate this matter further.

Just one more thing: at the behest of the English government, I am now meant to hold an hour's talkshow on the radio every week. In doing so, I will initiate understanding between nations.

Again, my warmest thanks,

your brother,

Ludwig

ps: Tell Maxl I said hello, the old DS [Drecksau = filthy swine] affectionately meant?

---

[37] Two types of Viennese poundcake, made with short pastry and yeast respectively, and reflecting this in their form.

152 Paul to Ludwig

Vienna, IV. Argentinierstrasse 16.

1 May 1936

Dearest Lucky,

Although I usually just send you compendious nonsense, you are receiving the enclosed article,[38] because of the bits highlighted in red.

Warmest Yrs

Paul

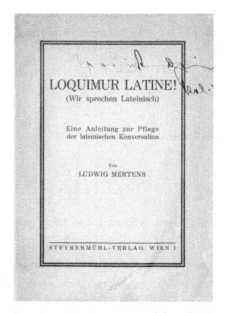

Loquimur Latine cover of handbook
send by Paul to Ludwig for his Nonsense
collection © The Brenner-Archiv.

---

[38] Enclosed was a brochure entitled *Loquimur Latine*, which lists examples of Latin conversations in modern times. The letter and the pamphlet are included in the Nonsense Collection. Ludwig replied: Pro calceo ingenti, quem mihi misisti, maximas gratias tibi ago. Stultitiae limes non notus est. Inanitas cerebrorum in dies impavescit. Warmest greetings Ludwig [Thank you very much for the immense piece of nonsense that you've sent me. Stupidity has no known limit. The emptiness of brains is more shocking from day to day. (ageo should be ago; impavescit does not exist as word, but expavescit means 'has been shocked'.)]

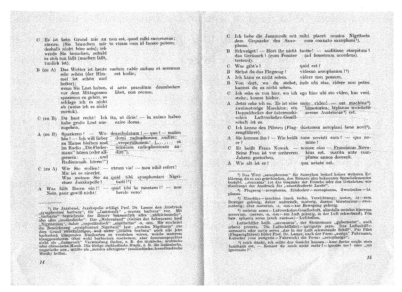

Loquimur Latine extract from a handbook send by Paul to Ludwig for his Nonsense collection © The Brenner-Archiv.

153 Margarete to Ludwig

11 July 1936

My dear, my good Ludwig,

There would be much, much to write. My lack of health is part of the reason I haven't written. This year I just can't seem to shake it off & that unsettles me more than I thought it would. I should be thinking: if it doesn't get any better, it doesn't really matter. But it's only every now and again that I really manage this attitude.

I've been back in Gmunden since yesterday, & Koder & Geiger will be coming on Saturday. I have had a great worry about Geiger. One day not long after you'd left, he came and told me of a friend who might be in need of some help. This friend's a gambler and gambles every night. I told him that I would of course need to know more if I'm to be able to help. Then it came out that he was this friend. You could've knocked me over with a feather, so unexpected was the news. This whole business was settled in about 14 days, but I was knocking at the knees for fear of dropping the ball on this one. Now, right before he's supposed to join the Voluntary Work Service, he has had a horrible experience that has hit him very hard. A young man with whom he had been working in the laboratory was burned in an explosion. He was in the same room & couldn't help him. I feel dreadfully sorry for Geiger. I can't imagine anything more horrible and insurmountable than such an experience.

Strange that Karl Kraus's death has hit so close to home for me. 'Close to home' is of course a stupid phrase. The thought that he could die just never occurred to me. I don't know why. I often thought of doing something nice for him & giving him, say, the *Der Zerrissene* manuscript I own, but I just kept letting the opportunity pass. Now I regret it.[39]

Yes & Schlick.[40] I'm not going to say anything about it. I think you already know what I think about the whole thing. One thing made me happy, though. Waismann told me that the students truly mourn and miss him.

Waismann was at my place. He called me (although I didn't know who he was) & said he wanted to speak with me about

---

[39] Kraus died on 12 June 1936 in Vienna. *Der Zerrissene* is a play by Johann Nestroy, one of Kraus's favourite writers.
[40] Moritz Schlick was murdered by a former student on the steps of the University of Vienna on 22 June 1936.

something concerning Schlick. He came, & it took quite some time before I even understood what led him to me in the first place. He wanted to ask me whether you might be willing to accept a teaching position in Vienna & whether our family, which he says is very influential, would let itself be used for this purpose. I said that we are not very influential, but even if we were, that we would never let ourselves be used like that & if we ever did, that you would strike us dead & that if you didn't strike us dead, then you would never consider it anyway etc. etc. He meant it all quite well & I was therefore very friendly in turn.

I've had some good news from Talla on the material level. A sure offer to go to Alaska & a large gift of money from old man Respinger. The way he wrote about it though didn't make me happy at all.

Thanks for your regards in Geiger's letter. Wollheim says you were well. May it really be so. There is little that I would like more. Stay healthy! Hugs and affection,

your Gretl

154 Margarete to Ludwig

26 September 1936

My dear, my good Luki,

Thank you very much for your kind letter and for the regards you had Geigerl pass on to me. The thought of your not being well is a sad and painful one for me. And a gall bladder infection at that. I have been imagining how nice it would be if I could come to your place and cook for you and put things to rights. That wouldn't be a stupid idea at all, believe me. —There was somewhat of a delay in settling the manuscript business, but now it seems to be perfectly clear that your manuscript is in the Alleegasse.[41] Waismann's identified it. To be sure, he thinks that some of it is missing. But he is probably wrong about that. (He'll be writing to you about it himself.) Nothing could be found at the Schlicks' place. —I've been in Vienna for a couple of days now. My children are in America again. I won't write anything about my troubles. I have already done and said everything I could, and now I just have to wait and hope. You can imagine how difficult that is for me and how very healthy it is all the same.

Adieu my dear. Get well. I would like that very much.

Hugs and affection,

your Gretl

ps: I've received a <u>nice</u> letter from Talla. The fact that he spends all his free time revising 'Mining and ingeneering' in preparation for Alaska is having the best influence on him.

155 Margarete to Ludwig

29 [November] 1936[42]

My dear, my good Luki,

I wanted to write to you tonight, but then comes a message from Wollheim that you are well and have sent your regards. I am overjoyed. May you <u>stay</u> healthy my dear! —Thank you very much for your latest, kind letter, which has once again crossed with mine. I am very curious about the presents from London. I probably

---

[41] See Letter 161 for the list of 'manuscripts', which, eighteen months later, were in the Alleegasse. The list is possibly based on Waismann's 'expertise'. It seems that Ludwig wanted to determine whether a manuscript known to Waismann and possibly lent to Schlick (presumably in a typewritten version) was safe and secure with his family.

[42] The transcript is dated 29 September 1936, but the date of Letter 154 and the allusion to Christmas make the 29 November more likely.

won't understand a thing. But your kitchen clock is a jewel in every respect. *Son ramage se rapporte á son plumage.*[43] —It's great that you're coming for Christmas. Something to look forward to! Yes, I too will be in Vienna this time, and Wedi will be with me. Am I happy that I'll be getting a manuscript instead of an 'indescribably beautiful' Saki bottle. I will gladly hold the manuscript in reverence. —We're all well here. It's not always easy with Geigerl, and I will be needing your advice, but that can wait till Christmas. I just remembered how much I am looking forward to going shopping with you and to your rucksack. —Keep well my dear,

hugs and affection,

your Gretl

156 Margarete to Ludwig

3 December 1936

My dear, my good Luki,

I am grateful that I can for once say: I think of you with tender love. I do it often, but I haven't ever dared say it.

If your confession has brought you some relief, then I am grateful to God that he has made it possible for you to make it.

I passed it on to Lenka in as fitting a manner as I could.

Surely you know that I could counter every one of your confessed sins with the same or ones far worse in kind.

Everyone is looking forward to your coming before long, me in particular.

Hugs my dear,

your Gretl

---

[43] 'Its notes are as fine as its feathers' (quoting Lafontaine).

157 Max to Ludwig

Vienna, 17 March 1937

Dear Luki!

You were finally right for a change, calling me an old d.s. in your birthday card, for which wonderful isn't the right word: that is, if old d.s.'s are – and I for one believe they are – the kind of creatures that are hardly or not at all capable of thinking of reasonable things. It's been 14 days now that I've been in possession of your ever so kind birthday wishes and the two books from you which Lenka put on the gift table for me, and I haven't thanked you for them yet, although the other birthday wishes hardly made me as happy as yours did! Only my age and the forgetfulness that comes with it are to blame, that and a 6-day stay at the Hochreit, from which I just returned yesterday evening and where I became conscious of my sin in a moment of clarity. My thanks for your friendly thoughts and your wishes and gifts are, however, no less affectionate because I am giving them to you only today. Accept them, please, friendly and good as you always are and don't judge your old brother-in-law too harshly! For he is always and especially happy to get the titles and wishes you give, which never fail to arrive on the 3rd of March, and asks that you – completely in contrast to his friends here whom he has been petitioning to ignore his birthday with ever greater succes – send him a few friendly words (they can even be swear words à la Luki) on this day next year.

Here everyone and everything is, knock on wood, in good health and in order. All 8 of the Stockerts will be going to the Hochreit for Easter; Lenka and I will be staying here with Pussy waiting for the new baby to arrive.

I hope you're well! When will you be here next? Looking forward to seeing you again and asking for your forgiveness because of my delay in writing you this letter, your

devoted brother-in-law,

Max

ps: Also, please forgive any mistakes I've made in typing!

Max Salzer, Oskar Wollheim, Leopoldine, Alois Hänisch (Seccession artist), Helene, Ludwig, Felix Salzer © *The Brenner-Archiv.*

158 Ludwig to Max

Monday, 23 March [1937]

Dear Maxl!

You old Hsrg!*[44] Your kind letter made me so happy that I can't help myself and just have to thank you for it. The books were, of course, Helene's idea, as nothing better occurred to me than flowers

---

[44] Original reads 'Hxszhrzn', which transcribes as 'Schasian'. 'Hsrg' follows the same rule, given that g = t.

and nibbles. —I've been meaning to tell you that a wee thing of a book written by me will be published in the near future, entitled *The Philosopher's Handbook*, dedicated to you and your wife. It will be printed on thin hygienic paper with non-bleeding printer ink, and every sheet can be ripped out individually.—

I'm glad that you are up at the Hochreit. Be sure to have a good time <u>and stay healthy</u>! I hope to come to Vienna again in the spring and am looking forward to seeing you.

Your Ludwig

ps: Give everyone my regards.

There's still snow and ice here, but it's not cold today, and the sun was shining, and it was splendid.

* This word is written in a code that your dear wife may perhaps be able to decipher.

159 Ludwig to Paul

Skjolden i. Sogn
14 October 1937

Dear Paul!

A few days ago, young Hermann Hänsel was at my place to talk about his studies. For reasons, which I can't explain here, but which are decent through and through, he would like to suspend his studies (philology) & to do his military service now. That is, he wants, if it's possible, to enlist immediately after his return to Vienna (in about 14 days), instead of attending university again. But neither of us knows what the enlistment dates are. What is more, however, Hermann H. has not yet discussed this matter with his father, but has indeed written to him, though I don't know whether he will give Hermann his consent to enlist. I, therefore, gave H.H. a letter addressed to you, which he should give to you after he has discussed the matter with his father (in the event the latter gives his consent), & in this letter I ask you to advise H.H. & to help him, if you can, by recommending him to some military person – because, in my opinion, he deserves patronage of this kind. After H. left, he sent me a letter from a stage along his route, asking me to send you a letter by post regarding his business, as it might otherwise become too late & perhaps impossible to do something for him if you learn about the matter only in 14 days (Hermann H. is doing the entire route by bike).

So my request to you is this: please contact Director Hänsel, show him this letter, ask him whether Hermann has his consent to do his military service now instead of completing his studies; & if that's the case, please pull some strings for him – if that's at all possible – so that he may enlist now. I believe Hermann H. is a very serious, honest & capable young man worthy of your support.

Forgive this imposition, warmest regards, your

Ludwig, who is very well.

ps: I hope this letter isn't too unclear. Your Ludwig.

160 Margarete to Ludwig

1 December 1937

My dear, my good Luki,

Thank you for the two letters. I have often replied to and been thankful for the first one in my thoughts. The Marrows have been procured.

Everyone is looking forward to your next visit & myself most of all, as I really believe, which is not meant as a degradation of their feelings, but as an elevation of mine.

Will you be dictating again? I am looking forward to that & to the hot soup, which always goes especially well with it.

Everything is still the same with me & I have despite my best efforts, <u>really</u> my best efforts, only been capable of very brief moments of decency. But that's how people are. Keep well my dear, be healthy, & may things go well for you. Yes, I am really looking forward to seeing you again!

Hugs and love from
Gretl

161 Ludwig to Hermine

[February 1938]

or the like.[45] Not that I believe that, but one had better find out. [. . .] If there is a definite risk, then I would take my m.ss to Cambridge only when I myself next travel from Vienna to Cambridge.[46] But I should <u>prefer</u> it, if they could be sent now. If you have them sent now, please have a small, but strong <u>box made for them, perhaps</u> with hinges and a padlock, if that is possible and does not cause any trouble for the shipping. The thing is that in the library my m.ss will be accessible to no one other than myself and <u>one other person</u>. —Furthermore, the manuscripts are

---

[45] At least one page is missing.

[46] See *Cambridge Letters* (p. 137) for Ludwig's decision to keep his manuscripts in the Trinity College library. Perhaps the thought of changing professions was behind this decision and perhaps also the dangerous situation in Austria at the time. This letter was probably written in Dublin when Ludwig was occupied by thoughts of changing professions: he considered becoming a psychiatrist. Given that the German takeover followed shortly after this letter, it is no wonder that the manuscripts were not sent to England. Nearly all eventually found their way into the Austrian National Library and the Trinity College library.

the following: nine numbered volumes of handwritten and two packages of typewritten material.[47]

An m.s wrapped in paper, and I believe sealed, is also in your custody; please do <u>not</u> send this with the others. Please let me know if anything's still unclear.

The address the m.ss are to be sent to is:

> The Librarian
>
> Trinity College, Cambridge
>
> England

Should there be no time to have the jug sent to Max (if nothing can be done about the postal scales), I'll just give him flowers for now and the jug some other time.

I'm pretty busy, and things are going well. Give all friends my regards!!

Your brother,

Ludwig

List of manuscripts (handwritten)

i	volume	Philosophical Remarks
ii.	volume	Philosophical Remarks
iv.	volume	Philosophical Remarks
v.	volume	Remarks
vi.	volume	Philosophical Remarks
vii.	volume	Remarks on Philosophy
viii.	volume	Remarks on Philosophical Grammar

---

[47] There is a handwritten version (clearly by Hermine) and a typewritten version of this list with insignificant variations: e.g., 'typed' (ms) instead of 'typewritten' (ts). Another manuscript – in different handwriting, but on Hermine's letterhead from her apartment in the Argentinerstrasse (Alleegasse) – was found among Ludwig's papers in Cambridge. This list may have been compiled by Waismann in 1936 (see Letter 153). In the typewritten version, all named writings bear a handwritten checkmark, except for the 'Table of contents' and '1 (package) without a label'.

ix.	volume	Philosophical Grammar
x.	volume	Philosophical Grammar

No. 1? (no title)

Philosophical Observations

No. 5 (no title)

Logisch-philosophische Abhandlung

'Table of contents' (appended, a portion of the table of contents in the typescript with an additional 24 pages of typewritten material)

Typewritten manuscripts:

1 package entitled 'old carbon copies'

1 package entitled 'new carbon copies'

1 package with no title, apparently carbon copies arranged by subject.[48]

---

[48] These seem to be lost. The *Logisch-philosophische Abhandlung* has been in the Bodleian Library, Oxford, since 1967. It is to be noted that Ludwig no longer had access to these manuscripts during the totality of his later creative period.

7

SECOND WORLD WAR: MARCH 1938 TO MAY 1945

1939 saw Ludwig occupied with the difficulties of his family. Immediately after receiving British citizenship he travelled to Vienna, from there to Berlin and back to Vienna. In the summer he went to New York to meet with his brother Paul, then to Zurich again. In October he took up the chair in Cambridge, to which he had been appointed in January.

During the war, Ludwig could mostly only receive 'Red Cross' letters from his sisters in Austria. Gretl spent the war years in the United States and wrote to him relatively frequently. Only a few letters, throwing light on family ties, are reproduced here. Ludwig's answers to these letters are not preserved.

Until October 1941 Ludwig led a regular life as a professor. Then suddenly Francis Skinner died. The war had also taken a new turn with Hitler's invasion of the Soviet Union. At this time Ludwig took up a position as technical assistant in a London hospital. He visited Cambridge only at weekends and held a few seminars there. Wittgenstein completely suspended his teaching activities. In April 1943 the research group to which he was assigned, was transferred to Newcastle, in the north of England.

In January 1944 he gave up his position as technical assistant and moved to Swansea in Wales, near his former pupil and later editor, Rush Rhees. Here Ludwig dedicated himself to writing and thought of publishing his works. In October 1944 he returned to Cambridge and resumed his lectures.

In the second half of 1945 he received the first letters from his sisters in Austria.

162 Ludwig to Paul

> East Rd
> Cambridge
> 30 March 1938

My dear Paul!

Just to be sure I am writing to you too, at Mining's request, to say: I will not join you in your petition, but am convinced of its justification for all of you.

Of course, you could list my war service, etc.; only this must not lead to any misunderstanding – as if I were thereby automatically involved in your petition.[1]

> With love & best wishes,
> your Ludwig

---

[1] The request involved filing an application with the Nazi authorities under the racial laws seeking privileged status – based upon the family history from the mid-nineteenth century through 1938.

163 Ludwig to Helene

81 East Rd
Cambridge
16 June 1938

Helenchen!

Just a line to tell you that I am thinking of you and Max and hope that you're holding your heads up. Mariechen wrote to me saying that you're having problems with your throat again. I hope your health won't be acting up too much. I'm well, as always.

I hope it'll be possible for me to come and visit you in the summer.[2]

My warmest regards to you and Maxl.

Your Brother,
Ludwig

164 Ludwig to Paul

81 East Rd
Cambridge
5 July 1938

Dear Paul!

Just a line to tell you the obvious: that I'm thinking of you.

Warmest regards,
your Ludwig

ps: Please give my regards to Koder, and to Mining & to everyone else too, when you see them.

---

[2] Ludwig may have been hoping to receive British citizenship by the summer, which would not happen until April 1939.

165 Margarete to Ludwig

[Autumn 1938]

My dear, my good Ludwig,

Thank you for your letters – & you have never been so close to me as you are in these times. I imagine you could help in simplifying this complicated situation, which has been made more confused still by worry and illness.[3]

A lot has happened, but a lot of beautiful and good things too! Hugs and affection,

your Gretl

166 Hermine to Ludwig

Saturday, 15 October [1938]

My dearest Ludwig,

My most heartfelt thanks for your kind lines! Last Sunday Staake, Koder and I played Bruckner, and I believe we've never been so fired up and alive (or was it just me?). When shall we be able to play for you or better: <u>shall</u> we ever be able to play for you? The times are serious for the family, a massive settling of accounts and a testing time for all relationships, not to mention the danger from the outside. Sometimes, I see everything so clearly in my mind's eye and think: not one stone will be left on another. At other times everything is shrouded in darkness for me, and I see myself as a big

---

[3] The situation refers to Gretl's plan to procure Yugoslavian passports for Helene and Hermine, so that they could not be forced to stay in the country. The plan failed when the passports were discovered to be fakes. After being detained and interrogated, however, all three sisters were eventually acquitted. The situation had dire consequences for Gretl's and Helene's health.

child capable of laughing at anything. What's going on now is quite simply beyond my comprehension.

You're in Zurich today; I can't imagine any of it. Let's hope you succeed!![4]

Greti is beginning to feel somewhat better; she was in a miserable state – understandably so given everything she's been through. We constantly talk about the past and the future and often speak about how we miss you because what our family really needs right now is a man at the helm. Max is old and unfortunately very ill, Paul has failed us, Fritz[5] has neither depth nor weight. What good does it do that Greti has a big heart and worries about everyone; the problems are unsolvable.

Saturday, 22 October

8 days have passed; it was impossible to write, for external reasons and for internal ones too, as I can't quite imagine the Swiss affair clearly, despite your letter*.

*The words don't seem quite right.

It is as if a connecting link is missing between what has happened here and your meeting. Perhaps, that is primarily due to the situation having undergone such a fundamental change since the beginning of September: that is, since the beginning of the great maelstrom of danger. War has been averted and – with it – the most imminent other danger that prompted us to take action. Not even I can at a given moment clearly recall the previous situation and the decisions that resulted from it, let alone an outsider. But in the end that is more or less irrelevant. The main thing is the

---

[4] Ludwig's second journey to Zurich was in aid of an attempt to reach a compromise with the Reichsbank, under which – in exchange for a rather large portion of the family's foreign holdings – Paul could enter and leave the country freely and the rest of the family would be guaranteed leave to remain in the country without being harassed.

[5] Mariechen's husband, see *Familienerinnerungen*, p. 213f.

tranquilization and the hope that we shall be able to bear or stave off future developments, of which there are many still to come.[6]

It makes me very happy for Greti that Ji has come, and I myself have very good conversations with him as well. That can't be taken for granted, for events here have caused a division within the family. Some of the family seem <u>warm</u> towards Greti and me, for instance, Ji, Arvid, Clärchen, and others <u>cold</u>: the latter being Felix, Mariechen, Fritz. The cold ones are really those who can now say, with justice: we've been saying it from the start, etc., etc. And yet they don't seem to me quite at ease with themselves, although of course they don't admit it and so a degree of friction arises, which much preoccupies me.—It makes me very sad that you aren't well, my dearest Ludwig, and that I can't do anything for you! I don't even want to think about it, but will it help you if I do?

That's all for today except the warmest and most heartfelt regards and wishes, your sister,

Mining

ps: If I could only see and speak with you again; yet, precisely that has become the most distant of prospects and well-nigh an impossibility.

167 Margarete to Ludwig

Vienna, 1 November 1938

My dear, my good Luki,

I'm sorry to hear you were ill, & that terrible nauseous feeling, which was lingering so, will, I think, not have been so easy to overcome. You poor thing!

---

[6] The Munich Agreement was expected to avert war by permitting the German occupation of parts of Czechoslovakia, the *Sudetenland*, commencing on 10 October 1938.

Thank you <u>very much</u> for your kind letters. I believe I wouldn't have been able to answer them even if I were healthy. I have, as well as I could, read and taken them seriously, even the bits directed against me. (Which was not easy to do.) Now I could say with an (almost) pure heart: 'It's right, although it's all wrong'. You understand me, I'm sure.

There is still a lot I would like to know if I'm to understand your words as quoted to me by P., including why, back then, you couldn't bring him as far as you could this time. If we ever see each other again (and I <u>hope</u> we do!), you can tell me then.

I'm feeling better, but I'm still lying down. I much miss my kind doctor, who is no longer in Vienna.

Thank dear Skinner for me; one can always do with good thoughts and wishes. That's why I'm sending them to you two as well.

Hugs and affection,

your Gretl

168 Margarete to Ludwig

7 December 1938

My dear, my good Ludwig,

How nice that you're feeling better again! My thanks to you and Skinner. (It's as if his friendliness shines through the most ordinary of words.)

I have never thought & never spoken of you as much as I do now. You belong with us.

Arvid, who has turned up trumps, was at my place yesterday. I also saw Hänsel a couple of times; nowadays it's extremely, and even more, difficult to get on terms with him, but on the inside what really matters is as right as rain.

I can't even begin to imagine that you won't be here for Christmas. No rucksack, no last-minute fuss with chocolate and packets of Lebkuchen. Wedi and Hedwig[7] are coming; I probably wouldn't be doing anything of the sort otherwise.

I haven't heard anything good from New York. Helen seems to be less well & Tom has written to say that he wants to marry again.

I'm much better, and send a tender hug!

your sister,

Gretl

169 Hermine to Ludwig

[1939]

[8]My warmest thanks for your letter and for managing to do something so quickly for that couple! I spoke with them myself and had a very good impression of them; the wife is especially nice, although of course Jewish. Betty knows the two of them because her brother-in-law also works on the railway and holds the husband in very high regard. He has worked on the railway for 35 years, most recently as a station master, and was still in service when those horrible days in November came and took him off to Dachau. You can imagine that he, as a Jew, would not have been allowed to stay in the service of the state for another 8 months after the upheaval, if he had not been in someone's very good graces.*

*That's also why they were so sure of themselves; the bad elements had gone right at the outset and are now a source of damage for Jews abroad.

---

[7] Hedwig Schulze, employee, then secretary and housekeeper.
[8] The beginning and end of this letter are missing. Hermine is speaking about a Jewish couple and the Wittgensteins' efforts to obtain a permit for them to enter England.

Both are considered to be uncommonly hard-working, and, I believe, whoever employs them will have every reason to be happy with them, and I would really like it if they could be helped. Also: thank you very much for your wish; of course, no one can ever have enough of those two things and that just might turn out to be true in my case. If only we were so far that we could put that to the test. Another decision is supposed to be made about something today, but I haven't heard anything yet. Everyone is healthy, thank God, including our friends.

With love and best wishes,

170 Paul to Ludwig[9]

1939

The <u>Germans are extortioners,</u> and if one shows an extortionist one's weak side – it's all over [...] There is only one thing to do, namely, one must tell the Germans: you get so much and not a penny more, and that they will comply with! [...] One must consider what that means: life or starvation was at stake for [...] My German passport was practically expired [...] Since I came to America much too late, all available paid positions at conservatories had long been made off with. I cannot take a position other than that of piano teacher, for I am of no use for all others – what idiot would employ an impractical one-armed man, when the best qualified men with both arms in the hundreds are wandering about jobless? [...] And even if a well-paid position were available, as a visitor, I would not be able to take it, since, as a visitor, I am under the obligation to earn no money [...] I was sold down the river.

---

[9] Paul wrote this in English; it was likely intended to be read by Ludwig.

e 171　Samuel R. Wachtell to Ludwig

wachtell, manheim & group

one cedar street

new york

cable address

"Manwacht"

samuel r. wachtell

harold manheim

meyer group

July 14th 1939

Professor Ludwig Wittgenstein

On Board S.S. Queen Mary.

First, please permit me to extend to you my welcome on your arrival here. I feel specially moved to do so because I believed the visit inadvisable in the present state of the negotiations for the settlement of claims made by the Reichsbank.

You will understand I am sure, that my position was impersonal. It was motivated solely by my situation as counsel charged with protection of your brother Paul's interests.

The announcement of your trip to America was the latest of a series of efforts which had been made in order to exert pressure on your brother to yield to the demands of the Reichsbank. No doubt as a result of threats and intimidation, your sisters in Vienna have not merely supported these demands passively, but sent, through Dr. Schoene, letters and cablegrams urging compliance and intimating serious and impending dangers otherwise. I have no means of measuring the degree of pressure applied against the sisters in Vienna and through them transmitted to you and Mrs. Stoneborough. But I am in a position to measure the pressure applied from all directions on Paul Wittgenstein.

That pressure has been unrelenting, in spite of the fact that Paul has made offers of compromise which are more than fair and which I am certain would have been acceptable to the Reichsbank had the latter not found it so easy to induce the sisters in Vienna to permit themselves to be used as instruments in the application of a pressure which has defeated itself by its own lack of moderation and sensible restraint.

Paul Wittgenstein will be very glad to see you, but made it a condition that I must see and talk to you first. This would save him the trouble and strain, heavy as well as unnecessary, of acquainting you with the facts, circumstances and considerations which have led him to leave the matter in my hands and to be guided by my impersonal advice. He has suggested to me therefore that I get in touch with you and arrange a time, at your convenience, to open my file for your examination and to inform you fully about everything that has taken place until now, so that when you and Paul meet both of you may be saved any possible annoyances and disagreeable differences due to lack of knowledge on your part of the facts involved.

I propose that as soon as you have rested from the fatiguing formalities inseparable from an arrival through the Port of New York, you will telephone me and fix a time for our meeting. My telephone number is White Hall 3–1354, and you may reach me at any time after 10 o'clock Monday morning. I am holding free Monday afternoon and all day Tuesday until I hear from you. When you will be at my office I shall endeavor to reach Paul over the long distance telephone so that you and he may arrange for your meeting.

A draft of this letter was sent on to your brother for his approval. The draft was returned to me with some slight alterations to which I have naturally given effect. While therefore, the stylization of the letter is my own, it expresses substantially your brother's thoughts.

With kind regards, I am,

Sincerely yours,

Samuel R. Wachtell

172 Margarete to Ludwig

[End of 1939]

My dear, my good Ludwig,

Oh, if these lines could just find you & if they could find you in as good a state of mind as possible & bring you but a bit of all the love we are always thinking of you with!

We are all healthy here. I needn't tell you how much of a relief the 'mixed race' solution is.

I'll stay on here. It's become clear to me that this is the right thing to do. In moments of clarity, I also know that what happens now will be decided for me. In the meantime, I'll just live from day to day.

Our good Georg[10] started his training yesterday. Betka[11] is exemplary.

Oscar[12] is a worry. His lease has been terminated for June. I'm thinking about taking him in at that point. There are many reasons to do so & many reasons not to do so as well, but it will eventually become clear. Making plans now is nonsense.

Anton & Alfred[13] were on the outside up until a few days ago because the miserable Konrad[14] created incredible difficulties during the wind-down.[15]

---

[10] Georg Schönborn-Buchheim, friend of the family. Gretl rented the first floor of the Palais Schönborn in the 1920s.

[11] Georg's wife.

[12] Oskar Wollheim.

[13] Anton is Anton Groller; Alfred is probably Alfred Indra, the family solicitor.

[14] Konrad is Konrad Bloch, Swiss solicitor retained by Wistag (see note 224).

[15] The wind-down in question concerns the wind-down of Wistag A.G.u.Co. Kommandit-gesellschaft, a Swiss limited partnership whose general partner was Wistag Aktiengesellschaft, in which the Wittgenstein family had invested significant sums of the family fortune. The family eventually entered into a settlement with the Reichsbank in exchange for preferential treatment.

I hope you're well & that we'll be able to see each other again!

Tender hugs,

your Gretl

ps: I am much better health-wise.

173 Margarete to Ludwig

[Christmas 1939]

My dear, my good Luki,

You know how much my thoughts & love are with you. That you're not here makes me sad. It makes everyone sad, but especially me. We speak of you all the time, & something good and loving always comes out.

Everyone is healthy, friends & family, & I believe you would be happy with everything.

I am supposed to leave soon, because of my passport, but I cannot believe that I won't be spared in some way from having to do so.

Should I <u>have</u> to move on, then I will do everything I can over there to make it possible for me to return here.

Oskar will probably be able to stay in his apartment. Georg sends you his love.

Merry Christmas, my dear! A loving hug!

your Gretl

174 Margarete to Ludwig

[1940]

My dear, my good Ludwig,

I've been here[16] for 14 days now & haven't written to you yet. Whenever I'm not feeling well, there's a maelstrom in me & it's impossible for me to distinguish between what's important and what's not. I just keep thinking: quick, quick, this & then that. It's like going upstairs. When you're feeling fine, you can take it slowly. When you're not, you think: 'My God, I still have to climb those', & you run just to get it over with.

I would have infinitely liked to have seen & spoken with you, but I was not allowed to go to England. (Everything is so monstrously difficult now.) I don't know whether any one country knows just what's banned & impossible in another![17]

Yes, I would have <u>infinitely</u> liked to have seen & spoken with you. First and foremost of course because I know nothing about how you are & would like to know <u>everything</u>. But also in order to get advice and clarity for myself. In order to have a discussion.

I haven't heard anything from home. They're not allowed to send cables, letters are being intercepted. I now believe I'll be returning to Vienna again, unless I'm unable to push through the passport I need to do so.

There is a lot to do here & lots of worries.

---

[16] Gretl has moved to New York City.
[17] The remainder of this paragraph appears to be missing.

Of course I don't see Paul, but things seem to be going much better for him, according to Helen, whom he often visits.[18]

The negotiations in Zurich are still not over. Bloch[19] keeps creating new difficulties, & Ji's small fortune continues to shrink.

I often see Lixi & his wife, whom I like very much & who is very good for him.

Let me hear something from you, my dear and good Ludwig. I think of you with love.

Yours,

Gretl

Margaret in New York in the 1940s
© *The Stonborough Family.*

---

[18] Paul was of the view that his sisters ought to leave Austria, as he had done. Nor did he want to give the Reichsbank anything more than was absolutely necessary. This all led to difficulties regarding the compensatory payment and to a falling out between Paul and his siblings. Ludwig travelled to New York in August to undertake one last attempt to get Paul to reconsider. See the Introduction page.

[19] See Letter 172 and the corresponding note above.

175 Hermine to Ludwig

[April 1940]

My dearest Luki, I wish you all the best anyone could think to wish for your birthday! For myself, I wish I could see you again soon, which I need and am utterly longing for! In my last letter I wrote to you saying that everyone is keeping well and this, thank God, remains the case. Oskar will be coming today, Rudolf tomorrow and Kauders the day after tomorrow[20] – we do this every week and find it very comfortable. I had a letter from Greti, in which she expressed her hope of coming, but which actually sounds dreary; I believe she's suffering quite a bit from the fact that no one besides Ji really needs her and that Pierre[21] is certainly being raised in a completely different spirit than the one she would like. It's hard on her. Of course, I've heard nothing from Paul. His things should be ready for shipment sometime over the next few days, as the authorities have finally finished reviewing everything; it can't come soon enough for me, and I fear that some impediments will crop up at the last minute. My dearest Luki, I think of you often. Warmest regards from

Mining

---

[20] Oskar is Oskar Wollheim; Koder, Rudolf Koder; and Otto, Otto Kauders. Wollheim had Jewish ancestry, and Dr Kauders (first assistant at the Pyschiatrische Klinik in Vienna) believed that he was subject to the Racial Laws given that his grandmother was Jewish. The Wittgenstein family did not avoid these friends at all but saw them regularly.
[21] Pierre Stonborough, Tommy's son.

176 Margarete to Ludwig

The Gotham
5th Ave. at 55th St.
New York City
[1940]

'Oh my dear, my good Ludwig!'
That is really what I would like to say to you. Yes & then that I think of you with love & would like to hear from you.

I haven't had any news from home for weeks & my letters there have presumably been destroyed en route as well. (Did you receive my letter from here?)

I am working on procuring a passport from the State Dept. for entering foreign territory in a state of war. I hope I get it, for I believe I belong at home. Then I will still need permission to enter the country, which may be even more difficult to obtain.—Please God!

My inner state here is not a good one.

Love to Skinner.—Hugs from an overflowing heart,

yours, with love,
Gretl

rct 177 Ludwig to Hermine

enquirer

Name: Wittgenstein

Christian name: Ludwig

Address: Trinity College, Cambridge

Relationship of Enquirer to Addressee: Brother

The Enquirer desires news of the Addressee and asks that the following message should be transmitted to him.

Dear Mining,

I am well. Happy about Maxl's response. Get Rudolf a birthday present. All the best to everyone. Give Georg my warmest regards.

Ludwig
Date: 9 April 1940
addressee

Name: Wittgenstein

Christian name: Hermine

Address: 4 Argentinerstrasse 16, Vienna, Germany

[Reply overleaf]

Dearest Ludwig,

Your message brought us all endless joy. We too are very well. Sundays celebrated as we used to. Thinking of you with love.

Hermine

rct 178 Ludwig to Helene[22]

enquirer

Name: Wittgenstein
Christian name: Ludwig
Relationship of Enquirer to Addressee: Brother
The Enquirer desires news of the Addressee and asks that the following message should be transmitted to him.
Dear Helene,
Think daily of you and Max. Tell Rudolf and Oskar and all friends everything imaginable
Warmest,

Ludwig
Date: 13 June 1940
addressee

Name: Salzer
Christian name: Helene
Address: 4 Brahmsplatz 4, Vienna, Germany

[Reply overleaf][23]

Dear Ludwig, we and all friends thank you for the kind lines, send you our warmest regards. We are healthy and in good spirits. Think of you lots.

Helene

---

[22] missing
[23] Helene's reply is stamped 27 November 1940.

rct 179 Ludwig to Max

November 1940

enquirer

Name: Professor Wittgenstein

Christian name: Ludwig

Relationship of Enquirer to Addressee: Brother-in-law

The Enquirer desires news of the Addressee and asks that the following message should be transmitted to him.

Am extremely well. Think daily of you, Helene and everyone. Give Arvid, Oskar and all friends my warmest regards.

Your Ludwig

Date: 13 August 1940

addressee

Name: Dr Salzer

Christian name: Max

Address: 4 Brahmsplatz 4, Vienna, Germany

[Reply overleaf][24]

Professor Ludwig Wittgenstein

Cambridge, England

We and all friends are well, think of you a lot and send you our warmest regards.

Max and Helene

20 November

---

[24] Max's reply is stamped 12 December 1940.

e 180 Margarete to Ludwig

the Elbow Beach
Paget
Bermuda

3 January 1941
address as usual
417 Park Avenue
New York City

My dear & good Ludwig,

It did me ever so much good to get your cable. Thank you for it my dear! I have an unappeasable hunger for news of those that I love.—From home I have <u>not</u> heard for several weeks. the post usually comes in batches, so I <u>hope</u> to find several letters at my return to New York. (We Ji & I are here only for a few days recovering from a slight siege of illness.).

At Christmas I saw you so vividly & felt full of thankfulness for the many happy Christmasses we had had together.

I also thought that you often said of my house that somehow, it was not going to last long; & now it will probably be taken away from me very soon. I loved it & I had good & beautiful times in it, so it's allright. I had a Christmas tree in my apartment & Helen, Pierre, Lixi & his wife, Karban[25] & Ji, Jochen & I were together & I think it was allright. Lixi was better than I had seen him in a long time. I had a long talk with him before, & I began to understand his attitude of grumpyness & lack of affection & interest. He explained to me how all his values had to be revalued & how he felt a certain

---

[25] Othmar Karban, one of John Stonborough's school friends.

grudge against the old environment & did not want to be reminded of it. I told him that I could understand his position, but on the other hand he should not be an idiot & throw the old ties away. I think he felt better after coughing everything up & on Christmas Eve he was very nearly his old self again.

Did you get my packages? Did I tell you that I got a particularly nice letter from Geigerl. He seems to have found a very nice wife. He wrote how often he thought of you & how he had worried about you & how glad he was that there was good news from you.

I sometimes hear your quick step & the servus[26] & my heart is heavy. May you, may we. God bless you my dear & keep you. Well thank you again for the cable. Yes & for so many other things!

Love from

Gretl

All sorts of messages to Skinner

e 181 Margarete to Ludwig

margaret stonborough

417 park avenue

new york city

[Autumn/Winter 1941]

My dear, my good Ludwig,

I have not written for some time. The reason for that is certainly not that I think less often, or less lovingly, of you. I felt deeply about dear Skinners death. I will always remember his dear & kind face. His tender face. I am bitterly sad for you.

---

[26] 'Servus' is an Austrian greeting.

The news that you are now working at a hospital did not surprise me. May the work be of the right kind to help you. But how astonishing that you don't understand Mins letter to you. I suppose you don't realize neither the strain under which she lives, nor the fact, that in suppressing what she thinks is unsuitable, she loses her naturalness. Hers is by nature a descriptive way of writing.

Last week Paul has had a third child, a son. I hear he is very happy about it.

Ossy and Louise are now both installed in Cuba. I had hoped to be able to have them come here in February but I am afraid this wont be possible now. I will try to go there for a visit. This is very important & I do hope I will succeed in overcoming all the obstacles.

I have not had any news from home for many weeks & I fear I will have to live without them for much longer. I am still sending them letters hoping against hope that they will reach them.

I will send you loving & wishing thoughts for Christmas. The memory of the evening in the Allg is most vivid. I think of them with a grateful heart & with love for everybody concerned. May you keep well my dear!

Bless you

> Your loving sister
> Gretl

e 182 Margarete to Ludwig

[May 1942?]

My good & dear Luki,

I meant to follow up my short letter with a long one in a few days & now over a fortnight has passed without my doing it. ('Only no preambles', as dear Baumayer used to say.) Apart from a lot of work

& lack of strength, there is also my incurable vice of never being able to distinguish the important from the unimportant. And the more tired I am, the more incapable to do so.

My cable to you came from Washington, where I had gone to a hearing of a committee in behalf of Ossys visa to the u.s.a. There are endless difficulties, owing to the fact that he has not only no family in the u.s.a. who would need him, but a sister on the other side. On top of that, I, his sponsor, am a naturalized American. Nothing but handicaps. It will be a miracle if I succeed. If I dont, then I will go to Cuba this Winter (health permitting) & stay with him for a while. I feel so badly about his having to stay in all this heat!

I want to add a few words to what I said in my last letter. <u>Please</u> write me a line about your health.[27] Operation, recuperation & present health. <u>I am very much worried</u> in spite of your cables. Because those that you sent me while you were in a very bad state of health sounded just as reassuring. Ji told me that he kept back his tears when he saw you last.

I have had a letter from Pro's sister[28] through Selle & I know now that she died from a gas poisoning in her bath. It is an immense relief for me, that she got my letter thanking her for all her devotion & telling her of my great affection for her.

Something else I heard from Selle.[29] Marys eldest boy is in the Ski Troops. the family seems to be well in all this Nightmare.

---

[27] Ludwig had gallstones removed during an operation on 27 April 1942.

[28] Berthe Prohaska, Gretl's former secretary and life-long socialist and admirer of Tolstoy. She remained in Vienna.

[29] Mlle Elisabeth Leuba, former governess of the Stonborough and Zastrow boys. She had returned to Switzerland by the date of this letter, supplied the family with news and information, aided in the manuscript matter mentioned in Letter 187 and even kept the contact with Ludwig intact.

I forgot to tell you an astonishing coincidence in speaking about Jis fiancée. Lady Morrison-Bell, his future mother in law was a great friend of Fanny Davies. (They are a very music-loving family.) I had a really good & touching letter from her, telling me how fond they are of Ji & how glad they are to have him as a son in law. It seems to me a piece of rare luck considering the difference of nationality & upbringing.

Ji will have to leave sooner than he thought at first. He will marry before leaving. Knowing him & her, I approve of it.

Another thing that seems to me very important. Most important. Ji says, that you did not understand Min's letters. That makes me very unhappy. How is that possible? You above all must know how deep her feelings are for you & what she goes through now & how incapable she is of coping with her situation without you or me helping her to see her way. She could not write real letters now to save her soul. She sits in her life now, like she used to sit in a taxi, tied in knots. Nobody in her entourage has the key to straighten her out. Surely you know what I mean.

My health is a bit better & the doctors have decided not to operate. If I could only get well enough to do some sort of a job.

To come back once more to Mins letters I want to say that people who are used to writing descriptive letters like she, have a much harder time anyway nowadays than you have.

When I think of us all my heart aches.

May you be well my dear! Bless you

Your loving sister
Gretl

Margaret's wartime apartment in New York
© *The Stonborough Family.*

e 183 Margarete to Ludwig

> Mrs Jerome Stonborough
> 563 Park Avenue
> New York City
> u.s.a.
> [End of 1942]

My dear, my good Ludwig,

Thank you very much my dear for your good letter. It was well doing [wohltuend= it did me good].

Well, Oscar has arrived at last! The excitement before I got him in, was great. It looked practically hopeless for many month & the idea, that I would have to tell him, that he could not come, was horrible to me. You will understand that. He arrived looking, very thin & much in need of being fed, but on the whole quite hale & healthy & strong. Full of enterprise & not a bit aged mentally. In a way he even seemed better than he used to be at home. I felt 'over all measures' relieved!

Now I have – as expected – some difficulties with him. His complete dependency on me here makes things worse. I have now for the first time understood the nature of his trouble & with it, my incapacity of dealing with it. He <u>wants</u> to be maltreated.

From my family I get few but good news. That they were able to go to the Highright[30] means a lot & makes me happy. I live a great deal in the old days. Oscar brought me some photos. I knew them all, but now I appreciate them. There is one of Aunt Clara standing before the entrance of Laxborough house. It is quite small but it seems to me as if it spoke volumes.

I got the Schumann records & I love them. Was that the quartett that you listened to in Zürich, when they closed the shop & would not let you hear the end? Do you remember what you once said about the Haydn Variations that go so near me. You said: 'In the highest & cleanest cell'. I often think of that, when I play them. (Because the words that <u>I</u> remember that you said, are not of the type of those of mine that <u>you</u> remember.)

Ji is still in Canada. His wife caught a bad pneumonia & is with me now on the way to recovery. Beside her I have a sick boy with me & a friend who shares my apartment.

I am happy when you write that you are well. May it be really so!

---

[30] The 'Highright' is of course the Hochreit.

When you read this letter please don't look at it critically. I will never be able to write the letters that you would like me to write. But the feeling, that you will overlook the little wheat in my letter in your dislike for the chaff, makes me uneasy & keeps me from writing oftener.

The little wheat being the love for you & the longing to see you & the deep wishes for you.

Bless you, my dear.

Gretl

Mrs Jerome Stonborough
563 Park Avenue
New York City
usa

e 184 Margarete to Ludwig

[End of 1942]

My dear, my good Luki,

It was so good to get your last letter. It made me very happy. I suppose one gets over sensitive in these times & I am sometimes afraid to open a letter of the people I love for fear that it could contain a word that might hurt or distort my precious memories. (That does not sound very clear but you will understand).

It meant a lot to me to hear something about your work. I had always hoped that you would once have an occasion to apply your brains to medicine. It seems to me that your type of brains & the schooling that your métier had given you would be invaluable for that science. Yes & your way of feeling invaluable for sick people.

I am sending this letter, with some other stuff, through a friend, whom I love dearly & who has been very good to me. Her name is

Blanca Kronacker-Deym.[31] She might seem a little off-putting to you at first, but I hope very much that you will like her. She has lived with me for the last year & she has also met Paul & has had a good talk with him in spite of the fact that he knew that she lived with me.

I had gone to a concert of his with her. I felt I wanted to see him (unseen by him) & also to hear him. He looks well & astonishingly young & is sympathetic as always on the podium. But his playing has become much worse. I suppose that is to be expected, because he insists on trying to do, what really cannot be done. It is a violation.

Yes, he is sick like Clotide & Tom, but how different the same sickness appears on such different seed beds.

Tom may come through England soon & it is my greatest wish that you could see him & talk to him & get an impression. This would mean so much to me. I have worked very hard & with pains & I have learnt a lot & have realized my errors & limitations.

I think you should think of Koder in the way you used to. How unhappy would he be, how deeply would he feel it, if you didn't. It would be more bitter for him than if you had died. You know well with how much of himself he is bound to you. With the deepest & best in him.

I think you have (like Tante Clara) a tendency to underrate the affections of other people for you.

With Oscar I have great difficulties. It is as if he had lost all his natural heart & as if only his artificial tendencies survived. He is quite happy, but it is a sad sight & it makes a really good & natural relationship practically impossible.

---

[31] An aristocratic lady, who shared Gretl's flat in New York (see Letter ([146])). Presumably, she was visiting her husband at the time, a wealthy Belgian who held a government position in London.

My heart is very full when I think of you. Full of love & wishes & hopes that I may see you again. Bless you my dear, my good one & keep you well.

Your loving sister
Gretl

rct 185 Hermine to Ludwig

Sender: Hermine Wittgenstein
Argentinerstrasze 16 Vienna iv/50
requests that the following be transmitted to
Addressee: Dr Ludwig Wittgenstein, Trinity College, Cambridge England
(Maximum number of 25 words!)
Family and friends healthy and in best spirits. Thinking of you and sending you all our love and warmest regards.

Hermine Wittgenstein
Date: 3 January 1943

e 186 Margarete to Ludwig

14 March 1944

My dear, my good Luki,
Thank you for your very welcome letter. How glad I was to get it! I am somehow relieved that you left N.[32] although I knew little about your life there in spite of your assurances that you were well.

---

[32] Newcastle.

And I am happy about the publishing of your books. Apart from other reasons I feel as if somebody was doing something sane, for sanitys sake amidst encircling insanity. Perhaps this is something like what you meant when you wrote it was 'the right moment'.

I am having a difficult time, as Blanca is really sick with a very bad depression. I had to call in a nerve specialist to give her the necessary sedatives. I love her very dearly & I hate to see her suffer. It is a horrible suffering & no persuasion helps. The latter is so hard to realize. I always catch myself trying.

Your dream was again most typical. I would have known it as yours anywhere among strange dreams I think. Was I teaching futile 'piffle'? (My dreams were always free of such puns) The 'harness' reminded me of something you told me long ago, of a descent on a funicular & you tied yourself to the board with a belt. Do you remember?

Ji sent me a happy cable about your meeting with Veronica. Yes I too like her. I like her very much although I realize that she has a hard & bitter kernel under the soft cover. Marguerite & Olive, each in a different way, had one too. It is somehow associated with eigensinn [self-will] & I wish I know whether it could be melted & how.

Blanca gave Paul your message. He seemed pleased & talked about you to her.

Keep well my dear. I think of you lovingly & I often put my hand on yours.

Bless you
Gretl

Blanca sends a message
March 14–44

e 187 Margarete to Ludwig

[Mid–1944]

My dear, my good Luki,

Thank you for your good letter & thank you very much indeed for your warning & advice. I know exactly what you meant & I hope to be able to keep it in my mind. <u>I really do.</u>

I put your order about your manuscript into my testament in case I should predecease you before the end of the war.

What you write about Paul is right but it applies to Lixi too. He too is now living a somewhat reduced, but human life which he would never have achieved without breaking with his family. Because he also has in a way broken with his family although not in such a fundamental way. And although our part of his blood spoilt the soup it has anyway given him his very real love for music. (I think you would be honestly charmed with the way he now plays the piano.) I didn't know whether I am right, but Schumann's Childrens Scenes, a few small Brahms, two moments musicals by Schubert he plays so that even you would nod your head. Also the choice of his program has changed so as to fit his real style.

I am worried about the money situation of my two sisters after the war. The more money they would have over here the better. I wonder whether it would not be a good idea to have the manuscripts that my brother deposited sent to me. Somebody could take them along & I could sell them. First I would have to get Paul's permission. My lawyer can approach his & also find out which ones belong to him.[33]

---

[33] The Wittgensteins inherited a rich collection of musicians' letters and manuscripts, including some of Mozart's, Beethoven's, Mendelsohn's and Brahms's. Around the time of this letter, Ludwig deposited a portion of this collection at a bank in Cambridge.

I am trying very hard to get a job that takes me on the other side; I am longing to see you.

Bless you my dear one. May you keep well & may we see each other again.

Your loving sister
Gretl

e 188 Hermine to Ludwig[34]

[April/May 1945]

My dearest Brother,

It seems so wonderful to be able to write to you after so many years and after all that we had reason to be afraid of during these last months![35] We even can hope now to see you again and we are looking forward to this moment with a heart full of Love, Lenka and I. We spoke of you very very often and we always knew that our cares and worries were yours. You cannot imagine what a relief it was for us all when Ji's compatriots drew nearer; from this moment we could hope to see you and Gretl again. I personally had never been afraid because I have no imagination and I am not sure at all, whether it was the right thing for me to come here and leave all my friends behind. But as I had not conceived the idea and could never have done the thing alone, but was sent here like a parcel by my family and as better people than I am thought it right, I suppose I may enjoy the security and the many good things here.

---

[34] This letter was written from Gmunden, in Upper Austria, where Hermine and Helene spent the last years of the war.

[35] Upper Austria was liberated by American troops, John 'Ji' Stonborough's compatriots. This letter and Letter 189 were probably brought by Ji, who – though enlisted in the Canadian army – made a brief visit to Gmunden as soon as it was possible to do so after the fighting was over. In any event, this letter and Letter 189 were not sent by post.

If we could but have news from all our friends we left! If we could but hope, that they had not suffered much! If we could [but] hope to see them again! We are completely cut off from them all and I am afraid they had to suffer great hardships while we were living here in security and peace.

We have no news either of Mary's two sons; we just hope for the best, that would be their having been taken prisoners by your or Ji's compatriots.

My dearest brother I send you our love and I kiss you with a longing

your loving sister
Mining

e 189 Helene to Ludwig

[April/May 1945]

My dear Ludwig,

Not a day passes but that Mining and I talk about you; our loving thoughts are always with you.

Please do not worry about us, we are quite well really and in best spirits and ever so happy to be here.[36] To see you <u>again</u> will be our greatest joy.

Lovingly yours,

Helene

---

[36] In Gmunden.

e 190 Margarete to Ludwig

563 Park Ave. New York City

Mrs Jerome Stonborough

12 May 1945

My dear, my good Luki

I had a long letter from Marguerite today. A detailed account of Talla's death.[37] It is hard for me to understand her reactions & I cannot follow them uncritically. But I believe that her love for Talla will from now on grow more & more; unhampered by what had not fitted into the picture she had wanted to make of him. This may sound callous but it isn't, it is only sad.

But my heart bleeds for Mima. Curiously enough my feeling for her had grown in these years of absence although I have never had a word from her.

Thank you for your letter my dear. At the time it arrived I could not help smiling at your advice not to advise Mima. First of all I stand in no advising relationship to her. Secondly even if I were I would not advise her & thirdly even if I did she would naturally not listen to my advice, (or to anybody else for that matter.) I smiled because I honestly believe that you overrate my idiocy when you have not seen me for some time.

As to the matter of my writing to you about my sons I did not say, or at least I did not <u>mean</u> to say that my terminology produced our disagreement on that subject. What I meant to say was, that my knowledge of your reaction to my terminology (which I suppose represents my attitude) prevents me to pour out my troubles & worries to you. Because, although I quite agree with you on our

---

[37] Talla was shot dead by a poacher at his farm in Chile.

fundamental differences, I still believe that you can help & advise me. I have always found your judgement & advice precious after I had stripped it of its disagreeable trappings so to say. These trappings are the part of your personality that is so profoundly different from my own. I dont understand it but I respect it deeply. You know I may be quite wrong, but I do believe that I am quite able 'to believe that a really intelligent man can disagree with me on fundamentals and he need not be either blinded by prejudice, or unable to understand my terminology'. But do we really disagree on fundamentals? I dont believe it. there is a deep disagreement & a deep agreement too. I am not clever enough to do more than feel it.

I am taking a week rest away from New York as my heart has been a bit troublesome. Yes 'honor & anxiety'!

All my love my dear, my tender love & may we see each other again.

Gretl

May 12–45

8

LUDWIG'S LAST LETTERS: JANUARY 1946 TO APRIL 1951

Wittgenstein gave his last lectures in Cambridge in the Easter term of 1947. In October he laid down his professorship but continued to work on what was to be published as his *Philosophical Investigations*. In the winter of 1947, he visited his former student Maurice O'Connor Drury in Dublin and began a one-and-a-half-year stay in Ireland.

In April and at Christmas 1949 he visited his sick sister Hermine in Vienna. In July he travelled to the United States to visit a former Cambridge scholarship student, Norman Malcolm in Ithaca; illness cut short his stay there. In October Wittgenstein returned to England, where his cancer was diagnosed. He now stayed with friends in Oxford and in Cambridge, among others with G. H. von Wright. He spent the autumn of 1950 with Ben Richards in Norway. After a stay in Vienna, he returned to Cambridge in February 1951, where he died in the house of Dr Bevan on 29 April 1951.

191 Ludwig to Helene

Trinity College
Cambridge
31 January 1946

Dear Helenchen!

I received a letter from Mining yesterday, the first one via normal post. You know I think of you all often and blether with you <u>countless</u> times in my head! Maybe we'll see each other again soon. It's difficult for me to write <u>because</u> so much has happened. I saw Gretl about three weeks ago and will see her again in a few weeks. She's in the north right now at her daughter-in-law's. I believe everything's going very well for her there.

I'm healthy, as usual.—I'm sorry to hear that the house in the Alleegasse has been damaged. But as long as it's habitable, then that, in itself, is good luck indeed.

Franz Brücke[1] is a prisoner of war. I hear from him every now and then and send him books. He is not doing badly.—I believe, when we see each other we shall find that we haven't changed.—

Your loving brother,
Ludwig

---

[1] Grandson of Ludwig's aunt Milly Wittgenstein (1854–1939) and Theodor Brücke.

192 Ludwig to Helene

Trinity College
Cambridge
30 March 1946

Dear Helene!

Just a few lines to tell you that I think of you often. I know that, physically, it's bearable for you all. But that of course means very little, and anyone can be miserable even if they have enough to eat and aren't freezing. And knowing that others are worse off isn't any help <u>at all</u>.—I wish you all the best.

Yesterday two acquaintances of mine played Bruckner's 7th Symphony for me (four-handed).[2] They play badly, but not without understanding. I haven't heard that symphony for years, and it impressed me <u>greatly</u> when I heard it again.

I don't write much, not because I don't think of you much, but because it's difficult for me to write at the moment. My health is still excellent.

Please give my regards to all friends you're able to reach.

Your loving brother,
Ludwig

---

[2] Very probably G. E. Moore and his son Tim, who had been intending to play a four-handed version of Bruckner's 7th for Ludwig since the autumn of 1945 (letter from Moore to Ludwig of 5 August 1945 (cld 332)).

193 Ludwig to Helene

Trinity College
Cambridge
26 July 1946

Dear Helene!

I would very much like to write to you; but there's nothing to write. I'm still well, and there is nothing happening in my life worth telling. I pray, things are not going <u>too</u> badly for you. I think of you all with longing and yearning.—Your loving

brother,
Ludwig

ps: Tell Postl I said hello.

194 Ludwig to Helene

Trinity College
Cambridge
24 November 1946

Dear Helene!

I think of you all a lot – and of you in particular whenever I want to blether, and that's often. A few days ago I said to myself 'My father, my father now or never he seizes me [after Goethe "Erlkönig"]' and thought of you immediately.—Mining wrote to me saying it's not impossible that she'll one day live in the Kundmanngasse.[3] I couldn't want anything more – regardless of what she hangs on the walls, even if she covers the windows with curtains. For anything is better than that that house, which cost so much, should just stand there devoid of any meaning whatsoever. After all, it was built for the

---

[3] In fact it was Gretl who eventually moved back into her house in the Kundmanngasse.

family. And even if it befits to Gretl and, in a certain sense, not the rest of you, then that is a <u>family</u> difference and nothing more.—It's sad that we have to live so completely cut off from one another. It's certain that Gretl will go to any and all lengths to get to Austria in order to be with you all. And she is doing it to give her own life meaning again. Hence, there can be no talk of cleverness or a lack thereof.—I can't write anything about when we'll be able to see each other again, as unfortunately there is too much uncertainty here.

I hope you're not <u>too</u> discontent with your fate!

As always, your loving brother,

Ludwig

195 Ludwig to Helene

16 January 1947

Dear Helene!

Thank you for your letter of 7th January. How happy I, too, would be if I were able to see you all again. Maybe it'll be possible at some point over the summer. I received a letter from Koder today, and one from Lydia from Thumersbach. You have all been through incomparably more than I have, and yet you have a greater will to live than I do, as I often just vegetate.

I hardly ever listen to music, but I did hear Brahms's 2nd piano concert on the radio just a few days ago. I <u>didn't</u> find it very moving. And the 2nd and 4th movements left me entirely cold. I gave a friend of mine, who plays the piano a little, a few of Schumann's piano pieces for Christmas, and he played a few bars from *Kreisleriana* for me. I thought: how extraordinarily noble!

Tell Mining and Koder I said hello. I hope things are going as well for you as they can for anyone right now!

Your loving brother,

Ludwig

196 Ludwig to Helene

Trinity College
Cambridge
4 February 1947[4]

Helenchen, my uncle!

(What must the censor think!) Some time ago, I received your kind
letter of 10 February. Strange as it may sound, I should like you to
be able to move back to Vienna soon. I know just what disadvantages
that would bring – or I can at least suspect what some of those
would be – but it would, nonetheless, be a good feeling to know
that you were home again.—I haven't heard any music for some
time now.

I would really like to hear Schumann quartets again. Just recently
the beginning of the one I mean occurred to me – the introduction
– and I was quite delighted. Unfortunately someone a few floors
below my rooms plays the piano, and the miserable strumming
(mostly Beethoven) disturbs me a lot. Strangely, it sometimes stifles
my breathing, of all things; it's a horrible feeling. 'It's stinking music
from down below', Labor once said; but I would prefer a real stench
by far.—The cold here has eased up a bit, but it is no doubt still
terrible where you are. May you and Mining stay healthy!

Tell everyone I said hello, warmest regards,

your loving brother,
Ludwig

---

[4] Ludwig writes the date only in numbers ('4.2.47'). He may have meant to write '4.3.47' (i.e.,
'4 March 1947'). Given the playful and joking nature of this letter, however, it is possible that
some joke is meant.

197 Ludwig to Helene

As from: Trinity College
Cambridge
22 July 1947

Dear Helene!

It has been a very, very long time since you've heard from me or I from you. I had a lot to do and was often far too depressed to write. I'm now on holiday in Wales, where I always feel much better than I do in Cambridge. It is very beautiful here, I mean the sea and the region, and the people here are much nicer than they are in England. I hope to be allowed to travel to Vienna in September. It is, I believe, as good as certain that I'll be approved. I'll be receiving my 'permit' at some point towards the end of August. Shall I be able to see you then? I certainly hope so.

I recently heard gramophone records of Schubert's Symphony in C major at a friend's house. I've long believed that the last movement falls somewhat flat when compared to the others; but a few years ago someone with a very deep understanding told me that the last movement made quite an impression on him. And I too have always been greatly impressed. (The performance was partially mediocre, partially bad.)

Please give the Sjögrens my regards, the lot of them. Tell Arvid that he'll probably get money from me in October, but probably not before that.—If you write to me, write to my Trinity College, etc., address, even though I'm not there at the moment. Everything will be forwarded to me.—I'll be traveling to Ireland in August to stay with a friend for two weeks.

May you not experience too much inner or outer discord.

Your loving brother,
Ludwig

198 Hermine to Ludwig

Prof. Ludwig Wittgenstein
Trinity College
Cambridge
England

18 October 1947

My dearest Ludwig,

I have to thank you straight away for your kind letter, because it made me very happy. Yes, it was nice for all of us to spend time with you, and I'm still living off the effects.—Hänsel's been to my place already, and I believe that talking does him good; he's coming again tomorrow, and I hope he'll come to see me every week as a matter of routine, as we did in the past. Sometimes he would read something to me, and towards the end we were beginning to read Shakespeare: that is, I was reading to him.*

*He wouldn't be the right author now, I believe.

Right after you left, I tried to change the self-portrait myself; it's actually a concession, for I really don't have any way of indicating a mere change in colour, and – oddly enough – something like that can be an impediment for me, but of course you are completely right. This year I made a small improvement with pencil to the reproduction of the stairwell drawing, which I wasn't able to decide on at the time because it would have required a minor change to a perspective line, and I just didn't hit upon this sacrilegious idea.

A few days ago Koder and I had an enormous treat: we heard Bach's *The Art of Fugue*, played four-handed so sublimely and movingly that we were at a complete loss of words. What a shame that the concert didn't take place while you were here; that would certainly have been something for you. One Professor

Seidhofer, who set the four-handed piece himself, played it with one Dr Dichler, and it seemed to me that only in Austria could someone play so movingly. Aunt Clara once told a foreigner, whom she held in high regard (I don't know who it was any more) that she'd show him something that personified Austria, and she had Baumayer play something.

Imagine: the gramophone wasn't broken at all, the voltage stabiliser was just out of place. Isn't that annoying?

Keep well, my good Ludwig, may everything you've undertaken go well! May you stay healthy and may we see each other again, that is what I want from the very bottom of my heart.

Your sister,

Mining

199 Ludwig to Helene

17 November 1947

Dear Helene,

Thank you for your letter. It was a great relief to hear that Koder is not seriously ill. I hope the vitamins from Sweden will arrive for him before very long. I also advised you once to take vitamin b1, and I'm completely convinced that you need it and that a lack of it is, at least partially, to blame for your anxiety. That may sound stupid to you, but it's not. I'm sending you a preparation via Jochen.[5] I'm leaving Cambridge tomorrow and will travel to Ireland in 14 days. Until further notice my address there will be:

---

[5] One of Gretl's two foster children; the other was Wedigo von Zastrow. Wedi fell in the war fighting for the Germans, while Jochen came to Austria with the American occupation forces.

c/o Dr Drury

Saint Patrick's Hospital

James's Street

Eire, Dublin.

Please give this address to all friends!—Hoping that you're reasonably well.

Give everyone my regards!

Your loving brother,

Ludwig

ps: All post will be forwarded to me from Cambridge.

200 Ludwig to Helene

c/o Dr Drury

Saint Patrick's Hospital

James's Street

Eire, Dublin

[undated]

Helenchen!

Thank you for the message regarding August. You know I wasn't expecting it.—I'm sorry to hear that the performance of Brahms's *Requiem* wasn't better. Presumably it was the same miserable timpanist I heard? But of course the conductor is primarily to blame. I can imagine that a very chaste Brahms doesn't suit Karajan very well. But maybe it's not that way at all.—The difficulty with blethering is that everything depends on the tone, and that can't be captured in writing. Hence, at most, I would have to send you gramophone records. To be sure, I am thinking of introducing a thoroughly precise phonetic notation, but then the censor wouldn't know what to make of it. I can vividly imagine him trying and ptactising to pronounce the words correctly.

Things are going well for me. I hope they're not going badly for you.

Your loving brother,

Ludwig

201 Ludwig to Helene

Kilpatrick House

Red Cross

Wicklow Eire

10 January 1948

Dear Helene!

Thank you for your letter. It's good that you're taking vitamin B, because it's <u>certain,</u> and not some illusion as is the case with so many medicines, that it works. I'm keeping well. The winter's been quite mild so far, even though it's been pretty wet too. The region here wouldn't attract me so if the colours weren't as wonderful as they often are. It must, I believe, be something in the atmosphere as it's not just the grass that's wonderful, but the browns too, and the sky and the sea. I feel a great deal better than in Cambridge. Give everyone around you my regards, and Mariechen and her family as well.

Your loving brother,

Ludwig

ps: I learned from a few lines and a small parcel that Marguerite[6] is now in England. I don't know why or for how long, but was

---

[6] Ludwig knew quite little of Marguerite's life at this time; but his concern for her is evinced by a letter to her of 13 August 1946: 'May you be well and may you find some kind of work that puts you in contact with people in a manner befitting a human being. I mean: not as a lady.' Ludwig obviously believed that the conditions for such contact would more likely be found in Chile than in Europe.

amazed because I thought Mima was on her way to see her: I mean in Chile. Did that not happen? I would be very sorry if it didn't.

202 Ludwig to Helene

Kilpatrick House
Red Cross
Wicklow Eire
20 February 1948

Dear Helene!

Please let me know whether Jochen is still in Vienna, and whether he will be staying there for a while and what his address is. Arvid wrote to me, in response to my query, that he probably won't be able to send you a vitamin preparation. If Jochen is still in Vienna, then I will try to send it to him through a friend in England, unless you've received it in the meantime. I'm well, and I think of you often – and almost always by way of blethering. I would be interested to know how Brahms's third was performed (I mean for the gramophone recording). Actually, the only movement that <u>says</u> anything to me now is the <u>fourth</u>. I would very much like to hear it. I believe, it sounds as if written for the orchestra much more than the middle movements do, in particular. And it seems to me that its sonority isn't <u>arid</u>. Of course I don't know what the reason for that is.

Give Koder my regards!

Your loving brother,
Ludwig

ps: If you see Jochen, please ask him whether he will send Hedwig Schulze parcels for me, as I've forgotten whether I asked him

<u>precisely that</u>. Please let me know what his answer is. If it's affirmative, then all is well; if he still hasn't done it, then would he please do so in future.

203 Ludwig to Helene

Kilpatrick House
Red Cross
Wicklow Eire
15 March 1948

Dear Helene!

Thank you for your letter. With any luck, you'll receive the parcel from Lixl's wife soon. I asked you for Jochen's address in Vienna because I could send something to him, as an American, more reliably than to you.—Hardly a day goes by that I don't think of you. And although it mostly happens in conjunction with blethering, you of course know that blethering is just as necessary for me as any vitamins are. May you remember that often.—I'm working an awful lot and am often very tired. The winter was the mildest I've ever seen, and just a few days ago it was as warm as in summertime.

Something strange happened to me about 2 months ago: almost no music at all goes through my mind, except the scherzo from *Midsummer Night's Dream*! It is of course <u>very</u> beautiful, but certainly not a piece of music close to me; nor does it suit my temperament. As such, there has to be reasons outside of music for why it occurs to me as constantly as it does. Freud would perhaps say, and perhaps rightly so, that I am just trying to tell myself that 'I'm an ass' because the part that races through my mind most often is the part where the ass brays.

I hope that Gretl will be able to travel to you soon. Hoping that you're reasonably well! Give my regards to Koder and everyone else!

Your loving brother,

Ludwig

ps: You write that you're all now used to music with stark contrasts. I <u>believe</u>, I should find that extraordinarily repellent. I believe, I would have the greatest mistrust in such an attitude. But maybe not, and maybe I don't understand these modern times either.—I haven't received a letter from Jochen. If you see him, please ask him to keep Hedwig supplied with parcels from my money as well.

204 Ludwig to Helene

Rosro Cottage
Renvyle P.O.
County Galway
Eire
29 April 1948

Helenchen!

My warmest thanks for your gift. I haven't received it yet, but I've been notified that it's coming.

As you see, I have a new address. I arrived here (in the very west of Ireland) only yesterday and don't yet know how it's going to go here. I can only hope.

I can't write very much today – only that, as usual, I think of you all with love. Please thank Mining in my name for her kind letter and tell everyone what my new address is. Post sent to the old address will be forwarded to me. My warmest regards to everyone.

Your loving brother,

Ludwig

205 Ludwig to Helene

Ross's Hotel
Parkgate Street
Dublin
Eire
14 February 1949

Dear Helene!

Thank you for your letter of 10 February. About two days ago I had a letter from Gretl dated the <u>8th</u>, where she wrote saying that she spoke with Tommy and learned that Mining is 'partially paralysed and not entirely in her right mind and doesn't recognise anyone' (those are her words). Was Tommy's report premature? Please write with something. I will of course <u>not</u> doubt your report. May her condition develop mercifully, in one direction or the other! I would be very grateful to you for any and all details – even for your judgment that I shouldn't come now. <u>I am relying</u> on you to send for me if Mining should want it.

With any luck, that catarrh of yours will go away soon!—Give Koder my regards, if you see him. Wishing you everything you already know, your loving brother

Ludwig

ps: I wrote to Mining a few days ago (in the Argentinierstrasse). Don't hesitate to open the letter and read it to her if she can't read herself. My friend Drury has written to her as well.

206 Ludwig to Helene

Ross's Hotel
Parkgate Street
Dublin
Eire
21 March 1949

Dear Helene!

Thank you for your cable. Should you send me another one, please send it to <u>Dublin</u>, at the address above; <u>only the doctor's certificate is to be sent to Ickenham</u>. (Unless I let you know at some point that I have left here and I give you a new address.) If you cable <u>here</u> and send the certificate to Ickenham, then I will make the journey to England and find, or expect, the report <u>there</u>, since I need it for the authorities in <u>London</u>. I have understood the content of your cable, and you may be right that my coming is not advisable at the moment. You see Mining and have to make that judgment. But please take care not to assume the role of fate. And if, as I imagine is the case, you discuss these things with Gretl, then this warning applies to her as well.

In my opinion, you have to do the following: sound Mining out. You can be <u>very</u> diplomatic, and it will, therefore, be easy for you to go about it the right way. You can steer the discussion towards me and will no doubt know how best to find out whether she would like me to come. You shouldn't forget that Mining, even if she very much wants me to come, would never say as much of her own accord – if only because she knows that I would come, and she won't want my work to be interrupted on her account, etc. You can even tell her that I was planning to come to Vienna this time before autumn, in fact as early as spring. You'll know best what you can say without exciting her, and you'll see and let me know what her reaction is.

Please also consider that it is difficult for me to be here in complete uncertainty. Please also write to me with what the doctors' present diagnosis is. Should it be too difficult for you to write yourself, then please tell Koder precisely what he should tell me. May you exercise sound judgment, tempered with insight!

Your loving brother,

Ludwig

207 Ludwig to Helene

c/o Dr Richards

40 Swakeleys Rd

Ickenham

Uxbridge

3 July 1949

Dear Helene!

You haven't heard from me in a long time. For a variety of reasons, writing has become very difficult for me, and it will be difficult for me now as well. But you know I think of you all, as I always do.

As you see, I'm near London now and can buy you the gramophone records that we spoke about sometime within the next 2½ weeks before I leave for America. But before I buy them I would like you to confirm that you indeed still want them. Hence, please <u>cable</u> me as soon as you receive this letter with whether you still want them. You need cable only 'agreed', and I will buy you the records that seem to me the most suitable and will have them sent to you. Then I'll let you know the prices, and you can have the equivalent paid to me in American currency, perhaps through Karban, when I'm in America. I'm leaving on 21 July on the 'Queen Mary', and my new address will be:

        c/o Dr Malcolm
        1107 Hanshaw Rd
        Ithaca ny
        usa

I am planning to stay there for approximately 3 months. Please send your cable to me at the address stated above: Professor Wittgenstein, c/o Dr Richards, 40 Swakeleys Rd, etc.

Koder and Hänsel were sending me messages about Mining's condition at regular intervals, but I haven't heard anything from them for a while now. I also had a letter from you, but it took more than 3 weeks to reach Cambridge. I hope she's not suffering, at least not physically!

Tell her I think about her with love, as always. There is nothing more to say. Give everyone my warmest regards! I hope things are going reasonably well for you!

                                    Your loving brother,
                                    Ludwig

208 Ludwig to Helene

                                    c/o Dr Richards
                                    40 Swakeleys Rd
                                    Ickenham
                                    Uxbridge
                                    17 July 1949

Dear Helene!

I sent two packages of gramophone records to you today via airmail. Altogether everything cost 11½ pounds, the records alone were slightly more than £9. I sent them via airmail because I assumed they wouldn't be mishandled as much. The records are 10 Haydn quartets and are by far the best I could find. I wanted to send you the adagio and fugue by Mozart, of which there was a very beautiful performance under Busch. But that's not in print any more – in its stead, however, a performance of Karajan's with all the characteristic, horrible mistakes. You will also find a few faults with the Haydn quartets, but you will, I believe, be satisfied on the whole.

I had a letter from Koder today. The poor man has <u>a lot</u> of worries. Please give him my regards. I'll write to him soon. He said Mining's in the same condition that she was in a few weeks ago. You know I can't send her any news other than the old news that I do think of her, and how. And of you all.

I'll be leaving for America in 5 days. My address will be:

> c/o Dr Malcolm
> 1107 Hanshaw Rd
> Ithaca ny

With all the old wishes and feelings,

your brother,
Ludwig

209 Ludwig to Helene

1107 Hanshaw Rd
Ithaca ny
usa
22 August 1949

Dear Helene,

I'm glad to hear the gramophone records have arrived. I hope that they haven't been damaged and that you like them as much as I do.

Please wire me the money for them as soon as possible <u>here</u>. I need it pretty urgently. The people I'm staying with are very good and friendly, but I don't want them paying my doctor's bills.[7]

Tell everyone I said hello and Mining in particular, when you go to Vienna, and tell her that I'm thinking of her, and how.

Your loving brother,

Ludwig

210 Ludwig to Margarete

[September 1949][8]

[...] wrote to me saying that you are lying in bed with bronchitis. I hope you recover soon.—Shortly before I left for America, I found the letters from Busch and Frau Anderson in a bookshop in London. I read a few of them and had the same impression as of old.

Your loving brother,

Ludwig

ps: Yesterday I thought, I don't know why, of the house in the Kundmanngasse and how charmingly you furnished it and how agreeably. In this, we understand each other.

---

[7] The seriousness of Ludwig's condition, but not that he had cancer, had been identified in the United States. It was for this reason that Ludwig cut his stay short, which had originally been planned for three months.

[8] This letter was written on a page ripped out of a notebook, and the beginning is presumed lost. It is unclear whether this letter is one of Ludwig's drafts or whether it is in fact the letter sent to and received by Gretl.

211 Ludwig to Helene

c/o Prof. v. Wright
Strathaird
Lady Margaret Rd
Cambridge
28 November 1949

Dear Helene!

I am turning over the idea of coming to Vienna some time in the near future.[9] My health is fairly bad, and I am, for that reason, unable to work. I'm hoping for some peace and quiet in Vienna. I would probably have to lie down for part of the day, but wouldn't need any particular care. If I could have my old room (with the skylight) in the Alleegasse, then that would be good. I'm taking some medicine which, so the doctor says, will help me.

Please write or cable me with whether my plan is possible – assuming that I obtain permission to enter from the authorities in London.

With best wishes, your loving brother,

Ludwig

ps: I can't travel just yet, but maybe in a few weeks.

---

[9] Ludwig did in fact return to Vienna on 22 December 1949, where he stayed through March 1950. Hermine died on 10 February 1950, after having suffered protracted pain.

Wittgenstein and Von Wright © Cambridge Archive.

212 Ludwig to Helene

27 St. John Street

Oxford

26 January 1951

Dear Helene,

You haven't heard from me for a very long time. There was nothing to write, nor is there anything to write today. I'm writing only out of an instinct of sorts. Koder wrote to me saying that you're suffering very much from a weak pulse. I imagine that's quite nasty. Koder wrote that Dr Strasser is treating you. With any luck, he understands something of your condition and can help. I've always found there to be an enormous difference between doctors, with only a few of them knowing what – as one would think – each of them must have learnt. I haven't heard any music for a long time. I hope you're still playing four-handed with Koder, and maybe even I will be able to hear you both at some point in the near future.

Give Gretl, Betty[10] and all friends my regards when you see them. Warmest regards, your

brother,
Ludwig

76 Storeys Way, Cambridge, home of Ludwig's doctor where he passed his last months.

---

[10] A household employee, first of Hermine's, then (at the time of this letter) of Helene's.

213 Ludwig to Helene

76 Storeys Way
Cambridge
15 March 1951

Dear Helene!

I've been thinking about you a lot recently, wishing I could blether with you again. I was born a century too early because, in future, in 100 years, people will be able to ring Vienna from Cambridge at no great expense and blether for an hour on the phone. But then again, it just might be in your best interest that this is still not a possibility in this day and age.

I've received a reproduction of the Labor drawing, and it's unfortunately on glossy paper, the scale of reduction is badly chosen and the blacks on the photograph are so ugly that it's not as nice as it could be. But when I look at it through tissue paper, it's quite impressive all the same. I am going to try to have the reproduction photographed onto decent paper with somewhat smaller dimensions (about ¾ of the reproduction, perhaps). Of course, it would be better if one could just get decent reproductions of the original; one would have to <u>know</u> that nothing can happen to the original in the process (I mean, through carelessness, say); and that perhaps is not easily possible in this day and age.

I recently read that there is now a recording of Bach's concerto for three pianos in C major; I'm not sure which of the two that is. I hear only the beginning of one such concerto in my inner ear, but do not know the key signature. I'll try to listen to it tomorrow in a shop. Edwin Fischer plays one of the pianos and also conducts.

Give Betty, Koder and Hänsel my <u>warmest</u> regards when you see them. Hoping that you're tolerably well! As ever,

your brother,

Ludwig

214 Ludwig to Helene

76 Storeys Way

Cambridge

17 March 1951

Dear Helene!

This is just a ps to my letter from yesterday. I heard the concerto for three pianos, and it was performed wonderfully. (A single passage in the first movement doesn't seem very good to me.) I have the feeling Fischer is a great artist. If you want I'll order the 3 records and have them sent to you.

Your brother,

Ludwig

215 Ludwig to Helene

76 Storeys Way

Cambridge

10 April 1951

Dear Helene!

First, I have to give me my <u>warmest</u> thanks for sending you the records of the Bach concerto a few days ago, second, for having had the excellent idea of asking you for a smaller version of the Labor drawing.—The reproduction of the original is quite satisfactory (the other one is awful).

Could you send me another copy of the good version? I would be <u>very</u> grateful to myself if you would!

Now I can hardly go on writing because I am so touched by my gratitude.—Give all friends my regards.

Your brother,

Ludwig

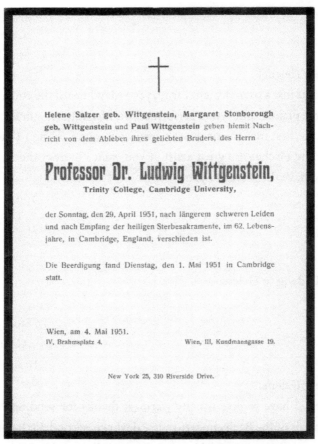

Death notice issued by Ludwig's family © Wittgenstein Initiative.

Appendix

Hermine to Ludwig[1]

The level at which I (Papa, Darwin, Kaiser Josef) stand is characterised by a feeling for the good and the absence of feeling for God: that is, by lack of religion. Tolstoy, too, occupied this level prior to his transformation; he was a completely decent human being, and that's the end of it.[2]

An entirely different level is the one in which feeling God and being in contact with the heavenly powers, which are one and the same thing, begins. And, to that extent, you were right: this contact is what's essential, since negating and stripping away all that's earthly,

[1] This manuscript sheet in Hermine's hand was among letters from her to Ludwig, written before 1927 and kept in Vienna. It is obviously addressed to him and expresses ideas that owe much to his influence. With slight variations it corresponds to a passage in her notebooks from that period, now published in the original German, 'Ludwig sagt . . .' edited by Mathias Iven (Berlin, H-E Verlag, 2015).

[2] Hermine has *Anna Karenina* in mind – Part VIII, end of Chapter XI, beginning of Chapter XII – in which Levin (obviously a character who represents Tolstoy himself) hears from a peasant that someone else: [lives for his soul and remembers God ... rightly in a godly way]'. This philosophy of life (which Levin interprets in his own mind as 'to live not for one's needs but for God') leaves a strong impression on Levin, which is similar to the one described by Hermine (quoted from [insert source]). In his *A Confession*, Tolstoy describes, absent any description of the details, the effect that the confession of a God-fearing peasant had had on him 'when a knowledge of faith revealed itself to me.' (Passages from Tolstoy are quoted in the The World's Classics translation of Louise and Aylmer Maude.)

which I believed was essential, is just the consequence of either this contact or the longing for it. At the moment in which a person is capable of talking about God of his own accord – he gives testimony of that contact and sets himself apart from other people.

The peasant's telling Tolstoy 'one must live for God' would have made little impression on him a year earlier. At that moment, however, it brought the accumulated powers of longing and discontent to the point of breakthrough, and he felt God. Through that feeling, he set himself apart from other people as well as from his past life, because now he had religion.

To be sure, in our day and age, religion, ethics and science could not be one and the same thing, since religion was as good as gone (not just detached, as Ernst[3] says).

---

[3] Probably Paul Ernst (1866–1933); See G. P. Baker and P. M. S. Hacker, *Wittgenstein, Understanding and Meaning* (Oxford, Blackwell, 1980, especially pp. 535 on), and P. Hübscher, *Der Einfluß von J. W. Goethe und P. Ernst auf L. Wittgenstein* (Bern, Peter Lang, 1985, pp. 55–82, 135f) for Ernst's influence on Ludwig. Ernst writes in 'Die Formbildende Kraft' (1931, p. 66): 'Even in religion, in thinking, we come upon the concept of "form", as in art' ('thinking' means 'science' here). In the 'Introduction', to *Erdachte Gespräche* (1931), it reads: 'the point of view of the pious man [is] impossible to today's world' (i.e., only the poet can answer its questions). But similar ideas also appear earlier: see P. Ernst, *Der Weg der Form* (1906) and his 'Nachwort' to Grimms' *Fairy Tales* (1910) – liked by Ludwig – where Ernst gives Tolstoy high praise.

Index